Life-Study of Genesis

Messages 92-109

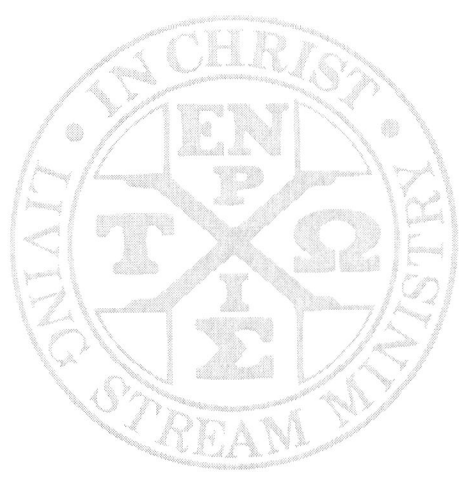

Witness Lee

Living Stream Ministry
Anaheim, CA • www.lsm.org

© 1977, 1978 Living Stream Ministry

All rights reserved. No part of this work may be reproduced or transmitted in any form or by any means—graphic, electronic, or mechanical, including photocopying, recording, or information storage and retrieval systems—without written permission from the publisher.

First Edition, August 1997.

ISBN 978-0-7363-0836-6
(Complete set, softcover)
ISBN 978-0-87083-915-3
(Messages 92-109, softcover)

Published by

Living Stream Ministry
2431 W. La Palma Ave., Anaheim, CA 92801 U.S.A.
P. O. Box 2121, Anaheim, CA 92814 U.S.A.

Printed in the United States of America
13 14 15 16 17 18 / 11 10 9 8 7 6 5

CONTENTS

MESSAGE NINETY-TWO   **BEING MATURED**   PAGE 1179
THE PROCESS
OF MATURITY (1)

f. Being Matured — 1) The Process of Maturity — a) The Dealings in the Last Stage — (1) Jacob Being Robbed of the Treasure of His Heart under God's Sovereign Hand

MESSAGE NINETY-THREE   **BEING MATURED**   PAGE 1191
THE PROCESS
OF MATURITY (2)

(2) Jacob Being Stricken with Famine — (3) Jacob Being Forced to Send His Sons to Egypt to Buy Grain — (4) Jacob's Second Son, Simeon, Being Detained in Egypt — (5) The Famine Becoming Severe — b) Jacob's Reaction

MESSAGE NINETY-FOUR   **BEING MATURED**   PAGE 1203
THE MANIFESTATION
OF MATURITY (1)

2) Manifestation of Maturity — a) No Blame at Hearing That Joseph Was Still Alive — b) Offering Sacrifices to God at Beersheba before Going to See Joseph — c) No Excitement Showing Looseness of Self at Seeing Joseph — d) No Begging after Arriving in Egypt — e) No Activity for Himself while Living in Egypt — f) Blessing People All the Time

MESSAGE NINETY-FIVE   **BLESSING**   PAGE 1213

    I. THE PRINCIPLE OF BLESSING   (1213)

    II. THE MEANING OF BLESSING   (1214)

    III. THE FIRST CASE OF BLESSING   (1215)

    IV. THE BLESSING OF THE PRIESTS   (1216)

    V. THE BLESSING OF THE APOSTLE   (1217)

    VI. THE LORD'S BLESSING CROSSING MAN'S NATURAL MANEUVERING   (1219)

    VII. MAN'S NATURAL CONCEPT HOLDING BACK THE LORD'S BLESSING HAND   (1221)

    VIII. JACOB'S SUPPLANTING HANDS BECOMING BLESSING HANDS   (1222)

MESSAGE NINETY-SIX   **THE SHIFTINGS OF THE BIRTHRIGHT IN THE SCRIPTURE**   **PAGE 1223**

    I. FROM ESAU TO JACOB   (1224)

    II. FROM ZARAH TO PHAREZ   (1227)

    III. FROM REUBEN TO JOSEPH   (1227)

    IV. FROM MANASSEH TO EPHRAIM   (1228)

    V. FROM ISRAEL TO THE CHURCH   (1229)

MESSAGE NINETY-SEVEN   **BEING MATURED THE MANIFESTATION OF MATURITY (2)**   **PAGE 1231**

    g) Prophesying with Blessing — (1) Four Requirements for Prophesying with Blessing — (2) Not a Gifted Prophet — (3) A God-constituted Person — (4) Jacob, the Father in the Flesh, and Israel, God's Mouth

MESSAGE NINETY-EIGHT   **BEING MATURED THE MANIFESTATION OF MATURITY (3)**   **PAGE 1243**

    (5) Concerning Reuben — (6) Concerning Simeon and Levi

| MESSAGE NINETY-NINE | BEING MATURED THE MANIFESTATION OF MATURITY (4) | PAGE 1257 |

(7) Concerning Judah — (8) Concerning Zebulun and Issachar

| MESSAGE ONE HUNDRED | THE SPIRITUAL SIGNIFICANCE OF THE BLESSING PROPHESIED CONCERNING JUDAH, ZEBULUN, AND ISSACHAR (1) | PAGE 1271 |

I. CONCERNING JUDAH—THE GLAD TIDINGS OF CHRIST (1273)

A. The Victory of Christ — B. The Kingdom of Christ — C. Rest in the Enjoyment of Christ's Riches in Life

| MESSAGE ONE HUNDRED ONE | THE SPIRITUAL SIGNIFICANCE OF THE BLESSING PROPHESIED CONCERNING JUDAH, ZEBULUN, AND ISSACHAR (2) | PAGE 1285 |

II. CONCERNING ZEBULUN—THE PREACHING OF CHRIST'S GLAD TIDINGS (1288)

A. Shipping Out the Riches of Christ — B. Reaching the Gentile World — C. Rejoicing in Going Out

III. CONCERNING ISSACHAR—THE CHURCH LIFE (1291)

A. Resting in the Church — B. Enjoying the Pleasant Christ — C. Issuing in Taskwork as a Tribute to the Master — D. Rejoicing in the Church Life

IV. THE CONSUMMATION (1294)

A. The Peoples Invited to the Mountain of God — B. Sacrifices of Righteousness Offered to God — C. The Church and the Kingdom Becoming Our Enjoyment

| MESSAGE ONE HUNDRED TWO | BEING MATURED THE MANIFESTATION OF MATURITY (5) | PAGE 1299 |

(9) Concerning Dan — (10) Concerning Gad — (11) Concerning Asher — (12) Concerning Naphtali

| MESSAGE ONE HUNDRED THREE | THE SPIRITUAL SIGNIFICANCE OF DAN, GAD, ASHER, AND NAPHTALI | PAGE 1315 |

I. THE APOSTASY OF DAN (1317)

A. Gaining More Christ by His Victorious Life — B. Being Individualistic and Independent — C. Setting Up a Divisive Center of Worship and Ordaining a Hired "Priest"

II. THE RECOVERY WITH GAD (1323)

A. Coming Back to the Victory of Christ — B. Enlarged by God — C. Crushing the Enemy by the Productive Life of Christ — D. Taking Care of the Brothers

III. THE SUFFICIENCY OF ASHER (1326)

A. The Exceeding Blessing and Surpassing Grace — B. The Rich Provision of Life — C. The Bountiful Supply of the Spirit for Our Daily Walk — D. The Absolute Rest with Peace, Strength, Security, and Sufficiency

IV. THE CONSUMMATION WITH NAPHTALI (1327)

A. Experiencing the Resurrected Christ and Uttering the Beautiful and Pleasant Words of Life — B. Satisfied with God's Grace and Full with God's Blessing — C. Taking the Earth for the Lord

| MESSAGE ONE HUNDRED FOUR | BEING MATURED THE MANIFESTATION OF MATURITY (6) | PAGE 1331 |

(13) Concerning Joseph — (14) Concerning Benjamin

| MESSAGE ONE HUNDRED FIVE | THE SPIRITUAL SIGNIFICANCE OF JOSEPH AND BENJAMIN (1) | PAGE 1343 |

    I. FRUITFUL   (1345)

        A. A Son of a Fruitful Tree — B. Branching over the Wall

    II. VICTORIOUS   (1351)

        A. Overcoming the Archers' Attack — B. Being Made Strong by the Mighty One — C. Tearing like a Wolf — D. Pushing like an Ox

    III. TRUSTING   (1355)

| MESSAGE ONE HUNDRED SIX | THE SPIRITUAL SIGNIFICANCE OF JOSEPH AND BENJAMIN (2) | PAGE 1357 |

    IV. BLESSED   (1357)

        A. With the Precious Things of Heaven — B. With the Dew — C. With the Deep, the Springs, Lying Beneath — D. With the Precious Fruits Brought Forth by the Sun — E. With the Precious Things Put Forth by the Moon — F. and G. With the Best Things of the Ancient Mountains and with the Precious Things of the Eternal Hills — H. With the Precious Things of the Earth and Its Fullness

| MESSAGE ONE HUNDRED SEVEN | THE SPIRITUAL SIGNIFICANCE OF JOSEPH AND BENJAMIN (3) | PAGE 1369 |

        I. With the Blessings of the Breasts and the Womb — J. With the Good Pleasure of Him Who Dwelt in the Bush

    V. DWELT   (1374)

        A. By the Lord between Benjamin's Shoulders — B. Benjamin Dwelling in Safety by the Lord

| MESSAGE ONE HUNDRED EIGHT | THE ULTIMATE CONSUMMATION OF GOD'S OPERATION IN THE BIBLE | PAGE 1381 |

I. THE UNIVERSAL BLESSING—THE NEW HEAVEN AND NEW EARTH   (1385)

A. All Things Made New — B. No More Sea — C. No More Tears, Death, Sorrow, Crying, and Pain — D. No More Curse — E. No More Night

II. THE ETERNAL DWELLING—THE NEW JERUSALEM   (1389)

A. The Tabernacle of God with Men — B. Constituted of God's Redeemed — C. God and the Lamb Being the Temple — D. God Being the Light, and the Lamb Being the Lamp — E. God's Throne Being the Source of Supply — F. The River of Water of Life with the Tree of Life Being the Supply — G. God's Authority, Face, and Name Being the Chief Enjoyment

| MESSAGE ONE HUNDRED NINE | BEING MATURED THE MANIFESTATION OF MATURITY (7) | PAGE 1393 |

h) Departing in an Excellent Way — (1) Asking Joseph to Put His Hand under His Thigh — (2) Considering Death as Sleep — (3) Charging Joseph Not to Bury Him in Egypt, but in the Good Land — (4) Worshipping God on the Top of His Staff — (5) Remembering Rachel's Sorrowful Death — (6) Realizing that God Had Shepherded Him All His Life Long — (7) Prophesying concerning His Twelve Sons — (8) Buried with High Honor

LIFE-STUDY OF GENESIS

MESSAGE NINETY-TWO

BEING MATURED
THE PROCESS OF MATURITY

(1)

In this message we come to the most pleasant section of the book of Genesis, chapters thirty-seven through fifty. All children like the stories in these chapters. When the writer came to this section, he changed his way of writing. The record of the first thirty-six chapters is brief and emphatic, but the record of the last fourteen chapters is very detailed. Chapter thirty-seven, for example, contains many details. This section is so detailed because it is very practical for our human life. No section in the book of Genesis is more practical than this last section of fourteen chapters.

Before we consider chapter thirty-seven, I would like to call your attention back to the beginning of this book. In the reading of any book we must understand the subject, the purpose, of that book. After reading through the book of Genesis, a book of fifty chapters, you still may not know the subject. What is the subject of this book? When I was young, I was told that Genesis covers two main things—God's creation and man's fall. Genesis begins with the words, "In the beginning God created," and it ends with the words, "He was put in a coffin in Egypt." I was told that because the first verse speaks of God's creation and the last verse speaks about Joseph's being put in a coffin in Egypt, Genesis is a book about God's creation and man's fall. Although this view is not wrong, it is a very inadequate understanding of this book.

It is not easy to understand the Bible. In fact, it is even difficult to understand ourselves. Although we have hair on our heads and ten toes on our feet, do hair and toes make a whole man? Is this a complete person? Certainly not. All the crucial parts and organs, such as the heart and the lungs, are between the hair and the toes. Likewise, the most important parts of Genesis are between the first verse and the last verse of the book.

Genesis 1:26 is a very crucial verse. "And God said, Let us make man in our image, after our likeness: and let them have dominion...." Notice two significant words here—image and dominion. Yes, man was created by God, and he fell. But we must consider in what way and for what purpose man was created. The Bible says that man was made in the image of God. Nothing is higher than God. Thus, man was made in the image of the highest One. Perhaps you have never regarded yourself this highly before. Because we bear the divine image, we should have a high regard for ourselves. We are not low creatures; we were made for the purpose of expressing God and exercising His dominion. The subject of Genesis is man bearing the image of God and exercising God's dominion over all things. We bear God's image that we might express Him, and we have God's dominion that we might represent Him. Therefore, we are God's expression and representation. This is the heart of Genesis.

In order to know this in a progressive way, we need all fifty chapters of this book. All the generations recorded in it—Adam, Abel, Enosh, Enoch, Noah, Abraham, Isaac, Jacob, and Joseph—are for one purpose: to show that God's economy in the universe is to express Himself through man. This is God's purpose, God's goal, and the desire of God's heart. God's purpose and economy are related to man.

The record of all the generations included in this book is a portrait of God's divine economy. In Adam we do not see much of God's expression and dominion. Although Abel believed in God, we do not clearly see in him God's expression and dominion. Enosh realized that he was fragile and weak, and he began to call on the name of the Lord. But in him we scarcely see God's expression or dominion. Enoch walked with God. Therefore, we see in him a little of God's expression; however, we see nothing of God's dominion. Although with Noah we do see a little of God's expression and dominion, it is rather vague; it is not definite, impressive, or clear. In Abraham we see less of God's expression and dominion than we do in Noah. Although many Christians have overly exalted Abraham, he was only on the first level of the doctrine of Christ. Abraham was the father of faith for justification, which is merely the beginning of the doctrine of Christ. Furthermore, we can hardly see God's expression and dominion in Isaac. Isaac, the one who inherited everything from his father, only cared for eating. As long as he was given something good to eat, he would grant his blessing blindly.

It is in Jacob that we see the expression of God. However, prior to the last fourteen chapters of this book, we do not see much of God's expression in Jacob. But in these last chapters we do see in him very much of the expression of God and the dominion of God. Although in this section Jacob was old in years, his spiritual eyes were very keen. Wherever he went, he perceived the real situation and blessed people accordingly. Moreover, his blessing became God's prophecy. Jacob truly bore the image of God and expressed Him. Even Pharaoh, the highest ruler at that time, was under Jacob's blessing. When Jacob was brought into the presence of Pharaoh, Jacob did not say, "Hello, how are you? How old are you?" Rather, he stretched forth his hand and blessed him (47:7, 10). This indicates that Pharaoh was under Jacob, the one who was God's expression.

Jacob's blessing upon the two sons of Joseph, Ephraim and Manasseh, was also a prophecy. Isaac, cheated by Jacob, blessed him blindly. However, Jacob's blessing of Ephraim and Manasseh was much different. Joseph brought his two sons to Jacob, expecting that Manasseh, the firstborn, would receive the birthright. But Jacob placed his right hand upon the head of Ephraim, the younger, "guiding his hands wittingly" (48:14). When Joseph attempted to move Jacob's hand from Ephraim's head to Manasseh's, Jacob refused and said, "I know it, my son, I know it" (48:19). Jacob seemed to be saying, "My son, you don't know what I am doing, but I know. I know God's heart. My blessing is God's expression and God's speaking. The word of my blessing is God's prophecy."

Here in Jacob we see a man who was one with God and who expressed God. Jacob's speaking was God's speaking. Do not think that speaking is an insignificant matter. According to the New Testament, the Son expressed the Father mainly by His speaking. The Lord Jesus said, "Do you not believe that I am in the Father, and the Father is in Me? The words which I speak to you, I do not speak from Myself; but the Father who abides in Me, He does His works"; and, "The word which you hear is not Mine, but the Father's who sent Me" (John 14:10, 24). Thus, to express God is mainly to speak for God and to speak Him forth to others.

We have seen that Jacob, God's expression, bore the image of God. But what about God's dominion? The book of Genesis ends with Joseph exercising dominion over the whole earth. Although Pharaoh was the king, he was merely a figurehead. The acting king was Joseph, who is a part of Jacob in the experience of life. In Jacob with Joseph we see the expression of God with the dominion of God. Never separate Joseph from Jacob. The record of the last fourteen chapters of Genesis mixes the two together. This indicates that Joseph is the reigning part of Jacob, and that Jacob and Joseph should not be considered as separate persons.

In this section Jacob was suffering, and Joseph was reigning. In chapter thirty-seven Joseph gave no impression that he was suffering. This chapter reveals that Jacob, not Joseph, was suffering. Some may argue and say, "When Joseph was cast into the pit, was he not suffering?" This is your interpretation, but this chapter does not tell us this. Jacob, on the contrary, suffered greatly. Although he did not weep at the death of Rachel, he wept sorrowfully when he concluded that Joseph had been devoured by a wild beast (vv. 33-35).

The record in the Bible has a purpose. Genesis, a book of God's image and dominion, shows a complete picture of how human beings can be remade and transformed to express God in His image and to represent Him with His dominion. The last fourteen chapters of Genesis indicate that after Jacob had become Israel, he bore the image of God and exercised the dominion of God. The book of Genesis is complete; it ends the way it begins. It begins and ends with God's image and dominion. In the closing chapters of Genesis, God must have been happy, and He could have said, "Now I have a man on earth expressing Me and representing Me. This man bears

My image and exercises My dominion. His words are My prophecy, and his actions are the exercise of My dominion." This is the subject of the book of Genesis.

f. Being Matured

1) The Process of Maturity

In chapter thirty-seven Jacob was an old man. With respect to both time and geography, he had journeyed a long way and had finally come to Hebron. Jacob had passed through many things. Probably no one in the Bible has passed through as many intermixed and complicated situations as Jacob did. He was dealt with by God to such an extent that he had lost nearly all he had cared for. At the time of chapter thirty-seven, Rachel had died, and Jacob was living in Hebron, enjoying the fellowship that his forefathers Abraham and Isaac had known there. It seems that Jacob had retired at Hebron. However, there is no retirement in the spiritual life, and God intervened to upset what appeared to be Jacob's retirement.

I believe that at Hebron Jacob tried his best to have a calm life. As Jacob was in fellowship there he may have had many memories. In the stillness he may have thought, "I shouldn't have grabbed Esau's heel. I shouldn't have cheated Esau or my father. Also, there was no need for me to lose my mother and to flee to my uncle Laban. Moreover, I didn't have to love Rachel so much. My, what trouble loving her caused me! Why was I so foolish? I shouldn't have been cheated by Laban. Why did I promise to work all those years to get Rachel? During the years I was with Laban, I had to suffer the heat and the cold." If you had been Jacob, what would you have done in your retirement? You might have said, "From now on, I simply want to lead a quiet life. There will be no more supplanting, no more heel-holding. Esau, Laban, and Rachel are all gone. Now is the time for me to be quiet and to enjoy life." Surely Jacob must have been enjoying a calm life there in Hebron.

Jacob loved Joseph more than all his other sons, and he made for him a coat of many colors (v. 3). If Jacob had not been in retirement, he would not have been able to make such a coat for Joseph. A busy father could not spend the time to do this. But Jacob was enjoying life and he had plenty of time to make the coat for his favorite son. This is a proof that he had retired. The mention of the coat of many colors is a little window through which we can see Jacob's character, desire, intention, goal, and disposition.

a) The Dealings in the Last Stage

After having had so many dealings under God's hand, Jacob was undoubtedly tired of human life. He was weary of supplanting, cheating, struggling, and fighting. His life was calm and he had a favorite son who was the treasure of his heart. Because of the partiality of his love for Joseph, he made him a coat of many colors. Was Jacob right in doing this? Why did he not make such a coat for Reuben, the oldest, or for Benjamin, the youngest? Although Reuben had defiled himself by committing adultery with Jacob's concubine, Benjamin was the baby of the family and was too young to have done anything wrong. Nevertheless, Jacob's heart was set firstly on Joseph and secondly on Benjamin. Jacob was partial. As we shall see, Jacob's partiality toward Joseph caused him to suffer.

Everything in this chapter is under the sovereign hand of God; nothing is coincidental. For example, immediately after Joseph's brothers had cast him into the pit, a company of Ishmaelites appeared on the scene, and his brothers decided to sell him to them. Then Joseph was taken to Egypt and sold to Potiphar, Pharaoh's chamberlain. All this was under God's sovereignty. In fact, even Jacob's partiality toward Joseph was under God's sovereignty. In chapter thirty-seven God exercised His sovereignty to deal with this partiality so that Jacob might mature.

Prior to this chapter, Jacob was a transformed person; however, he was not yet mature. To be transformed is to be changed in our natural life, whereas to be matured is to be filled with the divine life that changes us. We may be transformed in our natural life, yet not be filled with the divine life. Chapters thirty-seven through forty-five are a record of the process of Jacob's maturity. This process began in 37:1, and it lasted until 45:28. In the last five chapters of this book we see a Jacob who has fully matured. Probably in all his life Jacob never suffered as much as he did in these nine chapters. They are truly a story of Jacob's suffering. In these chapters we have the dealings in the last stage of Jacob's life. The sufferings he underwent here deeply touched his personal feelings. After these chapters, Jacob had no further dealings. Rather, he was fully matured, he was filled with the divine life, and he had the expression of God and the dominion of God.

For God's expression and dominion there is the need of maturity. Only a mature life can bear God's image and exercise His dominion. Even in chapter thirty-seven Jacob could not bear God's image or exercise God's dominion. Although he was transformed, he was not yet mature. His partiality toward Joseph proves that he was not mature. This partial love was a weak point. Do not think that a transformed person cannot be partial in his love or have other weak points. Therefore, God sovereignly placed Jacob under His hand that he might become mature.

(1) Jacob Being Robbed of the Treasure of His Heart under God's Sovereign Hand

In order to become mature, Jacob firstly had to suffer the loss of Joseph, the treasure of his heart. It seems impossible that Joseph could have been lost. He could easily have died of a certain illness, but how could Jacob have lost him? Although he was not to die, because he was still very useful, he had to be taken away from Jacob. Now we need to consider by what way Jacob's loss of Joseph took place.

(a) Joseph Bringing His Father Evil Reports of His Brothers

Verse 2 says that Joseph brought to his father evil reports regarding his brothers. Of all the twelve sons of Jacob, only two were good—Joseph, who was seventeen years of age, and his younger brother, Benjamin, who was still a small child. The other ten brothers were dirty and evil, and Joseph constantly brought to his father evil reports about them. The first of these ten brothers, Reuben, committed adultery with his father's concubine (35:22); and the fourth, Judah, committed fornication with his daughter-in-law, who was disguised as a harlot (38:12-26). Levi and Simeon were cruel, having avenged the defilement of their sister, Dinah, by slaying Hamor and Shechem and plundering their city (34:25-29). The fact that these brothers conspired to slay their own brother in the flesh indicates how sinful they were. It is difficult to believe that they were the sons of a chosen, holy family and that they were to become the fathers of the tribes of the children of Israel chosen of God. However, had his brothers been good instead of evil, Joseph would never have been lost.

(b) Israel Loving Joseph More Than All His Sons

As we have seen, "Israel loved Joseph more than all his sons, because he was the son of his old age: and he made him a coat of many colors" (v. 3, Heb.). Because of the partiality of Jacob's love for Joseph, he had to lose him in order to mature. The loss of Joseph was mainly due to Jacob's partial love for him.

(c) Joseph's Brothers Hating Him

Verse 4 says, "And when his brethren saw that their father loved him more than all his brethren, they hated him, and could not speak peaceably unto him." Jacob's partial love for Joseph caused his other sons to hate Joseph. Because a partial love for a child creates hatred among the other children, parents should avoid it. Our love must be equal and impartial. Joseph's brothers also hated him because he was good and because he gave evil reports about them to their father.

(d) Joseph Having Two Dreams that Caused
His Brothers to Hate Him More

Joseph had two dreams that caused his brothers to hate him even more (vv. 5-11). These dreams came from God. There were two dreams because two is the number of confirmation and testimony. Both dreams refer to one thing, for both the sheaves and the stars bowed down to Joseph. In our eyes Joseph's brothers, being adulterers, fornicators, murderers, and haters, should have been condemned to hell. But Joseph did not dream about thorns and robbers surrounding a gentle teenager. Rather, he dreamed of sheaves and stars. A sheaf is a bundle into which wheat is bound after reaping. This indicates that, in God's eyes, Jacob's sons were His crop on earth. Moreover, they were not a green crop; they were a ripened and harvested crop that had been bound into sheaves. In the second dream the members of Joseph's family are signified by the sun, the moon, and the eleven stars. They were bright lights shining in the heavens. We have pointed out in the life-study of Revelation that the sun, the moon, and the stars in Revelation 12 and Genesis 37 represent the totality of God's people. During Joseph's time, his family was the totality of God's people on earth. According to our view, they were evil and dirty, but according to God's view, they were bright and heavenly. Likewise, according to our human nature, we are ugly, evil, and unclean. Nevertheless, we have been chosen, redeemed, forgiven, regenerated, and transformed. Thus, we are God's farm, God's crop. Eventually, we shall be God's harvest; we shall be reaped by Him and become sheaves. Furthermore, we are heavenly lights. What a vision this is!

God was sovereign in giving Joseph these dreams, for they reveal the nature, the position, the function, and the goal of God's people on earth. God's people are His harvest and His lights. As the harvest, they have life, and as the heavenly hosts, they have light. In the first dream there is life, and in the second, light. Life and light are two characteristics of God's people.

In the first dream the sheaves bowed down to Joseph's sheaf, and in the second, the sun, the moon, and the eleven stars bowed down to him. When Joseph told his father and brothers about his second dream, Jacob rebuked him and said, "What is this dream that thou has dreamed? Shall I and thy mother and thy brethren indeed come to bow down ourselves to thee to the earth?" (v. 10). Joseph was not political; rather, he was genuine, frank, faithful, and straight. If he had not frankly told them about his dreams, there would have been no problem with this. In the church life we should be like Joseph, not like politicians. However, not many among us are frank, straight Josephs; instead, most of us are "wise" politicians.

You may have a dream, but you would never tell others about it. Joseph on the contrary was genuine, frank, open, and transparent; he was happy to tell his brothers about his dreams. But this provoked their hatred even more, and Joseph's transparency caused him to be "crucified." Many times I also have been "crucified" for my transparency. However, if I become political, I shall no longer be like Joseph. Humanly speaking, Joseph was wrong in telling his brothers about his dreams. If we had been Joseph, many of us probably would have said, "You know, I had a good dream last night." When others asked us about the dream, we would say, "Forgive me, I can't tell you about it." This is the political "wisdom" of today's Christians. Will you be a politician or a Joseph? If you are a Joseph, you will be "crucified" for your frankness. Because of Joseph's dreams, his brothers hated him more than ever.

(e) Joseph's Brothers Going Shepherding

Joseph's brothers went to feed their father's flock in Shechem (v. 12). Shepherding was their means of making a living. Through this livelihood of theirs they sovereignly had the opportunity to put Joseph away from Jacob.

(f) Joseph Sent to See His Brothers

Later Joseph was sent by his father to see his brothers (vv. 13-17). This also was sovereign of the Lord. The fact that Jacob sent Joseph to see his brothers is another indication that Jacob was enjoying life. If he had been busy, he would not have thought of sending Joseph to do this. But because he had nothing to do, he suddenly thought about his sons and was concerned for them. When Joseph was asked to go to his brothers, he was obedient. He did not gossip or speak idle words. Rather, he took his father's word and went to find his brothers.

(g) Joseph's Brothers Conspiring to Slay Him

When Joseph's brothers "saw him afar off, even before he came near unto them, they conspired against him to slay him" (v. 18). They gave Joseph a title, saying to one another,

"Behold, this master of dreams cometh" (v. 19, Heb.). They conspired together to slay Joseph and then to deceive their father about what had happened (v. 20).

(h) Reuben Wanting to Deliver Joseph out of His Brothers' Hands

Reuben, the eldest brother, wanted to deliver Joseph out of their hands. When he heard of their plot, "he delivered him out of their hands; and said, Let us not kill him....Shed no blood, but cast him into this pit that is in the wilderness, and lay no hand upon him" (vv. 21-22). Reuben's intention was to take him out of their hands and to deliver him to his father.

(i) Judah Proposing to Sell Him and Not to Slay Him

In Reuben's absence Judah, the fourth brother, proposed that instead of slaying Joseph, they sell him to the Ishmaelites (vv. 25-27). Judah said, "What profit is it if we slay our brother, and conceal his blood? Come, and let us sell him to the Ishmaelites, and let not our hand be upon him; for he is our brother and our flesh" (vv. 26-27).

(j) Joseph Being Sold to Ishmaelites of Midian

Joseph was sold to Ishmaelites from Midian (v. 28). Ishmael was the son of Abraham by Hagar, and Midian was the son of Abraham by his last wife, Keturah. Both the Ishmaelites and the Midianites represent the flesh. Hatred is related to the flesh, and the flesh is connected to the world represented by Egypt. Due to his brothers' hatred, Joseph was handed over to the flesh, and the flesh brought him down to Egypt. But God is sovereign over all. In His sovereignty, He used everything, including the flesh and the hatred of Joseph's brothers. Every negative thing in this chapter—the hatred, the flesh, Pharaoh, and Pharaoh's chamberlain, Potiphar—was sovereignly used by God to fulfill His purpose.

(k) Jacob Losing the Treasure of His Heart

Through God's sovereignty, which was exercised in all these seemingly coincidental matters, Jacob lost the treasure of his heart (vv. 31-35). After the death of Rachel, Jacob's heart was wholly set upon Joseph. Suddenly and much to his surprise, Joseph was snatched away. Jacob's sons deceived him into believing that Joseph had been devoured by an evil beast (vv. 32-33). When Jacob heard this news, he "rent his clothes, and put sackcloth upon his loins, and mourned for his son many days" (v. 34). To Jacob, there was nothing more on earth. He was not only broken; he had been robbed to the point where he had nothing left. Although his children tried to comfort him, he refused to be comforted and said, "I will go down into Sheol unto my son mourning" (v. 35, Heb.). Jacob was utterly despondent, and nothing could comfort him. He had lost his heart treasure. How deep and personal was this dealing!

In principle, sooner or later we all shall pass through such a dealing. Do not be frightened at the prospect of this. Praise the Lord that we not only have chapter thirty-seven, but also chapter forty-seven, where we see a glorious result. Chapter thirty-seven is simply a narrow underpass. Jacob had to walk this narrow underpass and experience a suffering that touched his heart profoundly that he might mature. Nothing in his entire life touched him as personally and as deeply as the loss of Joseph.

(1) The Midianites Bringing Joseph to Egypt and Selling Him to Potiphar

Joseph, however, was not lost. God was preserving him in Egypt. Joseph's being brought to Egypt was actually his transfer from "high school" to the "university." In Egypt he would receive his higher education, the education which would prepare him for kingship. Jacob, of course, did not know this. In Jacob's eyes, Joseph had been devoured by a beast. But in God's eyes Joseph was being prepared for kingship. Therefore, God could say, "Jacob, there is no need to mourn. Instead, you must rejoice because your son is in Egypt being prepared to be a king."

LIFE-STUDY OF GENESIS

MESSAGE NINETY-THREE

BEING MATURED
THE PROCESS OF MATURITY

(2)

Before we consider further Jacob's dealings at Hebron, we need to point out the difference between transformation and maturity. The last stage of transformation is maturity. Maturity means the fullness of life. When one is mature, he has no shortage of life. The more life we have, the more mature we are. An infant is obviously not mature, but a grown man is mature. For a human being to be mature means that his life has come into fullness.

Transformation is a metabolic change in life. Thus, transformation is not a matter of fullness; it is a matter of change. Plants do not require transformation, because they are simply plants. But we, the children of God, need transformation. Only through transformation can we reach maturity. We have a natural life, but this life is not good for God's economy. Although our natural life does not need to be replaced, it does need to be metabolically changed. We must not only have an outward change in appearance, but also an inward change in nature. Although our human life is necessary for God's economy, it should not remain a natural human life; it should be a human life that has been transformed in nature so that the divine life may be mingled with the transformed human life to become one. This is a deep matter.

At least two verses in the New Testament unveil the matter of transformation. Romans 12:2 says, "Do not be conformed to this age, but be transformed by the renewing of the mind." The Greek word translated "transformed" in this verse also appears in 2 Corinthians 3:18. According to the Greek, this verse should be rendered, "And we all with unveiled face, beholding and reflecting as a mirror the glory of the Lord, are being transformed into the same image from glory to glory, even as from the Lord Spirit." The word "transformed" in these verses indicates that in our Christian life we need a metabolic change. We do not need outward correction and alteration; rather, we need an inward change in nature and in life.

This metabolic change begins with regeneration. When we were saved, we were not only justified and our sins forgiven; we were also regenerated. At regeneration a new life, the divine life, was put into our spirit. From the time of our regeneration, this life has been transforming our natural life. As the divine life changes our natural life, it imparts more and more of the divine life into our being. Therefore, transformation is the change of our natural life. When this change reaches the point of fullness, the time of maturity has come. To repeat, the last stage of transformation is maturity. Maturity is not a matter of our being changed; it is a matter of having the divine life imparted to us again and again until we have the fullness of life.

Let us now apply this matter to Jacob. Although Jacob underwent many changes between chapters twenty-five and thirty-seven, we do not see any further change in him after chapter thirty-seven. In chapter twenty-five Jacob was a supplanter, a heel-holder. As we read from chapter twenty-six to thirty-six, which covers a period of approximately twenty-five years, we see how Jacob changed. Everything that happened to him during these years was for his transformation. When in chapter thirty-seven Jacob lost his beloved son, Joseph, he was absolutely different from the person he was in chapter twenty-seven. In a spiritual sense, the Jacob in chapter twenty-seven had several hands to use in grasping whatever he wanted. He grasped what belonged to his father, to Esau, and, later on, to Laban. However, in chapter thirty-seven Jacob did not even use his own two hands. The Jacob in this chapter seems to have no skill or ability; instead, it seems that he is not able to do anything. This indicates that he has absolutely changed. From chapter thirty-seven until the end of this book, we do not see any further change in this man. In these chapters we see a person who has not only been changed; we see a person who is full of life. In chapter thirty-seven we see neither change nor the fullness of life. The change took place before this chapter, and the fullness of life was reached after it.

I would ask you to read chapters twenty-seven, thirty-seven, and forty-seven once again. In chapter twenty-seven we see a supplanter. He had many hands, he was able to do everything, and no one could defeat him. Whoever came in contact with Jacob—his father, his brother, or his uncle—was the loser. Jacob, on the contrary, always came out ahead. He made a gain from his brother, from his father, and from his uncle. He even made a gain from Rachel, Leah, and their two maids. However, at the time of Rachel's death, Jacob began to suffer loss. But even this loss produced a gain, and that gain was Benjamin. In chapter thirty-seven Jacob underwent another loss, the loss of Joseph. In this chapter Jacob did not gain anything. From this point onward, Jacob lost one thing after another. Eventually, in chapter forty-seven, he gained the fullness of life. The fullness of life is blessing, which is the overflow of life. When you are filled past the brim with life, this life will overflow into others. This overflow is the blessing. Therefore, in chapter twenty-seven we see a supplanter; in chapter thirty-seven, a transformed man; and in chapter forty-seven, a mature person. Jacob's transformation began at the time God came in to touch him (32:25), and it continued until chapter thirty-seven, when the process of transformation was relatively complete. However, in this chapter Jacob did not yet have maturity, the fullness of life. In order to gain this, he had to experience the dealings in the last stage, the dealings at Hebron.

Now we must consider how Jacob, a transformed person, could be filled with life. Human beings are vessels. However, unlike jars and bottles, we are not vessels without feeling, sense, or will. If you want to fill a bottle with a certain liquid, the bottle has no opinion or feeling about it. There is no need to have the consent of the bottle before we fill it. But it is difficult to put something in us living vessels because we are filled with opinions, desires, and intentions. Parents know how difficult it is to put medicine into their children. Likewise, it is not an easy matter for God to put His life into us.

Now I want to point out a hidden matter in this book. Jacob's first dealing in the last stage was the loss of Joseph. Joseph was seventeen years old when he was sold (37:2), and he was thirty years old when he stood before Pharaoh (41:46). Following this, there were the seven plenteous years. It was probably one or two years later that Jacob sent his sons to Egypt to buy grain. Therefore, from the selling of Joseph to the sending of Jacob's sons to Egypt was a period of at least twenty years. The Bible does not afford us any record of what Jacob did during these years. It only gives us an account of what Joseph experienced. As far as the record of Jacob is concerned, this period of twenty years was a time of silence.

What do you think Jacob was doing during this time? If you had been Jacob, what would you have done? I have considered this matter very much, and I think I have discovered something. During these years Jacob had nothing to do. He had no lack and he had no ambition. Jacob had cared only for Rachel, not for Leah and the two maids. After Rachel died, Jacob's heart was set on Joseph, who was taken away from him about a year later. After Joseph was taken away, Jacob had virtually nothing left. Therefore, during these silent years he was a person without any ambitions, interests, or things to do. This must have been the time God imparted Himself into Jacob more and more. How different were these twenty years from the twenty years with Laban! During the twenty years with Laban (31:41), Jacob had struggled against Laban and had been concerned about dealing with Rachel, Leah, the maids, and all his children. But in these twenty years at Hebron Jacob was released from any bondage or occupation. He was not only retired—he was free.

The only thing that could not be taken away from Jacob was God's presence. At Hebron Jacob constantly lived in fellowship with God. Through the loss of Joseph, Jacob became a jar that was absolutely open to God. Joseph's presence might have been a hindrance to Jacob's openness to God. But now, after the loss of Joseph, Jacob was free from every frustration and was completely open to the Lord. Undoubtedly, Jacob thought about Joseph day after day. He had concluded that Joseph had been devoured by an evil beast, but this had not been confirmed. Hence, Jacob might have thought that perhaps he would see Joseph again. This pressed Jacob to God and opened him up to God. The more he thought about Joseph, the more open he was. During all these years, Jacob was a jar open to the heavens, and the heavenly rain was continuously falling into him. In this period of time Jacob was daily in the presence of God, being filled with the divine life.

(2) Jacob Being Stricken with Famine

Suddenly, beyond Jacob's control, he was struck with famine, for "the famine was in the land of Canaan" (42:5). God used this famine to deal with Jacob and to lift up Joseph. We have seen that in the twenty years between the loss of Joseph and the coming of this famine, Jacob had nothing to do. He probably felt that his life was over and that he was waiting to go to his people, that is, to die. He never thought that he would go to Egypt to have another new beginning. Of course, he never considered that Joseph would be there waiting for him. Jacob might have thought, "What new thing can happen to me? I am old, I have had four wives, and I have many children and grandchildren. My life is over." But as he was thinking this, God's hand suddenly came upon him, and Jacob was stricken by famine. What an exercise this severe famine must have been to Jacob's entire being! Before the famine struck, he was at peace; he was not short of anything. But suddenly there was no food. As the head of such a large family, he was certainly exercised about what to do in the midst of this famine. God used it to press Jacob.

God also used this famine to uplift Joseph. To Joseph, the famine was a great thing. If there had been no famine after the seven plenteous years, Pharaoh would have said to Joseph, "Joseph, you have fooled me in interpreting my dream. After the seven years of plenty, the famine has not come." But the famine did come, and it was Joseph's power and authority. The seven years of plenty were a partial fulfillment of Pharaoh's dream, but Joseph's interpretation of that dream had not been completely confirmed. Pharaoh was probably waiting to see what would happen after the seven years of plenty. If the famine had not come, he might have executed Joseph. Thus, Joseph needed the seven years of famine in order to be uplifted. This famine was Joseph's glory. God used it to crown him. Joseph's reign was a type of the millennium, of God's heavenly reign over the earth.

(3) Jacob Being Forced to Send His Sons to Egypt to Buy Grain

Because of the famine, Jacob was forced to send his ten sons to Egypt to buy grain (42:1-3). He had lost Joseph, and now he had to send away ten of his remaining eleven sons. In ancient times it was a long journey from Hebron to Egypt; it took about eight to ten days to travel this distance. After the ten sons had left for Egypt, only the youngest, Benjamin, who was in his early twenties, remained with Jacob. The ten sons must have been away from Jacob for nearly a month. This period of time was a great exercise to this old man. He might have thought, "Now my ten sons are gone. I wonder what will happen to them. Will they return safely? Will they be able to buy food and bring it home with them?" What an exercise this was to Jacob! This dealing was not for Jacob's transformation; it was for his maturity. God used it to fill Jacob with the very element of the divine life.

(4) Jacob's Second Son, Simeon, Being Detained in Egypt

When Jacob's sons returned from Egypt with the grain, Jacob learned that Simeon had been detained in Egypt (42:24, 36). This also was a suffering and an exercise to him. When we consider these chapters again on Joseph's side, the reigning side, we shall see how wise Joseph was. He did not keep the money, but rather had it put into the bags of grain (42:25). When one of them discovered that his money had been put in the mouth of his sack, he told his brothers about it, "and their heart failed them, and they were afraid, saying one to another, What is this that God hath done unto us?" (42:28). When they returned home and discovered "every man's bundle of money was in his sack," they all, including

Jacob, were afraid (42:35). Jacob seemed to say, "What is this? One of my sons has been detained, and you have brought back the grain, but the money is in your sacks. Suppose we finish this grain, and the famine continues. What shall we do then? We will have to go back to Egypt to buy more grain. But what shall we do with this money?" Jacob also learned the sad news that Benjamin had to go to Egypt. After he heard this, he said, "Me have ye bereaved of my children: Joseph is not, and Simeon is not, and ye will take Benjamin away: all these things are against me" (42:36). Although Reuben promised to bring Benjamin back to Jacob, Jacob did not listen to him. Rather, he said, "My son shall not go down with you; for his brother is dead, and he is left alone" (42:38).

(5) The Famine Becoming Severe

Genesis 43:1 and 2 say, "And the famine was severe in the land. And it came to pass, when they had eaten up the grain which they had brought out of Egypt, their father said unto them, Go again, buy us a little food" (Heb.). At this point Judah reminded Jacob that in order to buy food again in Egypt, they had to take Benjamin with them. Thus, due to the severity of the famine, Jacob was forced to send his youngest son with his brothers to Egypt to buy grain (42:4, 36; 43:1-15). What a suffering this was to Jacob! God was emptying this jar, taking everything away from him. After Benjamin went with his brothers to Egypt, Jacob was left alone without any of his sons. Joseph had been taken away, Simeon had been detained in Egypt, and now all the others had also gone down to Egypt. Perhaps that night Jacob said, "What do I have left? All my twelve sons are gone, and I don't know what will happen to them. On the first trip one of my sons was detained. I cannot say how many will be detained the second time." Although this was a great suffering to Jacob, the main point here is not his suffering—it is the fact that he was being emptied out by God. God took away everything that had previously filled him, and now Jacob was completely empty. But, as we shall see, on the day Jacob received the good news about Joseph, he was completely filled with the fullness of life.

God had taken away Rachel, Joseph, Simeon, and finally all the remaining ten sons, including Benjamin. When Benjamin was with his brothers in Egypt being reconciled to Joseph, Joseph was very happy. Jacob, however, was at home alone, being emptied out by the Lord. Night after night Jacob probably had the deep sense that he was an empty vessel. Everything that had once filled him had been taken away. This was altogether sovereign of the Lord. The Lord was preparing him to be filled with the divine life.

Let us now consider the situation from Joseph's point of view. The way Joseph dealt with his brothers was also sovereign of the Lord. Joseph detained Simeon and then had all the money bags returned to the others (42:24-25). What was Joseph's purpose in detaining Simeon? Why did he not detain one of the other brothers? I believe that Simeon was the leader of the conspiracy against Joseph. Simeon was cruel. He and Levi had killed Hamor and Shechem and destroyed their city (34:25-29). In 49:5 Jacob said, "Simeon and Levi are brethren; their swords are weapons of violence" (Heb.). I also believe that Simeon took the lead in proposing that Joseph be killed. Although Joseph's brothers did not recognize him, he was very clear about them. When he first saw them, he gave them a difficult time in order to touch their conscience. They said to one another, "We are verily guilty concerning our brother, in that we saw the anguish of his soul, when he besought us, and we would not hear; therefore is this distress come upon us" (42:21). Then Joseph "took from them Simeon, and bound him before their eyes" (42:24). This must have caused Simeon to consider what he had done to Joseph. During his imprisonment, Simeon might have thought, "Why am I the only one being detained? Oh, I never should have done that to Joseph." What Joseph did to Simeon was truly sovereign of the Lord.

Not even when the brothers came to Egypt the second time did Joseph reveal himself to them immediately. If I had been he, I would have said, "I am Joseph. How good it is that you have come back with Benjamin, my brother. Please return home and tell my father about me." Instead of doing this, Joseph had a feast prepared for his brothers (43:16). This surprised them and caused them to be afraid. After the feast, Joseph commanded that his brothers' sacks be filled with food, that their money be put in the mouth of the sacks, and that his silver cup be placed in the sack of the youngest. Surely Joseph's brothers must have been happy to leave Egypt. But Joseph's steward overtook them and accused them of stealing his master's cup. When the cup was found in Benjamin's sack, the brothers "rent their clothes" and returned to the city (44:13). They must have been terrified. Joseph, however, was not punishing them; he was touching their conscience. It was only after all this that Joseph made himself known to his brothers.

God sovereignly did not allow the good news about Joseph to reach Jacob at an early date. As Joseph and his brothers were happy together in Egypt, Jacob was suffering in Canaan, waiting for his sons to return. The longer Jacob's sons remained in Egypt, the more he suffered. But the more Jacob suffered, the better it was for him. Jacob's long wait for the return of his sons was surely a trial. This was under the sovereign hand of God to prolong Jacob's suffering that he might be emptied of everything. When the good news came to Jacob, he was absolutely empty.

Our preoccupations frustrate the growth of life. Due to these preoccupations, there is not much room in our being for the divine life. But when Jacob heard the news about Joseph in Egypt, he had been emptied of every preoccupation. Nothing was occupying his inner being. Rachel had died, his twelve sons had gone away, and Jacob had been utterly emptied out. He was so empty that when the good news came, he was not excited by it. In fact, his heart was even rather cold (45:26, Heb.). When the news came regarding Joseph, Jacob had not only been transformed; he was completely filled with the divine life. He had become mature.

Jacob's history must also become our biography. We must believe that everything in our daily life is under God's sovereign hand. Everything that happened to Jacob was for his transformation and maturity. In order to be transformed, Jacob had to be pressed into situations that gave him no choice except to undergo a change. Like Jacob, after we have been changed, God will sovereignly use persons, things, and events to empty us of everything that has filled us and to take away every preoccupation so that we may have an increased capacity to be filled with God.

If we read the book of Genesis again and again, we shall see that the two main aspects of Jacob's experience are transformation and maturity. It is not simply a matter of being chosen, called, saved, and regenerated. We still need the process of transformation and the process of maturity. However, few Christians pay attention to these matters. For this reason, God's economy has been frustrated among His children. Because there is such a lack of transformation and maturity among God's people, we have not yet seen the accomplishment of His eternal purpose. But this lack is now being made up in the Lord's recovery, which today is the recovery of Christ as life and of the church as our living. In the coming days many saints in the Lord's recovery will be transformed. Even now, some are in the process of maturity. The Lord is working among us, on us, and in us to transform us and to cause us to mature.

When I was young, I read a number of books about overcoming sin, but I did not read one book about transformation. With us today it is not simply a matter of overcoming sin. Even if you overcome every sin, you still need to be transformed. If we are not transformed, the overcoming of sin does not mean very much for God's economy. For God's economy we do not merely need the overcoming of sin; we also need the transformation of our being and the fullness of His life. God is concerned about transformation and maturity. This is His need today.

Along with maturity, we also have the aspect of reigning. The mature life becomes the reigning life. We have pointed out that Jacob and Joseph should not be considered as two separate persons, but as two aspects of a complete person who has the fullness of experience. We all should have the aspect of maturity and the aspect of reigning. Actually, it was not Joseph who was reigning in Egypt—it was Jacob, Israel. If you could have asked an Egyptian who was reigning over him, he would have said that a Hebrew, an Israelite, was reigning.

Israel was reigning in Egypt because Israel had matured in life. Only a matured life can be used by God for His kingdom, for His reigning.

From Jacob's experience we see that everything that happens to us is under God's sovereignty for our transformation and maturity. Nothing is accidental. God's eternal purpose can only be accomplished through our transformation and maturity. Jacob's experience is an excellent illustration of this.

b) Jacob's Reaction

Jacob actually did not react to all these dealings in the last stage for his maturity. He no longer had his own activity. Rather, without any struggle, he absolutely submitted to his circumstances. He took all the situations as they happened (43:11, 13). Concerning the probable loss of his sons, he said, "If I be bereaved of my children, I am bereaved" (43:14). What submission this was!

In his early days Jacob always trusted in his own skill and ability. However, after the dealings in the last stage, his trust was no longer in himself, but in God. Jacob had come to know God's mercy. In his experiences through all his life, he eventually realized that it was God's mercy, not his skill and ability, that had counted in his situations. And he had also learned that this merciful God is all-sufficient, not only almighty, to meet his needs in every kind of situation. Hence, Jacob said to his sons, "God all-sufficient give you mercy before the man" (43:14, Heb.). Now his trust and rest are altogether in the mercy of his all-sufficient God, no longer in himself and in his ability. Here we see a man who has been fully transformed for maturity.

LIFE-STUDY OF GENESIS

MESSAGE NINETY-FOUR

BEING MATURED
THE MANIFESTATION OF MATURITY

(1)

In the last message we pointed out the difference between transformation and maturity. Transformation is the metabolic change in life, and maturity is the fullness in life. Maturity is the last stage of transformation. As we are being transformed, we are also being filled with life. The more we are transformed, the more we are filled with life. No one can be filled with life without being transformed. The degree of the filling is in proportion to the degree of transformation. When we have been completely transformed, we shall be filled with life in its fullness.

From chapter twenty-five to chapter thirty-two we see no change in Jacob's life. According to the record of chapter twenty-five, Jacob began supplanting even before he was born. Jacob's transformation began from the time God touched him. This took place in chapter thirty-two. Although in chapters twenty-five to thirty-two there is no transformation, no change in life, these chapters are full of dealings. Remember, Jacob spent twenty years under the hand of Laban. During those years he suffered one dealing after another. After those twenty years of dealings, one night, at Peniel, the Lord came and touched Jacob's strongest part, his thigh, and Jacob became lame. That marked the beginning of Jacob's transformation, and the process of transformation continued from chapter thirty-two to chapter thirty-seven. In these chapters we see a picture of how Jacob was being transformed. However, after the time Jacob lost Joseph in chapter thirty-seven, we see no further change in Jacob's life. The reason for this is that at that time his transformation was nearly completed. Thus, in chapter thirty-seven Jacob's maturity began.

There are three distinct periods in Jacob's life: the period of dealings, the period of transformation, and the period of maturity. If you compare three chapters, twenty-seven, thirty-seven, and forty-seven, you will see the dealings, the transformation, and the maturity. In chapter forty-seven Jacob's maturity reaches its peak and it is fully manifested. In this message we shall consider the manifestation of Jacob's maturity.

2) Manifestation of Maturity

a) No Blame at Hearing That Joseph Was Still Alive

The first sign of Jacob's maturity is the fact that he did not blame his sons when he heard the news about Joseph's being alive in Egypt (45:21-28). Although they had conspired to kill Joseph, eventually sold him into slavery, and lied to their father about him, Jacob did not blame them. If he had not been mature, he would have said, "What have you done to me? Don't you know that you nearly killed me?" But, according to the record of chapter forty-five, Jacob did not blame anyone.

Genesis 45:26 and 27 mention Jacob's heart and his spirit. Although some so-called Christians think that the spirit and the heart are the same, we know by the true light of the Bible that the heart is the heart and that the spirit is the spirit. Verse 26 says that "Jacob's heart became numb" (Heb.), and verse 27 says that "the spirit of Jacob their father revived." When Jacob heard the good news concerning Joseph, his heart became numb. Some versions say that his heart became cold. The Hebrew word means numb, having no feeling or sense. Although Jacob's heart was numb, his spirit revived.

We need to be like Jacob. In certain situations, our heart should be numb, and our spirit should be revived. Recently, many of the young people have been getting "drunk" with Christ. But I would ask them these questions: Is your heart numb? Have you been revived in your spirit or in your heart? I am not certain that they have been revived in the spirit.

Perhaps their excitement is a mixture of the spirit and the heart. This mixture indicates that there has been no division between soul and spirit. According to Hebrews 4:12, the spirit must be divided from the soul. A mature saint is one who is revived, living, and excited in spirit, but numb in heart. Although we should be hot in spirit, we should be cold in heart. Our spirit must be a stove full of blazing fire, but our heart must be a refrigerator.

When we are young in our spiritual life, we are revived mainly in heart, and we are numb in spirit. The younger you are, the more you are revived in heart and numb in spirit. But as you grow, you become somewhat numb in heart and revived in spirit. In chapter forty-five we see that Jacob was a mature saint. Hence, the Bible says that his heart was numb, but that his spirit revived. This was a manifestation of his maturity. Such a saying about the heart and the spirit can be found only in the Bible, not in any secular writings.

Because Jacob's heart became numb and because his spirit was revived, he did not blame anyone or anything. In his heart there was no feeling, sense, or reaction. His soul life was completely deadened, and his heart was like wood. Because Jacob's soul and spirit had been divided, the good news concerning Joseph issued in the reviving of his spirit, not in the stirring up of his heart.

Do not think that I intend to cool down the excitement of the young people. No, the young people must be excited. Children are children, fathers are fathers, and grandfathers are grandfathers. How childish for a grandfather to be easily excited! It is the children who should be excited. If they are not, they may be physically or mentally ill. Healthy children are always easily excited.

When I returned from a recent trip to Europe, I brought back some souvenirs for two of my grandchildren. To the one, a boy of seven years of age, I gave a nutcracker, and to the other, a boy less than four years of age, I gave a little toy car. These boys were so excited that they could hardly eat, sleep, or stand still. The older boy even brought his nutcracker to school to show his teacher and classmates. We were very happy to see the excitement of our grandsons, for it was an indication that they are living and healthy. However, suppose I gave such a gift to one of the elders and, in his excitement, he showed it to the other elders. If he did this, I would doubt that he was the proper brother to be an elder. It is wrong for an older person to be excited like this. The young people, on the contrary, are young people, and they need to be excited.

Because Jacob was not excited, he did not blame others regarding the loss of Joseph. No one can learn this merely by being taught. Teaching about it simply does not work. If I teach my seven-year-old grandson not to blame his brother, it will be of no avail. As soon as I turn my back, he will blame his younger brother. Because he is at the blaming age and has a blaming life, he cannot keep from blaming others. Of course, this does not mean that we should not train our children. We must discipline them. But learning not to blame others depends on the growth of life, not upon outward teachings.

In Genesis chapter forty-five we see a saint who did not pretend, perform, or act. Because he had come into maturity, his heart was numb, and he did not blame others. Some may think that verse 26 indicates that Jacob's heart was shocked at the good news and that it became numb because of the shock. I do not believe this. When a young person receives some shocking news, his mind, emotion, and will continue to be active. They are not numb in the least. I have seen some who were severely shocked, yet their soul was very active. But when Jacob, an old man, received the good news about Joseph, he had no reaction: his heart was numb. This is a sign of Jacob's maturity in life.

Young people, do not try to imitate this maturity. There is no need to perform. You are young people, not fathers or grandfathers. Therefore, do not try to behave like a grandfather. Do not act as if you were numb in heart and revived in spirit. I appreciate it when my grandchildren are excited, for that behavior is genuine, natural, and spontaneous. It is not a performance. The young people should not be troubled by this message on the manifestation of maturity. I say again, the young need to be excited. If a young person is not excited, he is not normal. Do not pretend to be more mature than you are. Pretending only kills.

b) Offering Sacrifices to God at Beersheba before Going to See Joseph

Genesis 46:1 says, "And Israel took his journey with all that he had, and came to Beersheba, and offered sacrifices unto the God of his father Isaac." In 35:1 God told Jacob to arise and go up to Bethel and to make an altar there unto God. But in 46:1 Jacob went to Beersheba to offer sacrifices on his own initiative. This verse does not say that he offered a sacrifice; it says that he "offered sacrifices." He went to Beersheba for the purpose of offering sacrifices to God. This verse does not tell us that Jacob prayed, praised, or gave thanks to God. Rather, it says that he offered sacrifices. He did so that he might have true fellowship with God. Using New Testament terms, Jacob offered for God's satisfaction the Christ he had experienced in many aspects. This is the worship God desires to receive from us. But this worship is related to our growth in life. When we are matured, we shall frequently worship God in this way. God did not ask Jacob to go to Beersheba and offer sacrifices. Jacob went there of his own accord to offer Christ for God's satisfaction.

The next verse says, "And God spake unto Israel in the visions of the night." Notice that this verse does not speak of a vision but of visions. During that night in Beersheba, God appeared to Jacob at least twice and spoke to him. When we are young in life, we often say, "Lord, what is Your mind? Please tell me what You want me to do." However, in chapter forty-six Jacob did not say this. Instead of asking God for guidance, he offered sacrifices for His satisfaction. Then, during the night, God appeared to him. Here we see the kind of fellowship a saint mature in life has with God. There is no praying, praising, giving of thanks, or seeking. Instead, there is the offering of Christ to God for God's satisfaction. In this kind of worship, Jacob had fellowship with God, and God appeared to him. This surely is another manifestation of Jacob's maturity.

We cannot imitate Jacob's degree of life. Our degree of life is always related to our growth in life. If we do not have the growth, we simply cannot have the degree. Although you may pretend, perform, or act, you still do not have the degree of life you are imitating. Therefore, we all need to grow. When we grow into a certain degree of life, spontaneously we shall have the manifestation of life related to that degree of life.

c) No Excitement Showing Looseness of Self at Seeing Joseph

Another sign of Jacob's maturity was that he displayed no excitement showing looseness of self at seeing Joseph (46:28-30). Jacob was not excited, because his heart had become numb. It is all right for young people to be excited, but there should be no looseness in their excitement. There must still be a certain amount of control. Sometimes my grandchildren are so loose in their excitement that they are destructive. One of them became so excited that he even walked on the furniture. Children who display such looseness need to be disciplined. Nevertheless, you young people must be excited, and the churches and halls filled with young people must be exciting places. You may even "raise the roof" with your excitement.

The more the young people are excited, the better it is; for the more excited they are, the faster they grow. I have never seen a numb child grow. Children need to be active and excited. This indicates that they are living, healthy, and normal. I enjoy the excitement of the young people because it is a sign of their normality. This assures me that they will grow. However, in your excitement there should not be any looseness or lawlessness. In the midst of your excitement, your spirit may say, "Be careful. Don't do too much or go too far." This control is right.

Young people, I encourage you to be excited. Although I am an old man, I do not like to be in an old people's meeting. I prefer to attend the young people's meeting and stay in a church filled with young people. Although they may not yet have transformation and maturity, they are living. The presence of life gives me the assurance that growth, transformation, and maturity will eventually follow.

d) No Begging after Arriving in Egypt

After Jacob arrived in Egypt, he did not beg for anything. However, when he was young, he begged wherever he went. He not only begged; he supplanted others and robbed them.

Jacob expected to have everything for himself. If he stayed with you, what was in your pocket would sooner or later end up in his.

In the early years, Jacob robbed his father, his brother, his uncle, and even his wives. Eventually, when he was old, he himself was robbed and was bereft even of his sons. But, in his maturity, he did not beg for anything. According to his position after he arrived in Egypt, he had the standing to claim everything. However, he did not ask for anything. This is a strong sign of maturity. A mature person is not demanding. Instead of demanding, requiring, or asking, Jacob stretched forth his hands to bless others. If we beg, ask, and demand, it proves we are young in life. We, the saints, should not place demands on one another. However, this cannot be performed; it is the issue of the growth in life.

In any family the children are very demanding, much more demanding than anyone else. The grandfather, on the contrary, demands nothing; instead, he is constantly giving. But all day long the little children are asking for candy, cookies, and toys. My grandchildren are constantly asking their grandmother for things. The younger you are, the more demands you make. You may make demands of the elders, and of the brothers and sisters, but you never make demands of yourself. This proves that you are like a little baby. A baby does nothing except make demands. While the Lord may take some time to answer my prayer, the prayers of the babies are answered immediately. Making many demands is an indication that you are young.

Excessive praying may also be a sign of immaturity. Some young saints, thinking that the elders are not humble or diligent enough, pray for them in a childish way. Not praying for the elders in this way is a proof that you have grown up. Praying improperly for the elders indicates that you are young. The more you pray for them, the less mature you are. If you do not pray for the elders, then you must be grown up.

Many prayers for the church are also childish. Some saints pray, "Lord, I dare not tell you about the church. But, Lord, You know the situation. O Lord, do something about it." This kind of prayer is actually a condemnation of the church.

When you pray like this, you accuse the church. To pray this kind of prayer is to ask the Lord to deal with the church. You pray so much for the church because, in your eyes, the church does not satisfy your requirements. Paul, however, did not pray for the church in this manner. Fifty years ago, I also prayed in the way of blaming, begging, demanding, and accusing. But the Lord can testify for me that during the past six months I have not prayed for the elders in Anaheim. This does not mean that they are perfect; it means that I do not make demands of them and that I am not inwardly bothered by them.

Do not try to imitate this characteristic of maturity. Do not say, "Brother Lee told us that for six months he did not pray for the elders. From now on, I won't pray for them either." If you are able to keep from praying for the elders for six months, it is an indication that you have grown. It reveals that you are not begging or making demands.

e) No Activity for Himself while Living in Egypt

When Jacob went to Egypt, he did not engage in any activity for himself. This also is a manifestation of his maturity. Do not think that Jacob was lazy, tired, or lacked the energy to act. If he had not been able to do anything, he could have ordered his sons to do things for him. However, he did not do this. Rather, he was fully satisfied and rested absolutely in God's sovereignty. He did not depend upon his own endeavors. From his experience through the years, he had come to know that his destiny was in the hands of God, not in his own hands. As Jacob was about to bless the two sons of Joseph, he spoke of God as the One who had shepherded him all his life long (48:15-16, Heb.). Jacob's word in 48:15 and 16 is a reference to the Triune God. Here we see the Triune God in Jacob's experience, not in doctrine. In these verses Jacob said, "God, before whom my fathers Abraham and Isaac did walk, the God which shepherded me all my life long unto this day, the Angel which redeemed me from evil, bless the lads." Here we see a threefold mention of God: the God before whom Abraham and Isaac walked, the God who shepherded Jacob his whole life long, and the Angel who delivered him from evil. The God before whom Abraham and Isaac walked must be the Father; the God who shepherded Jacob his whole life must be the Spirit; and the Angel who redeemed him from all evil must be the Son. This is the Triune God in Jacob's experience.

Jacob experienced God's sovereign, shepherding care. Shepherding includes feeding. The shepherd meets every need of the sheep, who only eat and rest. Every provision for their existence comes from the shepherd. The example of the shepherd is a marvelous illustration of Jacob's realization that his destiny and existence were absolutely in the hands of the shepherding God. Thus, after he had matured and had arrived in Egypt, he did nothing for himself. This is another sign of the maturity of life.

f) Blessing People All the Time

Now we come to the strongest sign of Jacob's maturity: his blessing of others. The first thing Jacob did after arriving in Egypt was bless Pharaoh (47:7, 10). Although Pharaoh was the highest person on earth, he was under Jacob's blessing hand. According to Hebrews 7:7, "the lesser is blessed by the greater." Thus, the fact that Jacob blessed Pharaoh was a proof that he was greater than Pharaoh. After Jacob had been ushered into Pharaoh's presence, he did not speak to him in a polite, political way. He stretched forth his hand and blessed him. This is absolutely different from human culture and religion. As Jacob was leaving Pharaoh's presence, he blessed him again.

Blessing is the overflow of life, the overflow of God through someone's maturity in life. In order to bless others, we must be filled to the brim with life so that life overflows to them. Having such an overflow of life, Jacob blessed Pharaoh and the two sons of Joseph (48:8-20).

Jacob's father, Isaac, blessed blindly. But Jacob's blessing of his two grandsons, Ephraim and Manasseh, was full of insight. Although his physical eyes were dim, his spirit was clear (48:10). Joseph presented his sons to Jacob, placing Manasseh, the firstborn, at Jacob's right hand and Ephraim at Jacob's left hand. Joseph expected that Jacob would place his right hand upon Manasseh's head and his left hand upon Ephraim's head. But being very clear inwardly about what he was doing, Jacob crossed his hands and placed his right hand upon Ephraim's head. Joseph was not happy with this and he said, "Not so, my father: for this is the firstborn; put thy right hand upon his head" (48:18). But Jacob refused and said, "I know it, my son, I know it." Jacob guided his hands purposefully and intelligently. Unlike his father, Isaac, he did nothing blindly. Because he was mature and because he was one with God in life, he was clear in the spirit. In his spirit he knew that it was God's will to establish Ephraim above Manasseh.

Later we shall see that Jacob's mature life was filled with blessings. Jacob blessed his twelve sons, and those blessings were prophecies relating to the destiny of the twelve tribes of Israel. Jacob was so filled with life that he overflowed blessings to everyone he met. This is the strongest manifestation of Jacob's maturity in life.

LIFE-STUDY OF GENESIS

MESSAGE NINETY-FIVE

BLESSING

As we have pointed out many times, the book of Genesis is a book of seeds. Nearly every item in this book is a seed developed in the following books of the Bible. This is true also with the matter of blessing. In this message, another parenthesis in our life-study, we shall consider the seed of blessing sown in Genesis and its development in the Old Testament and the New Testament.

I. THE PRINCIPLE OF BLESSING

Hebrews 7:7 says, "But without any dispute the lesser is blessed by the greater." In this verse we see the principle of blessing: that the greater blesses the lesser. To be greater or lesser is not mainly a matter of age. It is a matter of the measure of Christ. We are greater or lesser according to our measure of Christ. In Matthew 11:11 the Lord Jesus said, "Truly I say to you, Among those born of women, there has not arisen a greater than John the Baptist; yet he who is smallest in the kingdom of the heavens is greater than he." Here the Lord Jesus says that John the Baptist was greater than all who had preceded him. However, the least in the kingdom of heaven is greater than John. The reason John was greater than his predecessors was that he was very close to Christ. Although Abraham was great, he did not see Christ. However, John the Baptist saw Him. But, although John was so close to Christ, he did not have Christ in him. Those in the kingdom of heaven are not only close to Christ; they have Christ within them. For this reason the least in the kingdom of heaven is greater than John. The great ones in the Old Testament could say that Christ was coming, and John the Baptist could say that Christ was in front of him. But all of us in the kingdom of heaven can say that Christ is within us. We can even say, "For to me to live is Christ" (Phil. 1:21). Hence, we are closer to Christ than John the Baptist and all who went before him.

Whether we are greater or lesser depends upon our measure of Christ. If you have more of Christ, you are greater. If you have less of Christ, you are lesser. If by having more of Christ we are greater than others, then we are qualified to bless them; for the greater always blesses the lesser. The reason for this is that the greater one has a larger measure of Christ to give to others. If you are greater than I, it means that you have a greater portion of Christ than I. If so, then you have something more of Christ to minister to me. To bless others means to minister Christ to them. Those who have just a small measure of Christ need the blessing of those who have a greater measure. We bless them with the very Christ in whom we participate and whom we enjoy. If we enjoy Christ more, then we have more of Christ to minister to others. This ministering of Christ is blessing.

II. THE MEANING OF BLESSING

It is rather difficult to give a proper definition of blessing. Years ago I could only say the blessing was asking or wishing something good for others. But after years of experience I can say that blessing is the overflow of God through someone's maturity in life. God cannot flow Himself into others without a human channel. If Christ had never been incarnated, God would not have been able to flow to man, because there would not have been a channel. God's flowing needs humanity as a channel. The only humanity God can use as the channel is one saturated and permeated with God. For this reason Jacob did not bless anyone until he had become mature. Jacob did not bless Laban or Esau. Even when he saw his brother Esau after the twenty years with Laban, he did not bless him. It was not until he went down into Egypt that he blessed Pharaoh, the highest ruler on earth (47:7, 10). At that time Jacob was filled with God. Through Jacob's blessing of Pharaoh God's blessing overflowed to Pharaoh.

A child two years of age cannot bless anyone; however, a child of seven or eight may perform some kind of blessing.

This illustrates the fact that blessing others depends upon maturity in life. Maturity in life is a matter of being filled with God. When you are full of God, you have the overflow of God, and thus you are able to bless everyone you meet. Years ago I could not say such a word about blessing. This understanding of blessing does not come from reading books; it comes only from experience.

III. THE FIRST CASE OF BLESSING

The first case of blessing in the Bible is Melchisedec's blessing of Abraham (14:18-20). Melchisedec was a type of Christ. Therefore, Melchisedec's coming to Abraham was Christ's coming to him. Melchisedec came to Abraham with bread and wine, just as the Lord also comes to us with bread and wine. Furthermore, Melchisedec came as the eternal priest, and Christ became a priest according to the eternal order of Melchisedec (Heb. 5:6). A priest brings people to God. If you would bless others, you must be God's priest. Later we shall see that in the Old Testament God commanded the priests to bless His people. Blessing is the overflow of God, and this overflow is brought to people through the priests. The first blessing was bestowed by a priest. We all need to be priests, those who bring people to God.

If we would bless others, we must be close to God ourselves. We must be priests who bring others to God. People need God's blessing because they are far away from Him. A priest eliminates the distance between God and the people; he brings those who are far off into the presence of God. On the shoulders of the high priest were two onyx stones engraved with the names of the twelve tribes of Israel, and on his breastplate there were twelve stones, also engraved with the names of the twelve tribes (Exo. 28:9-12, 15-21). Whenever the high priest entered into the Holy of Holies, he wore the breastplate and the shoulder plates. This indicated that he brought the people of Israel into the presence of God. We all realize that a priest serves God, but we may never have seen that he also eliminates the distance between the people and God. Before you are blessed by a priest, there may be a distance between you and God. But after he blesses you, this distance is taken away, and you are brought into the presence of God to share in the enjoyment of God. When Melchisedec blessed Abraham, that blessing brought him into the presence of God. Melchisedec even said, "Blessed be Abram of the most high God" (14:19). If you read Genesis 14 carefully, you will see that Melchisedec blessed Abraham with nothing other than God. He did not say, "Be blessed with a good house"; neither did he say, "Be blessed with two sons." Instead, he said, "Be blessed of the most high God." In this way, Melchisedec brought Abraham much closer to God.

IV. THE BLESSING OF THE PRIESTS

In Numbers 6:23-27 we see a pattern of blessing. Here God commanded the priests to bless the people by saying to them, "The Lord bless thee, and keep thee: the Lord make his face shine upon thee, and be gracious unto thee: the Lord lift up his countenance upon thee, and give thee peace." The blessing here is not onefold or twofold; it is threefold. The blessing is threefold because it is a matter of the dispensing of God into man. This involves the Trinity: the Father, the Son, and the Spirit. The Trinity is not a matter of doctrine; it is a matter of God's dispensing Himself into His people.

The first aspect of the blessing in Numbers 6 is related to God the Father's blessing and keeping power. The second aspect is related to the shining face of God the Son and His grace. The word "gracious" in Numbers 6:25 means more in Hebrew than the English word gracious conveys. The Hebrew meaning is to stoop in kindness to those who are inferior. This indicates that by becoming a man the second of the Trinity stooped in kindness to us, the inferior ones. When He became man, He surely stooped down from the heavens. This is grace.

I like the words "make his face shine upon thee." Have you not experienced this? Second Corinthians 4:6 says that the glory of God shines in the face of Jesus Christ. Jesus is the true light, which is God Himself (John 8:12, 1 John 1:5). God Himself as light shines over us in the face of Jesus Christ. Thus, the second aspect of the threefold blessing is related to

God the Son who stooped in kindness to visit us that we may have grace. John 1:14 says, "The Word became flesh and tabernacled among us...full of grace and reality." Because the Lord has stooped in kindness to us, we now have this blessing.

The third aspect of the blessing is related to God the Spirit's countenance and His peace. The lifting up of the Lord's countenance upon us and the giving of peace is certainly the gracious work of the third of the Trinity, the Spirit. Today the Spirit is constantly lifting up God's countenance over us and giving us peace. He gives peace not only in our environment, but also in our being—in our heart, in our spirit, and even in our mind. In the Spirit, through the Spirit, and with the Spirit we have peace. Others may be troubled in heart, mind, spirit, and environment, but we should not be troubled. Wherever we are, we have peace because the Spirit of God is with us and His countenance is uplifted over us.

In summary we may say that blessing is the bringing of people into the presence of God, into the very enjoyment of God. The threefold blessing in Numbers 6 is the pattern of blessing by the priests in the Old Testament. This pattern reveals that the proper blessing is to bring people into the presence of God, into the light of His face, and into the shining of His countenance that they may participate in His grace and may have peace. This surely is the proper blessing. How wonderful! How marvelous!

V. THE BLESSING OF THE APOSTLE

In 2 Corinthians 13:14 the Apostle Paul also gives a pattern of blessing. This verse says, "The grace of the Lord Jesus Christ, and the love of God, and the fellowship of the Holy Spirit be with you all." We have seen that a priest brings people to God. An apostle, however, brings God to people; he comes to people with God. In 2 Corinthians 13:14 we see a gracious visitation of the Triune God. In the blessing of the Apostle Paul, the Triune God comes to people for their enjoyment. This enjoyment is the love of God as the grace of Christ by the fellowship of the Holy Spirit. Love, grace, and fellowship are not three separate things; they are three aspects or stages of one thing. They are the three stages of God for our enjoyment. Love is within, grace is love expressed, and fellowship is the transmission of grace into us. Love is within God Himself. When this love is expressed, it is grace, and grace is transmitted in the fellowship. I may love a certain brother, but this love is within me. How can it be expressed? I may express it by giving him a Bible. The Bible represents grace as the expression of the love I have within me for this brother. In order to communicate this grace to him, I must actually hand the Bible to him. This is fellowship.

In the Old Testament the basic thought with respect to blessing is that of bringing people into God's presence. But in the New Testament the Apostle, coming with God, not only brought people into the presence of God; he also brought God into them. There is a great difference between the Old Testament pattern of blessing by the priests and the New Testament pattern of blessing by the Apostle. The New Testament blessing is much higher and deeper. On the one hand, to bless others is to bring them into the presence of God; on the other hand, it is to bring God into them as love, grace, and fellowship.

All Christians are familiar with the word blessing. One hymn even says, "Count your blessings, name them one by one." Undoubtedly, the concept of blessing expressed in this hymn is that blessing is a matter of being given a good wife, children, education, promotions, houses, and cars. According to this hymn, these are the blessings we should count one by one. More than thirty-five years ago, I sang this hymn during the last few hours of the year. I would gather some together and say, "Let us count the blessings of this past year, one by one." But the blessing according to the pure Word is much different from this. According to the Old Testament pattern of the blessing by the priest and the New Testament pattern of blessing by the Apostle, the proper blessing is to bring people into the presence of God and to bring God into them as grace, love, and fellowship that they may enjoy the Triune God, the Father, the Son, and the Spirit. Hence, blessing is a matter of enjoying the Triune God.

VI. THE LORD'S BLESSING CROSSING
MAN'S NATURAL MANEUVERING

Now we come to some practical points concerning blessing. The Lord's blessing crosses man's natural maneuvering (48:13-20). When Joseph brought his sons Manasseh and Ephraim to Jacob, he maneuvered the situation so that the firstborn, Manasseh, would be in front of Jacob's right hand. The father put the firstborn in front of the grandfather's right hand to receive the first blessing and the second in front of the left hand to receive the second blessing. Joseph's maneuvering was according to the natural concept. According to the natural concept, Joseph was right. However, Jacob crossed his hands. Although his eyes were dim, he was very clear in his spirit. Genesis 48:17 says, "And when Joseph saw that his father laid his right hand upon the head of Ephraim, it was evil in his eyes: and he held up his father's hand, to remove it from Ephraim's head unto Manasseh's head" (Heb.). Then Joseph said, "Not so, my father: for this is the firstborn: put thy right hand upon his head" (v. 18). Jacob refused and said, "I know it, my son, I know it" (v. 19). Thus, the Lord's blessing crossed man's maneuvering.

Because parents have their natural taste, natural choice, and natural concept, they are always maneuvering the situation. But maneuvering must be crossed out. I have done a good deal of maneuvering, even in the preaching of the gospel. As I considered the audience, including some who were brilliant and very promising, I said to myself, "These are the good ones." However, most of them never believed at all or else believed in a sloppy way. But others, whom I considered useless, believed in a good way and became useful.

Another kind of maneuvering is found in the church service. In the past we thought that certain ones were trustworthy, spiritual, and superior. But many times we were disappointed because they did not measure up to our expectations. Our maneuvering does not correspond to God's blessing. Maneuvering is our choosing, our selecting. More than thirty years ago I said, "These are very good. They are growing, they will be built up, and they will be one." Eventually, however, the best ones did not come from the group I had chosen; they came instead from another direction. This is an instance of the crossing of hands.

The Lord never places His hand according to our maneuvering. Therefore, in our families, in the preaching of the gospel, and in the church service, we must learn to keep our hands off. We should simply bring our two sons to God and trust them to His sovereign hand. We all are Josephs. We like to bring our Manasseh to the right hand of the Lord and our Ephraim to His left hand. But time after time the Lord crosses His hands. If you consider the church life and study church history, you will see that God's blessing is always sovereign, never subject to man's maneuvering. For example, Peter was a leading one in Jerusalem. Do you believe he prayed that Saul of Tarsus would become an apostle? Certainly not! Rather, Peter might have prayed, "Lord, Saul is too active. I ask You to bind him." But the Lord's hand crossed over the twelve Apostles and was placed upon Saul. Apart from Peter, James, and John, nothing is mentioned about the other Apostles in the book of Acts after the first chapter. But as Saul was on the way to Damascus, the Lord guided His hand purposely, and the blessing came upon him.

We parents should not have our own taste concerning our own children. We simply cannot tell which of them the Lord will choose. We cannot foresee which of our children will be saved. It absolutely does not depend on our maneuvering; it depends on the Lord's blessing.

In the church life I have come to have no trust in my choice. Often my hand has been held back in the choice of elders, deacons, and the leading ones in the church service because I have no trust in my discernment. Most of the time our choosing leads to maneuvering, and God's crossing hand comes in to bless the one we did not choose. Those who are parents and those who are leading ones in the church service must be careful about their choosing. Do not exercise any kind of maneuvering according to your likes and dislikes, for God's blessing always crosses our maneuvering.

There is something about Jacob's blessing of Ephraim which should be very encouraging to us all. Probably there have been times when you considered yourself hopeless and useless. During the past few months I heard of many who were disappointed and felt this way about themselves. Some even felt that life was meaningless. Some may have said, "I have believed in the Lord Jesus, and I have come into the church life. I know that I must function in the church, but I have not been chosen to do anything. Apparently, there is no hope for me. If I cannot function in the church, then life has no meaning." Be encouraged; you are not through. Among many churches, especially the large churches, there has been an atmosphere that made people feel they are not needed. Although in a large church only a few can be elders, everyone is still important. Do not maneuver your situation in any way, for the Lord's blessing hand will cross over to you.

Although we never know where the spiritual blessing will go, we do know that the blessing hand of the Lord always crosses man's natural maneuvering. You may say, "This is the firstborn," but He says, "I know it." The Lord's crossing His hands may be evil in your eyes, but it is altogether beautiful in His eyes. Blessing does not depend on your maneuvering; it depends on God's desire and selection. In any selection we make there is the possibility of maneuvering according to our taste or choice. Do not maneuver, and do not be disappointed. Rather, believe that the Lord's hand will cross over to you.

VII. MAN'S NATURAL CONCEPT HOLDING BACK THE LORD'S BLESSING HAND

We have seen that Joseph tried to hold back his father's blessing hand. This indicates that man's natural concept holds back the Lord's blessing hand. In the church life, the Lord will raise up many we do not like, and some of them will become the best elders. Surely I have had my human feelings, concepts, and tastes. But my natural concepts have been crossed out. We simply do not know from which direction Saul of Tarsus will come. The one you think is the best may turn out to be the worst. But one of the opposers will become today's Apostle Paul. Although you do not like him, the Lord likes him. Many will be raised up who do not fit your concept. Forget your selection. It will never work. If it did, there would be no need for predestination. This is the reason the New

Testament nowhere records the names of the children of the Apostles. Only the names of the spiritual sons are given. Paul called Timothy his "child in faith" (1 Tim. 1:2) and Titus his "genuine child according to the common faith" (Titus 1:4), and Peter spoke of "Mark my son" (1 Pet. 5:13). The names of the Apostles' children are not mentioned because not all of them were predestinated. Likewise, we must also admit that not all our children have been predestinated. However, do not allow the matter of predestination to cause you to neglect the preaching of the gospel. To do that is to go to an extreme. Do not maneuver anything. Simply bring the boys to God and let Him make the choice. Do not let your natural concept hold back the Lord's blessing hand.

VIII. JACOB'S SUPPLANTING HANDS BECOMING BLESSING HANDS

Jacob's supplanting hands eventually became blessing hands (25:26; 47:7, 10; 48:14-16). In chapter twenty-five we see that Jacob began his supplanting even when he was in his mother's womb. How skillful he was in supplanting! But in chapters forty-seven and forty-eight we see that these two supplanting hands have become blessing hands, bringing people into God's presence and ministering God into people so that they may enjoy Him. Would you have believed that Jacob's supplanting hands could become the blessing hands of a mature person? Here we see the growth and maturity in life. A supplanter, a heel-holder, became the greatest person on earth at the time. He was able to bless Pharaoh because he had become greater than Pharaoh. He became this kind of person by the way of life. We need the growth in life and the maturity in life so that we may be filled with Christ to become those who are able to bless others.

LIFE-STUDY OF GENESIS

MESSAGE NINETY-SIX

THE SHIFTINGS OF THE BIRTHRIGHT IN THE SCRIPTURE

Genesis is a book of seeds. In this message, a parenthesis in our life-study, we shall consider another one of these seeds—the seed of the shifting of the birthright.

Perhaps you have never imagined that the birthright could be shifted. The birthright is the special portion of the firstborn. In nearly every race of people, especially in ancient times, the firstborn in a family inherited a special portion. Among the ancient Jews, this portion was usually a double portion of the land. According to the Bible as a whole, the birthright includes the double portion of the land, the kingship, and the priesthood. The priesthood brings people to God, and the kingship brings God to the people. The book of Genesis reveals that this birthright can be shifted from the firstborn son to the second son. In this book there are at least four cases of the shifting of the birthright: from Esau to Jacob (25:22-26, 29-34); from Zarah to Pharez (38:27-30); from Reuben to Joseph (49:3-4; 1 Chron. 5:1); and from Manasseh to Ephraim (48:12-20).

Furthermore, in the New Testament the birthright is shifted from Israel to the church. In Luke chapter fifteen the Lord Jesus indicates by means of the parable of the prodigal son that the publicans and sinners are like the second son, and that the self-righteous Pharisees are like the first son (Luke 15:1-2, 11, 25-28). However, in Matthew 21:28-32 the Lord shifts the birthright from the Jews to the publicans and harlots. Here the Lord reveals that the publicans and harlots are like the firstborn son who at first did not obey his father's word but later repented and obeyed it. Then the Lord likened the Pharisees to the second son who said that he would fulfill his father's word, but who actually did not obey it. Originally, the Jews were the first son. At the beginning of the Lord's ministry, they were still first. But at the end of His ministry, the Lord Jesus shifted the birthright from the Jews to the church. His word in Matthew 21:28-32 was spoken at the end of His ministry. In these verses the Lord likened the publicans and the harlots to the firstborn. The church is composed of redeemed and regenerated sinners. In God's economy they are the ones who have received the birthright. Hence, Hebrews 12:23 speaks of the church of the firstborn.

I. FROM ESAU TO JACOB

In 25:22-26, 29-34 we see the shifting of the birthright from Esau to Jacob. Although Esau was the firstborn (v. 25), Jacob was predestinated to have the birthright (v. 23). The shifting of the birthright from Esau to Jacob reveals that receiving the birthright is a matter of predestination. It does not depend on our natural birth. Although you may be an Esau by birth, this does not mean that you are predestinated to have the birthright. This is absolutely a matter of God's sovereignty; it does not depend on us. As we consider the five cases of the shifting of the birthright, we must worship God for His sovereignty and say, "O Lord, we thank You for Your sovereignty. Everything depends on Your sovereign predestination."

Jacob, the one predestinated to have the birthright, was very covetous and did everything possible to get the birthright himself. When Jacob and Esau were still in their mother's womb, they were fighting over the birthright. I believe that this fight was initiated by Jacob. But, according to God's arrangement, Esau was stronger. If you read the Bible carefully, you will see that Esau, as a hunter, was strong and rather large in physical stature. Jacob, on the contrary, as one who stayed home with his mother, must have been rather small. I do not believe that a husky young man would always stay home with his mother. Because Jacob was smaller and weaker than Esau, he could not obtain the birthright by fighting for it with his physical strength. Although Jacob fought for the birthright in the womb, Esau defeated him, was born first, and gained the birthright. Jacob's struggle had been in vain.

Jacob, however, refused to give up the fight. I believe he stayed with his mother mainly for the purpose of conspiring with her to gain the birthright. Perhaps Jacob's mother eventually agreed to help him gain the birthright. In order to supplant his brother and gain the birthright, Jacob did two things. The first was to maneuver Esau into a situation where he was willing to sell the birthright to him (vv. 29-34). Jacob was exceedingly subtle and clever. He was very skillful. Through his cleverness he gained his mother's cooperation, and Rebekah, who was more clever than Isaac, stood with Jacob. This clever Jacob tempted Esau to sell his birthright.

Jacob probably observed Esau's activities over a period of time. He might have noticed that after hunting Esau was always hungry. Because hunting arouses one's appetite, a hunter enjoys a good meal after a hunt. Anyone who engages in exhausting activity, such as hard work or play, afterwards desires some hearty and nourishing food. Jacob analyzed the entire situation—the environment, Esau's psychology, and Esau's appetite after hunting. Jacob might have said to himself, "Aha! I have a way to get the birthright. While Esau is hunting, I shall prepare soup for him." Genesis 25:29 says, "And Jacob sod pottage: and Esau came from the field, and he was faint." Esau was hungry, and the soup had been prepared. Esau said to Jacob, "Feed me, I pray thee, with that same red pottage; for I am faint" (v. 30). To this, Jacob replied, "Sell me this day thy birthright" (v. 31). When a person is hungry, he will eat anything and pay any price for it. Thus, Esau said, "Behold, I am at the point to die: and what profit shall this birthright do to me?" (v. 32). Esau seemed to be saying, "The birthright is something for the future. What good does it do me now? But here is a bowl of soup in front of me. It is actual, present, and practical. Who knows when I shall have the birthright? I don't know when it will come. For now, I need something real and practical." Hence, Esau agreed to Jacob's proposal and sold his birthright. On the one hand, the birthright depends on God's sovereign predestination. But on the other hand, whether or not we shall have the birthright depends on our attitude and our deeds. Esau's attitude was poor, and his act was foolish. He was absolutely wrong to accept Jacob's offer. Nevertheless, using today's terms, he signed the contract and gave up his birthright.

Although Esau had sold the birthright, he did not have the standing to give the blessing of the birthright. This blessing was not in his hand; it was in the hand of Isaac, his father, the representative of God. Therefore, the second thing Jacob did to gain the birthright was to deceive his father into giving him the blessing of the birthright (27:18-29). Probably Jacob's maneuvering of Esau was initiated by Rebekah who, in all likelihood, had been maneuvering the whole situation. Jacob was the learner, and his mother was the tutor. After Esau had been maneuvered into selling the birthright to Jacob, Rebekah waited for the opportune time to help Jacob receive the blessing of the birthright from Isaac. Although this had to take place before Isaac died, it could not be too early. If it had been too early, Isaac's eyesight would still have been keen. Hence, Rebekah waited until Isaac's eyes were dim. When she heard that Isaac was about to bless Esau, Rebekah said to Jacob, "Now therefore, my son, obey my voice according to that which I command thee" (27:8). Rebekah seemed to be saying, "Now is the time to deceive your father." Jacob obeyed his mother and deceived Isaac into blessing him blindly. As a result, Jacob obtained not only the birthright, but also the blessing of the birthright.

Jacob's maneuvering, however, was unnecessary. If he had done no maneuvering or deceiving, God would have had a way to give him the birthright. Apparently, Jacob's maneuvering and deceiving helped him to acquire the birthright. Actually, it caused him to suffer. From the time Jacob deceived his father, he never saw his mother again. Although Rebekah loved Jacob, due to her cleverness she lost him and never saw him again. Jacob had to flee to Laban's home and suffer there under his hand for twenty years. Do not learn of Rebekah. If you do, you will suffer.

Through the case of the shifting of the birthright from Esau to Jacob, we see that the birthright depends on God's sovereignty. We also see that we should never maneuver or deceive in order to gain the birthright. In other words, there is no need for us to struggle for the birthright. Moreover, we should not be so loose as to sell our birthright. Although we may not be able to gain the birthright by our own effort, we can sell it if we have it. It was not because of his doing that Jacob gained the birthright, but Esau lost it because of his wrongdoing.

II. FROM ZARAH TO PHAREZ

In 38:27-30 we see the shifting of the birthright from Zarah to Pharez. This case illustrates the fact that the granting of the birthright does not depend on man's doing. Zarah was trying to come out first. He "put out his hand: and the midwife took and bound upon his hand a scarlet thread, saying, This came out first" (v. 28). But human doing cannot manage, direct, or guide the birthright. Although the midwife never thought that Pharez would be born first, Pharez was actually born first (v. 29). When he came out, the midwife said in surprise, "How hast thou broken forth?" (v. 29). The Hebrew here is very difficult to translate. It may be rendered, "Wherefore hast thou made a breach for thyself?" or, "How hast thou made a breach! Breach be upon thee!" or, "What a breach you have made for yourself!" The midwife had to admit that Pharez had obtained the birthright. Hence, receiving the birthright does not depend on man's maneuvering.

III. FROM REUBEN TO JOSEPH

The third case of the shifting of the birthright, the shifting from Reuben to Joseph (49:3-4; 1 Chron. 5:1), contains a strong warning. Reuben, the firstborn, lost the birthright because of his defilement. God had intended to give the birthright to Reuben, the firstborn, but Reuben lost it by indulging in defilement. The birthright was shifted from Reuben to Joseph, who fled from that kind of defilement (39:7-12). God is just. He took the birthright from the one who indulged in defilement and gave it to the one who fled from it. (Although the birthright was shifted from Reuben to Joseph, Joseph received only the double portion of the land. He did not receive the priesthood or the kingship. Rather, Levi received the priesthood and Judah, the kingship.)

Never think of fornication as something insignificant. God hates it. We live in an age of Sodom. The whole world today, including the United States and especially Sweden and France, is a Sodom. Many men and women live together without being married. Certainly this will bring in God's judgment. In the Bible God exercised a special judgment over Sodom because the people there indulged in lust without any restriction. Nothing offends God more than this indulgence. Nevertheless, many young people today, even young women, have no sense of shame regarding this. Indulging in fornication will always cause you to suffer loss. There will be no need for God to judge you deliberately because a natural judgment will come upon you spontaneously. The case of Reuben reveals that, although you may be predestinated to have the birthright, you may lose it by indulging in fornication.

Every Christian who commits fornication will lose his birthright. This birthright includes the full enjoyment of Christ with the priesthood and the kingship. To have the birthright is to have the right and the position to enjoy Christ in full. It is also to have the right to be priests and kings. If we lose our birthright, we lose the enjoyment of Christ. Any Christian who commits fornication loses this enjoyment immediately. This sin will also keep any believer from being a priest and a king. Furthermore, no fornicator will enter into the millennial kingdom to have the fullest enjoyment of Christ and to be a priest of God and a king with Christ (1 Cor. 6:9-10; Gal. 5:19-21; Eph. 5:5). Only the overcomers will share this enjoyment, be God's priests, and be the co-kings of Christ. Take heed: defilement may cause you to lose your birthright.

IV. FROM MANASSEH TO EPHRAIM

Now we come to the fourth case, the case of the shifting of the birthright from Manasseh to Ephraim (48:12-20). Manasseh was the firstborn (v. 14). When Joseph brought Ephraim and Manasseh to Jacob to be blessed by him, he tried to maneuver the blessing of the birthright according to the natural birth (vv. 13-17). However, Ephraim received the blessing of the birthright because Jacob crossed his blessing hands (vv. 14, 17-20). I have the strong feeling that Joseph's maneuvering of the situation reminded Jacob of the maneuvering he had done in his youth. He might have remembered how he had maneuvered his brother to obtain the birthright and deceived his father to receive the blessing. As Jacob crossed his right hand and placed it upon the head of Ephraim, the second son, he might have said to himself, "Jacob, there was no need for you to maneuver anything. Ephraim is not doing anything, yet you place your right hand upon him. Why did you maneuver so much when you were young?" I believe that, as Jacob crossed his hands, he had very deep feelings within him. If Joseph and his sons had not been present, Jacob might have openly expressed his regret. You may think that you are right in maneuvering certain situations. But after a number of years you will feel ashamed of what you have done and say, "What a shame it was to do those things!"

We must believe that Jacob did not guide his own hands. Certainly they were guided by the Spirit. The Spirit's guidance was a blessing to Ephraim, but it was a rebuke to Jacob. Perhaps the Lord said to him, "Jacob, you didn't need to do anything. Look at Ephraim. Although he is doing nothing, he is receiving the birthright. Why did you maneuver so much and cause yourself such suffering?" Like Jacob, I also did certain things when I was young, but I later regretted them. Young people, you need to realize that the blessing is not in your hands; it is in the hands of the old ones. Whether we shall cross our hands and place our right hand upon your head does not depend on you. It depends on us. If you want to receive the blessing, you must have the old ones. If you stay away from them, you will miss the blessing. The old ones will not bless you unless you honor them. Young people, you simply cannot go on without the blessing of the older ones. You desperately need their help.

V. FROM ISRAEL TO THE CHURCH

Now we come to the last case of the shifting of the birthright in the Scriptures, the shifting of the birthright from

Israel to the church. This is very important. In Exodus 4:22, the Lord said to Moses, "Thou shalt say unto Pharaoh, Thus saith the Lord, Israel is my son, even my firstborn." Although Israel was God's firstborn, Israel lost the birthright because of unbelief (Matt. 21:32; Rom. 11:20). According to Luke 15, in the beginning of His ministry the Lord still considered Israel, represented by the Pharisees, as the firstborn son and the publicans and sinners as the second son. But according to the enjoyment in Luke 15, it was the second son who received the birthright, for the second son enjoyed the fatted calf, which is Christ. This indicates a shifting of the birthright. By this we see that the Pharisees lost the enjoyment of Christ, but the repentant publicans and sinners gained this enjoyment. This means that they gained the birthright.

Toward the end of His ministry, in Matthew 21, the Lord indicated that the repentant publicans, harlots, and sinners, of whom the church was to be composed, were the first son and that the unbelieving Pharisees, representing Israel, were the second. Matthew 21:32 says, "For John came to you in the way of righteousness, and you did not believe him; but the tax collectors and the prostitutes believed him; and you, when you saw it, did not later regret it so as to believe him." Due to unbelief, Israel, the first son, was cut off, and the second son was grafted into the birthright. Thus, the repentant and believing sinners have become the constituent of the church, and the church today is called the church of the firstborn (Heb. 12:23). We in the church are a group of firstborn sons who possess the birthright. This birthright gives us the right to enjoy Christ to the fullest, to be priests of God, and to be co-kings of Christ. Although we have the birthright, the New Testament warns us of the possibility of losing it (Heb. 12:16-17). Be careful: you may lose your birthright.

LIFE-STUDY OF GENESIS

MESSAGE NINETY-SEVEN

BEING MATURED
THE MANIFESTATION OF MATURITY

(2)

g) Prophesying with Blessing

In this message we shall consider another manifestation of Jacob's maturity in life: his prophesying with blessing (49:1-28). Although we are familiar with what it means to prophesy, we may not be familiar with prophesying with blessing. Genesis 49 is the only chapter that reveals this matter. Although Moses' blessing in Deuteronomy 33 is close to what is found in Genesis 49, the blessing there is not as rich as the blessing here. Both portions of the Word are prophecies concerning Israel, but in Genesis 49 there is a richer blessing than in Deuteronomy 33.

The prophesying in chapter forty-nine is a manifestation of maturity, for our speaking always reveals where we are and how mature we are. A baby cannot speak at all, but a child over a year old may begin to say a few words. His speaking reveals that he is a small child. It is the same with other age groups: a young man speaks like a young man, a middle-aged person like a middle-aged person, and a grandfather like a grandfather. Hence, our speaking not only represents our age, but also the kind of person we are. If you are quick, you will not speak slowly. If you are slow, you will not speak quickly. If you are a high person, you will not speak in a low way, and if you are a low person, you will not speak on a high level. Thus, our speaking reveals what we are and where we are.

It has been said that the wisest thing to do is not to speak at all. If I stood before a group of people without saying anything, they would not know whether I was deep or shallow, quick or slow. I would be a mystery. However, during the past fourteen years, every fiber of my being has been revealed to you all through my speaking. Even children seven or eight years old know me rather well because they have listened to my speaking. Because I speak so much, I am not able to conceal myself. The best way to conceal yourself is not to speak. During my early years in the ministry, I was quite wise, for I never said anything in the conferences of the co-workers. Because that was my policy, I was a mystery to the other co-workers, and no one could understand me. Although it is difficult to speak, it is more difficult not to speak. When the opportunity presents itself, you simply will not be able to refrain from speaking. I doubt if you could stay with me for sixty minutes and not say a word. I am certain that after a few minutes you would be speaking.

Now let us briefly trace the matter of Jacob's speaking as it is revealed in Genesis. The first record of his speaking is in 25:31, where Jacob said to Esau, "Sell me this day thy birthright." Gaining the birthright was the desire of Jacob's heart; it was his dream and aspiration. For a long time he had been waiting for the opportunity to get it away from Esau. When the opportunity finally came, the first word out of Jacob's mouth recorded in Scripture was the word about selling the birthright.

In chapter twenty-seven Jacob spoke in a deceitful way to Isaac, his father (vv. 19-20, 23). In 27:19 Jacob lied to his father, saying, "I am Esau thy firstborn." When Isaac asked how he had found the venison so quickly, Jacob said, "Because the Lord thy God brought it to me." Then Isaac said, "The voice is Jacob's voice, but the hands are the hands of Esau" (v. 22), and he asked, "Art thou my very son Esau?" (v. 24). To this, Jacob replied, "I am." Thus, Jacob's speaking in chapter twenty-seven was absolute falsehood.

Jacob's speaking in chapters twenty-nine through thirty-two is full of self-interest, self-ambition, and self-gain. Through his speaking recorded in these chapters many aspects of the self are exposed. Jacob's speaking was so selfish that it almost seemed that he did not have a spirit. If we had a brother like that among us, we would doubt that he had been truly regenerated.

Jacob's speaking to his brother Esau in chapter thirty-three was a performance. In this chapter Jacob several times addressed Esau as, "My lord" (33:13-14). Deep within, Jacob never recognized Esau as his lord. The reason he addressed his brother in this way was that he was afraid Esau would kill him. Jacob was an actor, a politician, and his display of humility before Esau was a performance.

By the time of chapter thirty-five, however, Jacob's speaking had undergone a change. His speaking in this chapter begins to resemble that of a regenerated person, a child of God.

In the chapters that follow Jacob's loss of Joseph, Jacob spoke very little. This indicates that, as we grow in life, our speaking will firstly change in nature. The characteristic of our speaking will change. Eventually, the amount of our speaking will be greatly reduced. The more we grow, the less we shall speak. At present you may not be able to withstand the temptation to speak. But after some years have gone by and you have had much more growth in life, you will not speak no matter how great the temptation is.

We can trace Jacob's progress in life by following his progress in speaking. The change in his speaking reveals his growth. Eventually, Jacob grew to the point that, even when he lost Joseph, he had very little to say. However, many of us have a great deal to say over such insignificant matters as losing a pair of socks. If a young brother in the brothers' house loses a pair of socks, he may shout, "Where are my socks? What has happened to them?" But when Jacob lost Joseph, the treasure of his heart, he did not say very much. This was a healthy sign. But talking a great deal over a pair of socks is a sign of immaturity, a sign of childishness. Too much talking reveals that you are childish. In this we see that our speaking is a sign of how much we have grown. There are some among us who used to be quite talkative several years ago. But now they talk very little. I hope that after another period of time, they will hardly talk at all. The reason for their not talking will not be that they are unhappy; it will be the fact that they have grown in life. The more we grow, the less we talk.

Consider Jacob's reaction at hearing the news that Joseph was alive and in Egypt. He said very little; in fact, he said hardly anything at all. If we had been Jacob, we would either have been furious with the other sons, ready to beat them, or we would have been extremely excited, running from one son to another and saying, "Joseph is still living!" In either case, there would have been a great deal of talk. But Jacob said very little. Furthermore, he had little to say after he had gone down to Egypt. When Jacob was ushered into the presence of Pharaoh, he did not say anything. Rather, he simply blessed Pharaoh. There was nearly no talk, but there were strong blessings (47:7, 10).

Because of his maturity, Jacob's word in chapter forty-nine was very weighty. Every word he uttered here became a prophecy. Because this chapter is so deep, it is closed to many Christians. They have neither probed the depths of this chapter, nor do they know what it is talking about. In Genesis 49 we see a person who has fully matured. This man does not speak in a shallow, light, idle manner; he speaks in a way that is full of life and maturity. This indicates that our growth in life will be manifested in our speaking.

This message on prophesying with blessing is quite deep. It is not deep in doctrine; it is deep in experience. Although few among us have come to the level of this experience of life, this message is still needed as part of our life-study of Genesis. It will help us both in the growth of life and in the matter of speaking. Be impressed with the fact that your speaking reveals where you are. Whenever you are about to speak, you should say to yourself, "My speaking reveals me." Realizing this will help us a great deal.

Jacob's word in chapter forty-nine is the kind of word that cannot be found elsewhere. It is not a word of instruction, encouragement, or exhortation. Neither is it merely a weighty word nor just a word of prediction. Rather, it is a word of prophesying with blessing. Although it is a prophecy, it is a prophecy saturated with blessing. It is not easy to speak this kind of word. Isaiah was the highest among the prophets.

However, among the many prophecies in his book, it is difficult to find one prophecy with blessing. Isaiah prophesied, but he did not prophesy with blessing. But in Genesis 49 Jacob not only prophesied; he prophesied with blessing. His blessing flowed out of his prophetic word.

(1) Four Requirements for Prophesying with Blessing

(a) Knowing God

In order to prophesy with blessing, we must fulfill four requirements. The first requirement is to know God, the desire of God's heart, and the purpose of God. God, God's desire, and God's purpose are all revealed through Jacob's word in this chapter. The remainder of the Old Testament and all of the New Testament are the development of Genesis 49. In other words, nearly the whole Bible is the development of Jacob's word spoken in this chapter. How high, deep, and profound is this word! This chapter is a very rich seed, a seed that undergoes a marvelous development in the rest of the Scriptures. In order to speak such a word, we must know God, we must know God's heart, and we must know God's purpose.

(b) Knowing People

The second requirement is to know people, to know the actual situation of every person involved. You may think that, because it should be easy for a father to know his son, it was easy for Jacob to know his twelve sons. However, it is often very difficult for parents to truly know their children. Many times we know our children in a blind way like Isaac knew Jacob. Seemingly, we parents know our children; actually, we know neither what they are nor where they are. But Jacob had a thorough understanding of his sons. Every situation, condition, and hidden problem was clear in his sight. Likewise, if we would speak such a word in the church, we must know the church, the elders, and all the brothers and sisters. This is not easy. Although we meet together day after day, probably I do not know you too well. Although I have been meeting with the elders for a number of years, I still may not know them very well. We should not know people according to our mental understanding; rather, we must know them according to the spirit. Genesis 49 indicates that Jacob had a proper understanding of his sons. He knew their deeds, their situations, and their condition. Jacob was an expert in knowing people. He had a spiritual x-ray. As he was prophesying with blessing, this heavenly x-ray made the situation of each son crystal clear in his sight. His knowledge of his sons is expressed in his brief word about each one.

(c) Having the Riches

Although we may know God, God's heart, and God's purpose and although we may know the situation of others, we shall still not be able to bless them if we are poor. A certain dear one may be pure, absolute for God, and worthy of a rich blessing. However, if I am poor, what blessing can I grant to him? Spiritually speaking, I may just have a dime and I may need to keep two cents for myself. Thus, I could only give an eight-cent blessing. Jacob, however, was full of riches. Because he had no lack of riches, he could bless others. In fact, the capacity of those receiving his blessing fell far short of his riches.

(d) Having a Strong, Active Spirit

In addition to the three requirements already covered, we need a strong, active spirit. Jacob's word in this chapter was spoken as he was dying. When many Christians are about to die, not only their body, but their whole being is weak. Thus, they do not have a strong spirit to exercise in prophesying by blessing others. Although Jacob was dying physically, he was vigorous spiritually. In his body he was dying, but in his spirit he was strong and active. Therefore, in order to prophesy with blessing, we must have the knowledge of God, the knowledge of people and their situations, the riches of God, and a strong spirit.

(2) Not a Gifted Prophet

Due to the influence of today's Christianity, many think that only prophets can prophesy. But where is the verse saying that Jacob was a prophet? Jacob was not a gifted prophet predicting the things to come, but he still prophesied. In 49:1 Jacob said, "Gather yourselves together, that I may tell you that which shall befall you in the last days." This was the opening word of his prophecy.

Today many Christians are talking about the gifts. But what gift did Jacob have? I would say that the only gift he had was the gift of supplanting. In chapter forty-nine Jacob did not say "Reuben,...thus saith the Lord." Nevertheless, the most profound prophecy in the Bible is the one uttered by Jacob in this chapter. This is the only prophecy that requires the whole Bible for its development. Although it is such a deep prophecy, it was not spoken by a prophet or by a gifted person.

(3) A God-constituted Person

Jacob was not a gifted prophet; he was a God-constituted person. He was not constituted with gifts, with utterance, or even with function; he was constituted with God. Because he had been infused, saturated, and thoroughly permeated with God, his speaking was God's speaking. His word was God's word. Whether we consider his word a prophecy or a blessing, it is the kind of speaking that is lacking in the churches today. What the churches need today is the speaking of God-constituted persons.

At this point we need to consider some verses in 1 Corinthians 7. In 1940 I received great help from Brother Nee regarding these verses. In one of his talks he said that 1 Corinthians chapter seven reveals the peak of Paul's Christian experience. When I first heard this, I could not understand it, because it was very different from my concept. I was familiar with chapter seven of 1 Corinthians. I knew that it talked about marriage and virginity. Thus, I said to myself, "How can this chapter be the peak of the Apostle Paul's Christian experience?"

Brother Nee referred us to verses 10, 12, 25, and 40. In verse 10 Paul says, "But to the married I charge, not I but the Lord, A wife should not be separated from her husband." Here Paul was assured that the Lord's commandment was that

Christian wives should not leave their husbands. Because Paul was convinced that this was the Lord's commandment, he was bold.

But in verse 12 he said, "But to the rest I say, not the Lord." Regarding the matter of a brother having an unbelieving wife, Paul said, "I say, not the Lord." If I had been there, I would have said, "Brother Paul, if it is not the Lord, then you should not speak. Since you know that it is not the Lord, why do you speak? We don't want to hear you. You are just a saved sinner; you should not say anything by yourself." When I heard Brother Nee speak about this verse, I said to myself, "If it was not the Lord speaking, why did Paul keep on talking?" Nevertheless, the word Paul spoke was recorded in the New Testament and became the word of God. According to verse 12, Paul's word became an inspired word in the Holy Bible.

Moreover, in verse 25 Paul said, "Now concerning virgins I have no commandment of the Lord, but I give my opinion as having received mercy of the Lord to be faithful." If I had been there, I would have stopped him and said, "Brother Paul, since you don't have the commandment of God, please don't speak." Not only did Paul not have a commandment from the Lord; he even gave his opinion. We probably would have said, "Paul, we don't want to hear your opinion. We want to hear the word of the Lord." Although I had read 1 Corinthians 7 many times prior to hearing that word from Brother Nee, I had never seen these verses, and I was shocked when he pointed them out to us. Although Paul simply gave his opinion, for more than nineteen hundred years, his opinion has been regarded as the word of God. Thus, Paul's opinion became God's word.

Finally, in verse 40 Paul said, "But she is more blessed if she so remains, according to my opinion; but I think that I also have the Spirit of God." Here we see that Paul taught according to his opinion. According to Paul's opinion, a widow would be happier if she remained in her widowed condition. The reason Paul was bold to speak this way is given in verse 25: he had "received mercy of the Lord to be faithful." We need the mercy of the Lord to make us faithful to Him. If we have this mercy, we may be bold.

At the end of verse 40 Paul said, "But I think that I also have the Spirit of God." The little word "also" here means a great deal. Paul seemed to be saying, "I not only have my opinion; I also have the Spirit of God." Notice that Paul did not say, "I have the assurance," or "I believe"; rather, he said, "I think." This indicates that he was not certain. Although he did not have the assurance that he had the Spirit of God, we all recognize chapter seven of 1 Corinthians as the word of God. Eventually, as I was listening to Brother Nee that day in 1940, I agreed with his word that 1 Corinthians 7 records the peak of Paul's Christian experience. Paul's opinion was God's word.

In principle, it is the same with Jacob in Genesis 49. Whatever Jacob uttered in this chapter was God's word. Although it was his opinion, it was also the word of God. In 49:3 and 4 Jacob seemed to be saying, "Reuben, you are my firstborn; however, because you have been defiled, you cannot enjoy the preeminence of having the birthright." Jacob's word to Reuben was somewhat of a prediction, for it concerned the loss of the birthright; it was also somewhat of a curse, for it pointed out that Reuben was to be bereft of the birthright. This was not the speaking of a young man nor even of an ordinary human being. It was the utterance of a man who was filled with God, a man who had been constituted with God in his entire being. At the time of chapter forty-nine, Jacob was a God-man, a man filled, constituted, permeated, and even reorganized with God. Thus, whatever he spoke was God's word; whatever he thought was God's thought; and whatever opinion he expressed was God's opinion. Neither a young person nor a middle-aged person can speak this kind of word. It can only be uttered by one who has come to full maturity. Jacob's speaking in this chapter reveals that he had fully matured.

My burden in this message is to impress you all, especially the young people, with this fact that your speaking exposes where you are. If you have a lot to say when you lose your socks, that should remind you of your immaturity. This kind of reaction makes evident your need for the growth in life. Forget that pair of socks and seek to gain more life. If you have to say something, you should say, "I need more life." Do not say, "Where are my socks?" Rather, say, "Brothers, do you know where my growth in life is?" Whenever a brother asks about his socks, the others should say, "Here is your growth in life."

Many of us are talkative. We were born this way. It is our nature, disposition, and characteristic to be talkative. Whenever you are talkative you should be reminded that your talkativeness is a sign that you need to grow in life.

(4) Jacob, the Father in the Flesh, and Israel, God's Mouth

Genesis 49:2 says, "Gather yourselves together, and hear, ye sons of Jacob; and hearken unto Israel your father." This verse is in the form of Hebrew poetry, which is always written in pairs. The first part of the pair in verse 2 is, "Gather yourselves together, and hear, ye sons of Jacob," and the second part is, "And hearken unto Israel your father." The begetting father was Jacob, and the speaking father was Israel. All twelve sons were born of Jacob, the father in the flesh, a supplanter, a heel-holder, and a liar. But the blessing and prophesying father was no longer a Jacob; he was Israel. In his natural being, Jacob could never have uttered such a word. It was only because of his maturity that he was able to speak this kind of word. Jacob did not say to his sons, "Hearken unto Jacob your father"; he said, "Hearken unto Israel your father." Israel was not only a transformed person, but also one matured in the divine life. We all would enjoy hearing testimonies from those who were Jacobs many years ago but who are now Israels. We need more Israels, those who speak not only for God, but also with God. Whatever they say is God's utterance. In Genesis 49 Israel was fully permeated, saturated, constituted, and reorganized with God. Because he was one with God, whatever he spoke was the word of God. Therefore, in this chapter we have a prophecy that is permeated with blessing.

Verse 28 says, "All these are the twelve tribes of Israel: and this is it that their father spake unto them, and blessed them; every one according to his blessing he blessed them." Is this a prophecy or a blessing? Although it is a prophecy, it is prophecy filled with blessing.

The Jacob in chapter forty-nine is spiritually and divinely knowledgeable. He knows God, and he knows the situations of his sons. Furthermore, he has the necessary riches with which to prophesy and bless. Therefore, he can speak a prophecy permeated with all manner of blessing. In his speaking there is no error, opaqueness, darkness, emptiness, or vanity. Rather, his speaking is a rich, deep, profound prophecy permeated with blessing. This is absolutely different from the "Thus saith the Lord" common among Christians today. In just a few minutes you may receive the gift to speak that kind of prophecy. But it takes many years to grow to the stature where you can utter the kind of word spoken by Jacob in this chapter. This is not a matter of gift or function; it is a matter of growth and maturity.

To be mature is to be constituted with God. All that God is must be constituted into our being. Every fiber of our being must be reorganized and permeated with the element of God. When this has taken place, like Jacob, we shall be the kind of person who can prophesy with blessing. In this maturity we are divinely knowledgeable, knowing thoroughly the things of God and the situations of other people. In this maturity we also have the riches to speak a blessing prophecy.

LIFE-STUDY OF GENESIS

MESSAGE NINETY-EIGHT

BEING MATURED
THE MANIFESTATION OF MATURITY

(3)

In this message we shall continue with the subject of Jacob's prophesying with blessing (49:1-28). In the previous message we pointed out that although this word of prophecy was spoken by a man, it was nonetheless the word of God. Because, in his maturity, Jacob was one with God, whatever he said was God's word. Most Christians have a difficult time understanding Genesis 49. When I first began to study this chapter about fifty years ago, I found that it was not easy to learn the meaning of the prophecies recorded here. This is a very significant chapter, for it is virtually the conclusion of the book of Genesis.

According to the record of Genesis, the human race began with Adam and continued with Abel, Enosh, Enoch, Noah, Abraham, Isaac, and Jacob. Eventually, Jacob was no longer an individual, because he became the father of a house that was chosen by God. This house, the house of Jacob (46:27), was composed mainly of Jacob's twelve sons. Later, these twelve sons became the twelve tribes of the nation of Israel. This indicates that God's intention is to have a house, not individuals. The house of Israel was a type of the church, which is God's house today. In the Old Testament we have a house, the house of Israel, and in the New Testament we also have a house, the church of the living God (1 Tim. 3:15).

Whatever is spoken regarding the house of Israel is a type, a picture, and a shadow of the church. When I was with the Brethren teachers, they told us to differentiate those parts of the Bible that were for the children of Israel from those that were for the church. In a sense, this is correct, for we should not mix God's word concerning the house of Israel with His word concerning the church. However, because the church is a spiritual entity, it is difficult for us to understand it. Thus, we need the picture of the house of Israel in the Old Testament. The principle is that the Bible uses types and figures to portray spiritual things. Anything that is spiritual is mysterious. For example, because New Jerusalem is spiritual and mysterious, the Bible uses a city to illustrate it. Likewise, without the picture of the house of Israel, we would find it difficult to adequately comprehend the church. However, when we examine the picture in the Old Testament, we are able to understand many aspects of the church revealed in the New Testament. Therefore, what is spoken concerning the children of Israel is not only for them; it is also for us.

Based upon the principle of using types and pictures to portray spiritual realities, we must apply to ourselves all that is said about the twelve tribes of Israel. Physically speaking, of course, we are not the twelve tribes of Israel; however, spiritually speaking, we are the twelve tribes because they are pictures of us. If we want to know ourselves, we should look at the photograph of ourselves in these twelve tribes. Do not think that the prophecies in Genesis 49 are only concerned with the sons of Jacob. These prophecies probably concern us more than they do Jacob's twelve sons.

The number twelve is composed of three times four. Firstly, Jacob prophesied concerning his first three sons, Reuben, Simeon, and Levi (vv. 3-7). These three brothers are subdivided. Reuben stands alone, and Simeon and Levi are grouped together. According to their activities, Simeon and Levi were one.

Before we examine the significant aspects of Jacob's prophecy regarding Reuben, Simeon, and Levi, I wish to point out that according to Jacob's prophecy with blessing, it is possible for our natural status and disposition to be changed. Perhaps you were born good. But do not be proud of your goodness, for you may become bad. If you were born bad, you should not be disappointed. Rather, you should have the faith that you will become good. This is both a warning and an encouragement. As the firstborn, Reuben had the preeminence. However, he lost his preeminence, and his natural status, his status by birth, was changed. Therefore, we should neither be disappointed nor complacent. Instead, we should be careful lest we lose our birthright.

Moreover, although you were not actually born first, you may become the firstborn. Joseph was born eleventh, but he eventually became the first. In most cases of the shifting of the birthright in the Bible, the birthright is shifted from the first to the second. Upon hearing this word, a thoughtful person may say, "I was born neither number one nor number two. I was born number eleven. No matter how many times the birthright is shifted, it will never be shifted to me." But be confident and be encouraged. Although you may be number eleven, God still has a way to make you number one. He did it with Joseph. Be impressed with the fact that it is possible for your natural status to be changed either for the better or for the worse. Do not blame God for making you number eleven instead of number one. If we try to blame God in this way, He may say, "Dear child, read Genesis 49 again. Although you were born number eleven, your status can be changed to number one."

Throughout the years, I have been speaking to the elders about their disposition. I admit that my word on this matter has been strong and sharp as a two-edged sword piercing into the brothers. When the elders ask me how they can be more useful, I always tell them that their usefulness depends upon their disposition. I have often told them that their natural disposition is the main reason they are not useful. Many have been disappointed by this word. But here in Genesis 49 there is some good news for those who have been disappointed about their natural disposition. In this group of three brothers we see not only that our natural status may be changed, but also that our natural disposition can be used by God. However, as we shall see later in this message, God can use our disposition only if certain conditions are met.

Jacob put Simeon and Levi together in his prophecy because they were the same in character and disposition. Their disposition was exposed in chapter thirty-four, the chapter that records the defilement of their sister, Dinah, and their revenge on Hamor and Shechem. Simeon, Levi, and Dinah were all born of the same mother. Thus, these brothers dearly loved their sister. When they learned that she had been defiled, their disposition was exposed by the way they killed all the males in the city of Shechem, plundered the city, and even hamstrung the cattle. How cruel they were! The cruelty of Simeon and Levi terrified Jacob. In his entire life Jacob had never been as frightened as he was in chapter thirty-four. Nevertheless, in God's sovereignty, the events in that chapter were a great help to Jacob's maturity. These events were the strong sunshine that helped to burn Jacob into maturity. Therefore, in chapter thirty-five we see a real change in Jacob's life.

Jacob, however, could not forget what Simeon and Levi had done. Hence, in 49:6 Jacob said of them, "O my soul, come not thou into their secret; unto their company, my glory, be not thou united: for in their anger they slew a man, and in their self-will they hamstrung oxen" (Heb.). The word "glory" ("honor" in KJV) refers to the spirit. What Simeon and Levi had done made such a deep impression on Jacob's spirit that he could not grant them any blessing. In Deuteronomy 33, however, Moses did bless Levi. The blessing in Genesis 49 was by a father who had a loving concern for his sons. But the prophecy in Deuteronomy 33 was by an old man who represented the law. Whatever he prophesied was the judgment according to the law. Nevertheless, that judgment was filled with mercy, and Levi received a blessing.

Although Jacob loved his sons and was very concerned about them, he could not give a blessing to Simeon and Levi. Genesis 49:5 says, "Simeon and Levi are brethren; their swords are weapons of violence" (Heb.). The word regarding Simeon and Levi being brethren means that they were companions, that they formed one company. Their swords were weapons of violence. As we have pointed out, verse 6 reveals their cruelty. In verse 7 Jacob said, "Cursed be their anger, for it was fierce; and their wrath, for it was cruel: I will divide them in Jacob, and scatter them in Israel." Jacob did not say, "Cursed be Simeon and Levi"; rather, he said, "Cursed be their anger and their wrath." Although they deserved to be cursed, their father did not curse them; instead, he cursed their anger and exercised judgment over them to divide them. The best way to deal with those who are cruel is to scatter them. Regarding Simeon and Levi, Jacob seemed to say, "Simeon and Levi were too cruel. They showed no mercy or kindness. Yes, Hamor and Shechem were wrong in defiling Dinah. It would have been sufficient to kill them. Simeon and Levi didn't have to kill all the males of the city nor to hamstring their oxen. I will not allow them to stay together. The best thing to do is to scatter them."

(5) Concerning Reuben

(a) Being the Firstborn to Have the Preeminence
in Dignity and in Power

Let us now consider Jacob's word to Reuben. Because Reuben was corrupted, defiled, and full of germs, in Jacob's blessing with prophecy he is isolated from all the other brothers. Verse 3 says, "Reuben, thou art my firstborn, my might, and the firstfruits of my strength, the preeminence of dignity, and the preeminence of power" (Heb.). As the firstborn, Reuben had the preeminence in dignity and in power. Look at the words Jacob used to describe him: "my firstborn," "my might," "the firstfruits of my strength," "the preeminence of dignity," and "the preeminence of power."

(b) Having Lost the Preeminence of the Birthright
because of His Ebullition in Lust

Although Reuben had the preeminence of the birthright, he lost it because of his defilement. Verse 4 says, "Ebullient as water, thou shalt not have preeminence; because thou wentest up to thy father's bed; then defiledst thou it: he went up to my couch" (Heb.). The Hebrew word rendered "unstable" in the King James Version is very difficult to translate. I believe that the best rendering is "ebullient," which means boiling, to move violently. Reuben, who was boiling over with lust, moved violently to defile his father's bed. In doing that, Reuben went too far. That indulgence in lust caused him to lose his birthright. Because in his ebullience Reuben had defiled his father's bed, Jacob said that he would not have preeminence. Thus, the preeminence of the birthright was taken away from him.

As Jacob was prophesying regarding Reuben in chapter forty-nine, he undoubtedly remembered that he had already given the birthright to Joseph (48:5-6). Jacob did not give it to Joseph by accident; rather, he must have considered the matter for a long time. According to 48:5, Jacob said, "And now thy two sons, Ephraim and Manasseh, which were born unto thee in the land of Egypt before I came unto thee into Egypt, are mine; as Reuben and Simeon, they shall be mine." Furthermore, in 48:22, Jacob said, "Moreover I have given to thee one portion above thy brethren, which I took out of the hand of the Amorite with my sword and with my bow." Therefore, Joseph received two portions of the land, one portion for Ephraim and another for Manasseh. Eventually, this prophecy was fulfilled in Joshua 16 and 17. When the land was divided by lot, Joseph received two portions. This was not accomplished through human maneuvering; it was accomplished through lot, which was controlled by God for the fulfillment of Jacob's prophecy.

At this point I need to say a strong word, especially to the young people. Do not think that defilement is an insignificant matter. We were made by God in His image. Because we have the image of God, we are honorable, even according to our natural make-up. Although other sins may not damage our body, fornication causes direct damage to our physical body, a vessel of honor (1 Cor. 6:18; 1 Thes. 4:4). Because we have been regenerated, our body is now the temple of the Holy Spirit (1 Cor. 6:19). Therefore, not only do we bear the image of God in our physical body, but after regeneration our body is the temple of God. Therefore, you must keep your body in an honorable way. Nothing damages your body as much as fornication. The practice of the world today is utterly hellish, devilish, and satanic. How devilish it is for young people to have contact with one another without any restriction! I wish to warn all the young people, even the young brothers and sisters in the church life, to exercise certain restrictions upon their contact with one another.

As a young brother coming into the ministry, I went to

Shanghai to receive help from Brother Nee. During those days, Brother Nee had many long talks with me. The first instruction he gave me, as a brother in the Lord's ministry, was never to contact a member of the opposite sex alone, but, for my protection, to always have the presence of a third party. I have never forgotten this word; it has been a great help and protection to me. By the Lord's mercy, I have followed his word throughout the years.

We are fallen human beings, and we all have lusts. None of us can say that he does not have lust. In 1930 there was in my home province a particular so-called Pentecostal movement. A certain group declared that because they had received the baptism of the Holy Spirit, they no longer had any lusts. Thus, males and females began to live together. However, this practice resulted in fornication, and great shame was brought upon the Lord's name. Because of the fornication among this group, the door to the gospel was closed in that district for quite a period of time. Approximately fifteen years ago, the same kind of thing occurred in Korea. Many Korean Christians who had had so-called Pentecostal experiences began to contact one another without restriction, and the result was fornication.

Remember, you are still in the flesh. For a male and a female of the same age to be alone gives opportunity for the enemy to tempt them. Because your past experiences have already convinced you of this, there is no need for me to say too much. Never consider fornication as an unimportant matter. As we have seen, nothing damages your honorable physical body as much as fornication. What a shame it is that some of those in the government want to legalize homosexuality! To do this is to turn this country into a Sodom.

Reuben lost the preeminence of the birthright because of one sin. Today this preeminence is the top portion of the enjoyment of Christ. The double portion of the land signifies the top portion of the enjoyment of the riches of the all-inclusive Christ. Once anyone commits such an awful and terrible sin, he is through with the top enjoyment of Christ. Not only the young people but even those who are middle-aged must be aware of the danger of being alone with a member of the opposite sex. To do this is to take a great risk, for it opens the door for the subtle one to come in. You do not know how subtle and how evil your flesh is. The lusts in our flesh are terrible! Thus, we should have no trust in ourselves. Do not think that it is impossible for you to commit such a thing. The best protection is following the word I received from Brother Nee.

Do not say that my word is the word of a conservative Chinese man from the Far East, and that you live in modern America. As one who is over seventy years of age, I have passed through all the human experiences. Please take heed to my word regarding fornication. Again and again in the New Testament the Apostle Paul issued the warning that no fornicator would have any inheritance in the kingdom of God (1 Cor. 6:9-10; Gal. 5:19-21; Eph. 5:5). When we come to Matthew 5 in our life-study, we shall see how strict the Lord Jesus was regarding this matter. Never be loose in contacting members of the opposite sex. For the Lord's name, for the church's testimony, for your protection, and for the honor of your physical body, you must follow this principle of not being alone with a member of the opposite sex. If you follow this principle, you will be preserved. Remember, due to his defilement, Reuben's natural status, the status derived from birth, was altogether changed.

(c) In Danger of Dying and Decreasing

In Deuteronomy 33:6 Moses uttered a prophecy regarding Reuben. This prophecy, a judgment according to the law, was spoken through an experienced, sympathetic old man. Moses said, "Let Reuben live, and not die; and let not his men be few." This word implies that, according to the law, Reuben should have died. According to his sin, Reuben should have died (Ezek. 18:20). Although Reuben should have died, Moses was merciful in executing the judgment of the law. As an old judge, he judged the twelve tribes according to God's righteous law, but he nonetheless judged mercifully and sympathetically. Moses was concerned either that Reuben would die or that the number of his tribe would be greatly decreased. By this we see that fornication not only causes us to lose our birthright; it may also cause us to die or to be decreased. Therefore, we must flee fornication (1 Cor. 6:18).

Joseph received the birthright because he fled from the very defilement that Reuben indulged in (39:7-12). Joseph did not go in the house purposely to be with Potiphar's wife. He was a servant working in the house, and she tempted him. Joseph fled from this temptation. Whenever this temptation comes, the only way to deal with it is to flee. Do not talk or reason with the other party—run away. Reuben lost the birthright because of his defilement, and Joseph obtained it because of his purity. God is righteous, just, and fair. Reuben was on the dark side, and he lost; Joseph was on the bright side, and he gained. Because Reuben was in danger of dying, or at least of being reduced, Moses prayed that he would not die. Anyone in the church life who commits fornication will be in a very dangerous position. He will not only lose the top portion of the enjoyment of Christ; he will be in danger of dying or of being reduced. This is the experience of Reuben.

The birthright is composed not only of the double portion of the land, but also of the kingship and the priesthood. As the firstborn, Reuben should have inherited all three blessings. Due to his defilement, he lost not only the double portion of the land, but also the kingship and the priesthood. As we have seen, the double portion of the land was given to Joseph, the kingship was given to Judah (1 Chron. 5:2), and the priesthood was given to Levi (Deut. 33:8-10). This typifies that today, if we allow ourselves to be defiled, we shall lose the double portion of enjoying Christ, the kingship, and the priesthood.

(6) Concerning Simeon and Levi

(a) Receiving No Blessing because of Their Cruelty

We have seen that Simeon and Levi received no blessing because of their cruelty (34:25-30). Their cruelty in slaughtering and plundering the city of Shechem frightened their father to such an extent that he could not give them any blessing. Their indulgence in their disposition caused them to lose the father's blessing.

(b) To Be Scattered in Israel

Jacob was frightened by Simeon and Levi's cruel disposition. Hence, he would not allow them to dwell together. Rather, he exercised judgment over them to scatter them among the children of Israel so that they would not be able to behave cruelly according to their disposition.

(c) Simeon Being Omitted in Moses' Blessing

Simeon was omitted from Moses' blessing recorded in Deuteronomy. According to the righteous law of God, Simeon had no ground to be blessed. It is not an insignificant matter to be omitted from the record of God. Simeon was altogether too natural, never exercising any restriction over his natural disposition. I believe he was the one who initiated the plot to kill Joseph. Therefore, when Joseph's brothers came down to Egypt the first time, Joseph arranged for Simeon to be kept in prison. While he was in prison, Simeon might have said to himself, "I shouldn't have done that to Joseph." Simeon must have had a very cruel disposition. No matter what our disposition may be, we should not indulge in it. Simeon lost all the enjoyment of Christ through indulging in his disposition. He needed to share another's rich portion of Christ, the rich portion of Judah. Because "the part of the children of Judah was too much for them," Simeon was scattered among the people of Judah (Josh. 19:1, 9).

(d) Levi Receiving the Priesthood
because of His Faithfulness to the Lord

Although Simeon and Levi were companions, Levi eventually took the opportunity to have his natural disposition changed. Both Simeon and Levi had a disposition to kill others. But at the time the children of Israel worshipped the golden calf, Levi's killing disposition was used by God (Exo. 32:29). When Moses came down from the mountain with the tablets and saw the people worshipping the golden calf, he said, "Who is on the Lord's side? Let him come unto me" (Exo. 32:26). Out of all the tribes, only one tribe, the tribe of Levi, gathered together unto Moses. Why did Simeon not join Levi? They were of the same natural disposition. However, when

God's call came, one answered it, and the other refused to respond. This indicates that, although we may have a very ugly disposition, our disposition may still be useful in God's purpose. However, there are certain conditions that must be met. Firstly, we must consecrate ourselves; secondly, we must exercise our disposition against our natural likes and dislikes; and thirdly, we must use our disposition in a renewed, transformed way. Because the inhabitants of the city of Shechem were Levi's enemies, it was easy for him to kill them. But it was quite another matter to kill parents, brothers, sons, and relatives. In order to do this, you must exercise your disposition against your desire and use it in a new way, a way that is both for God and with God. Both Simeon and Levi, having a killing disposition, were able to slay others. However, the slaying of the men in Shechem did not require them to exercise their disposition against their own desire. Simeon did not join Levi in carrying out Moses' command because he was not willing to pay the price. Simeon might have said, "It was all right to kill the people of Shechem, but it is crazy to kill our brothers, our children, and our relatives. Yes, they all worshipped the idol. But God is merciful, and He will forgive them. Why must we kill them?" At that time, these two companions were separated. The one used his natural disposition for God, with God, and in a new way, and the other did not. Levi used his disposition in the way of transformation. Thus, Levi's natural disposition, his slaying disposition, was transformed.

Do not think it is impossible for your disposition to be used by God. It may be used by Him if you use it against your natural desire and in a transformed way. I have known some brothers whose will was very strong. Perhaps you would say that their will was stubborn. But because their stubborn will was used for God, with God, and in a new way, they were used by Him. God cannot use one whose will is like jelly. Such a will must be transformed into steel. The principle here is that our natural disposition can be changed and used by God. Levi not only slaughtered the men of Shechem, but also hamstrung their oxen. Through transformation work a disposition was not only used by God to kill the idol worshippers, but also to slay the sacrifices for offerings to God. Our natural disposition will be useful if three conditions are met: consecration, using it against our natural desire, and using it in a renewed and transformed way.

Because Levi's disposition was changed, he became a great blessing. God's Thummim and Urim were with him (Deut. 33:8), and he had the privilege of coming into the presence of God to serve Him. Although the double portion of the land is rich, the privilege of entering God's presence is intimate. The priesthood can be considered as the sweet portion of the birthright. Levi received this portion.

(e) The Scattering of Levi Becoming a Blessing to the Children of Israel

In 49:7 Jacob said that Levi should be scattered among the children of Israel. According to Joshua 21, this prophecy was fulfilled through the casting of lots. Because of Levi's faithfulness and absoluteness, Levi was scattered among the children of Israel. Moses, a God-man, was very happy with Levi. However, he could not annul the prophecy of Jacob; rather, he had to fulfill it. Therefore, the Lord said to Moses, "Command the children of Israel, that they give unto the Levites, of the inheritance of their possession, cities to dwell in; and ye shall give also unto the Levites suburbs for the cities round about them" (Num. 35:2). Each of the twelve tribes had to set aside some cities for the Levites. The selection of these cities was made by lot. There was no maneuvering in this matter, for the lot did not permit the exercise of any maneuvering. Altogether, the Levites were given forty-eight cities (Num. 35:6).

Out of these forty-eight cities, six were to be cities of refuge (Num. 35:6; Josh. 20:7-9). These cities were conveniently located throughout the land of Israel. Three were on the east side of the Jordan, and three were on the west side. A manslayer could easily flee to one of these cities of refuge. Therefore, the scattering of Levi according to the curse actually became a blessing. The Levites brought people to God and God to the people. Thus, in ancient times, it was a blessing to have some Levites in your city or in your territory (Judg. 17:7-13).

These cities of refuge are a type of Christ. We all are manslayers, and Christ is our city of refuge. Do you really think that you have never slain anyone? We all have slain our parents, our husband or wife, or our children. The brothers in the brothers' house have all slain one another. After we have slain someone, we need to flee to a city of refuge; that is, we must run to Christ.

The scattered Levites not only brought others to God; they also brought God's refuge to sinful people. We may apply this to our situation today. If we are true Levites, wherever we are, Christ will be present as a city of refuge for others. Our dwelling will be a city of refuge into which sinners can flee for salvation. In this way we bring God's refuge to sinful people. The sinners do not need to run to a cathedral; they simply need to flee to God's refuge, to the cities where God's priests dwell. In these days the saints in Anaheim are grouping together according to neighborhoods. I hope that each group will be a city of refuge and that many unbelievers will flee to this refuge. In this refuge those who have committed sins will find the covering they need. Because there are so few Levites, there are hardly any places of refuge in the city of Anaheim. We must be today's Levites. We must be desperate, absolute, and faithful to slay our fleshly desires so that we may be God's Levites, God's priests. If we are Levites, then wherever we live, our dwelling place will be a city of refuge into which sinners may run for salvation.

Through the cases of Reuben, Simeon, and Levi we see the possibility of either losing or gaining. Whether we shall lose or gain depends upon our attitude and upon our reaction to various situations. May God have mercy on us so that we may react in a way that will cause us to gain and not to lose.

LIFE-STUDY OF GENESIS

MESSAGE NINETY-NINE

BEING MATURED
THE MANIFESTATION OF MATURITY

(4)

In this message we come to 49:8-15, the most difficult section of this chapter. In order to understand these verses, we need a strong spirit and a clear mind.

As I pointed out in the last message, the twelve sons of Jacob are divided into four groups of three. This is not according to my opinion; it is absolutely according to the arrangement of the Bible. The books of Moses reveal that the twelve sons of Jacob are arranged in three different orders: the order according to birth, the order according to blessing, and the order according to encampment. Let us first consider the order according to birth. Jacob's twelve sons were born of four mothers. The first was Leah, Jacob's proper wife. The first four sons, Reuben, Simeon, Levi, and Judah, were born of Leah. The second mother was a maid named Bilhah. Jacob's fifth son, Dan, and his sixth, Naphtali, were born of her. Jacob's seventh and eighth sons, Gad and Asher, were born of another maid, Zilpah. The ninth and the tenth, Issachar and Zebulun, were also born of Leah. Finally, Joseph, the eleventh, and Benjamin, the twelfth, were born of Rachel. This is the order according to birth.

In the order according to blessing, the first three sons are Reuben, Simeon, and Levi, the same as in the order according to birth. They are followed by Judah, Zebulun, and Issachar. Thus, the first two groups in the order according to blessing include the six sons born of Leah. However, in the order according to birth Issachar precedes Zebulun, but in the order according to blessing Zebulun comes before Issachar. The third group includes Dan, Gad, Asher, and Naphtali.

According to birth, the order was Dan, Naphtali, Gad, and Asher, but according to blessing, it is Dan, Gad, Asher, and Naphtali. Later we shall see that Gad was moved from this group and replaced Levi in the group with Reuben for encamping. The fourth group is composed of the sons of Rachel, Joseph and Benjamin, the same according to blessing as according to birth. (In the encampment, Joseph became two tribes through Ephraim and Manasseh.)

In the book of Numbers we see the order according to encampment. This book reveals that the twelve tribes of Israel were encamped around the tabernacle. At that time, they were armies, and they camped as armies. The arrangement of the tribes around the tabernacle went from the east, to the south, to the west, and then to the north. According to the encamping order, Judah, Issachar, and Zebulun were on the east, toward the sun; Reuben, Simeon, and Gad on the south; Ephraim, Manasseh, and Benjamin on the west; and Dan, Asher, and Naphtali on the north. Gad was placed with Reuben and Simeon because Levi had been uplifted and taken into the tabernacle, the center of the camp. Ephraim, Manasseh, and Benjamin were the equivalent of Joseph and Benjamin. Through Ephraim and Manasseh, Joseph became two tribes to inherit the double portion of the land.

In the foregoing message we considered the first group in the order according to blessing in Genesis 49: Reuben, Simeon, and Levi. In that message we saw mainly the changing of the birthright and the transformation of the natural disposition. The outstanding feature of the first group is that it reveals that our natural status and disposition can be changed. In this message we come to the second group, composed of Judah, Zebulun, and Issachar. Verses 8 through 15 are very difficult to understand. In order to understand chapter forty-nine, we must know the Bible in black and white. Furthermore, we must know the history of the children of Israel, we must have the experience of Christ and the church life, and we must know how to allegorize the Bible. If you do not know how to allegorize the Scriptures and interpret the poetry of the Bible, how could you be able to understand such a portion as Genesis chapter forty-nine? In verse 9 Judah is likened first to a young lion and then to a lioness, and verse 11 speaks of the choice vine and of binding the foal to the vine. When those who oppose the allegorizing of the Bible read this portion of the Word, they will have no way to understand it. Verse 13 says that Zebulun will be a haven of ships and dwell at the haven of the sea; verse 14, that Issachar is a strong ass couching between the sheepfolds; and verse 15, that Issachar saw that "rest was good, and the land that it was pleasant." What does all this mean? Because this is so difficult, very few Christians have any understanding of it at all. The only way to understand it is to allegorize it.

However, it is not an easy matter to allegorize the Bible. In order to understand such a portion as 49:8-15, we need several things: the knowledge of the Bible in black and white; the knowledge of the history of the children of Israel; the experiences of Christ and the church life; the wisdom to allegorize the Bible; and the knowledge of how to apply the types to today's situation. When we have all this, then we shall be able to see the true significance of this portion of the Word.

The Bible is very economical. Not one word is wasted. Jacob's prophecy with blessing in chapter forty-nine is poetry. Poetry is the most thoughtful and meaningful form of writing. Jacob's utterance of prophecy with blessing is stately and filled with grandeur.

(7) Concerning Judah

As we consider these verses, we need to be impressed with the fact that in the first group, composed of Reuben, Simeon, and Levi, Christ has not yet come. We do not see Christ in Reuben, in Simeon, or in Levi. What we see in Levi is his absoluteness, his desperation, and his faithfulness. It was due to these characteristics that the Lord gave him the priesthood. Although Levi had the priesthood with the Urim and Thummim, we do not see Christ in him. Only when Judah comes does Christ appear. Judah typifies Christ. In fact, we may even substitute the name of Christ for Judah in this prophecy. Although Jacob had twelve sons, Christ came only out of Judah. In Revelation 5:5 He is called the Lion of the tribe of Judah. Hence, because Christ came out of Judah, He belongs to Judah. In order to understand verses 8 through 12, we must apply these verses to Christ and substitute the name of Christ for Judah.

We can all testify from our experience that once we were Reubens. Were you not a sinful Reuben before you were saved? Were you not, like Reuben, one boiling over with lust? We also were Simeons, those who were natural and filled with the natural disposition. Everything we did was according to our lusts and our disposition. But praise the Lord that we were saved and became a Levi! Now we are qualified to come into the presence of God and, with the Urim and Thummim, to receive God's vision and God's revelation. Furthermore, as priests, we can bring others into God's presence and learn the Lord's mind regarding them. Is not your experience somewhat like this? Although you may be the least among the saints, day by day you come into the presence of the Lord. As you stand in His presence, you sense that there is something shining and enlightening within you. This is the Urim and the Thummim. At times you bring others to the Lord and pray for them. Perhaps you say, "O Lord, remember my father, my brother-in-law, and my sister-in-law." This is the priesthood. Neither Reuben nor Simeon had a function like this. Only Levi did. And we also have it today. We are no longer Reuben and Simeon; rather, we are today's Levi.

However, although I had been a Levi for years, I can testify that I had little experience of Christ. Thus, in addition to the experience of Levi, we need the experience of Judah, that is, the experience of Christ. It is good to come into the presence of the Lord to receive enlightenment, revelation, and vision, and it is good to bring others into His presence. Nevertheless, we still need Christ as a young lion, the Lion of the tribe of Judah. Have you ever experienced Him as a strong lion? As the young lion, Christ is for fighting, for putting His hand on the neck of His enemies. To place the hand on the neck of our enemies means to defeat them, to subdue them, and to gain the victory over them.

(a) Praised and Worshipped by His Brothers

Verse 8 says, "Judah, thy brethren shall praise thee: thy hand shall be upon the neck of thine enemies; thy father's children shall bow down before thee" (Heb.). Here we are told that Judah's brothers will praise him and that his father's children will bow down before him. This means that Judah's brothers will praise and worship him for his victory. Does this actually refer to Judah or to Christ? It refers to Christ. Thus, I say again, we may substitute Christ for Judah and declare, "Christ, Thy brethren shall praise Thee, and Thy Father's children shall bow down before Thee."

(b) A Young Lion Conquering the Enemies and a Lion and a Lioness Resting in Conquest

Verse 9 says, "Judah is a young lion: from the prey, my son, thou art gone up," and verse 8 says, "Thy hand shall be upon the neck of thine enemies." We need to see the picture portrayed here. A lion dwells on the mountain. When he goes after some prey, he descends from the mountain. As he is waiting to seize his prey, he crouches. But after he has taken his prey, he brings it up the mountain with him. Thus, the words, "From the prey, my son, thou art gone up," mean that the lion has gone up the mountain to devour his prey. After eating it, the lion no longer crouches; instead, he couches, that is, he lies down. This indicates that, after swallowing up his prey, he is satisfied and lies down to rest.

We need to apply this picture to Christ. Christ was firstly the young lion crouching as He waited for His prey. After seizing His prey, He brought His captive to the heavens where He enjoyed him. This reminds us of Ephesians 4:8, which says, "When he ascended up on high, he led a train of vanquished foes" (Gk.). This train of vanquished foes was Christ's prey. Now, after enjoying the prey He has captured, He is satisfied and rests in the heavens. To put it in plain words, this means that Christ is now sitting on the throne in the heavens. But according to the poetry of verse 9, after devouring His prey, Christ was satisfied and couched to enjoy His rest.

Have you ever seen such a vision or experienced such a Christ? In your experience, do you have Christ as a young lion? Do you also have Him as the satisfied lion who lies down to rest? Years ago, when I was young, I was troubled by many kinds of enemies. But one day I saw that my enemies had already become a prey to my Christ. My temper, my problems, my weaknesses, and all my other enemies were Christ's prey. He went to the cross and captured them, and in resurrection He led a train of vanquished foes to the heavens for His enjoyment. Now, in the heavens, He is no longer fighting; He is couching. He is lying down to rest, and I am experiencing Him as a resting lion. He is couching, and I also am resting. Why should I be troubled by anything? I simply need to enjoy this victorious, satisfied, and resting Christ.

I know the situation of the brothers and sisters, especially of the young people. In the last message you learned that you were a Levi. However, during the past week, you have probably been troubled by some enemies. Perhaps an enemy came in through your roommate, your parents, your husband or wife, or your own disposition. But after you have read this message, I hope you will also be able to say that you are a Judah. Immediately after Levi, Judah appears. This means that Christ has come. Today our Christ is no longer the young lion; He is the resting lion. When the Apostle John was weeping because no one was qualified to open the scroll of God's mystery, an elder said to him, "Do not weep; behold, the Lion of the tribe of Judah, the Root of David, has overcome to open the scroll and its seven seals" (Rev. 5:5). This verse does not say that our Christ will overcome; it says that He has overcome already. He has captured the prey and swallowed him. Hallelujah, all the enemies have been devoured by Christ! Today Christ is not the fighting One; He is a couching One, the resting One sitting in the heavens. If you see this, you will forget your enemies, your temper, and the troubles caused by parents and children, and you will say, "Hallelujah! Lord, I worship You and praise You! Lord, You were the young, fighting lion. But today You are resting in the heavens as the victorious lion. And now I am partaking of all You have done."

Notice that, according to the Hebrew, verse 9 says, "He couches, he lies down as a lion, and as a lioness." Why does this verse first speak of a lion and then a lioness? The young lion is for fighting, for gaining the victory, and couching is the sign that the fighting lion has won the victory, has devoured the prey, and is now resting in satisfaction. Here we firstly have the young lion and then the couching lion. But what is the significance of the lioness? It is that the lion is about to bring forth many cubs, many baby lions. Thus, Christ is not only the fighting lion and the resting lion, but also the producing lioness. Christ is our mother lion, and we are all His lion cubs. In the last message we saw that we have become priests. In this message we need to see that we also have been made lion cubs. When the enemy troubles you, you should realize that you are a baby lion. Let the enemy challenge us all he wants. We are not merely priests; we are also lions. Christ is the producing lioness who has brought forth us as His many cubs.

The last part of verse 9 says, "Who shall rouse him up?" Some versions say, "Who dares to rouse him?" This means, "Who dares to defy Him?" Today, not only is Christ the lion; we also are lions.

(c) Producing Kings, Rulers, and Christ

Verse 10 says, "The sceptre shall not depart from Judah, nor the ruler's staff from between his feet, until Shiloh come; and unto him shall the obedience of the peoples be" (Heb.). The scepter here denotes the scepter of the kingship or of the kingdom. Psalm 45:6 says, "The sceptre of thy kingdom is a right sceptre." The scepter, a symbol of the kingdom, refers to the kingly authority of Christ. Thus, the scepter in verse 10 refers to Christ's kingdom, Christ's kingship. For the scepter never to depart from Judah means the kingship will never depart from Christ.

Hebrew poetry is written in pairs; hence, "the ruler's staff" in this verse is synonymous with "the sceptre." Undoubtedly the ruler here is Christ. The Hebrew word for ruler in this verse means lawgiver. Christ is the One who gives the law, for He has the staff and the scepter. He is the Ruler who has the authority, the staff and the scepter of the kingship.

This verse says that the ruler's staff will not depart from "between his feet." The words "between his feet" are a poetic term denoting seed or posterity. Thus, they refer to Judah's descendants. This means that the tribe of Judah will always have kings. According to 1 Chronicles 5:2, Judah has the kingship, and rulers come out of his posterity.

(d) Having Shiloh

This authority will continue until Shiloh comes. The word Shiloh means "Peace bringer." Most good Bible teachers agree that Shiloh refers to Christ in His second coming. When Christ comes the second time, He will come as the Prince of peace, as the One who brings peace. At that time, the whole earth will be filled with peace.

Verse 10 also says, "And unto him shall the obedience of the peoples be." The peoples here are equivalent to the nations. At the second coming of Christ, all nations will submit to Him and obey Him. Isaiah 2:1 through 3 and 11:10 indicate that from the beginning of the millennium at the Lord's second coming, all nations will obey Christ. They will come to Him to receive God's instructions.

(e) Rich in Wine and Milk

Verse 11 says, "Binding his foal unto the vine, and his ass's colt unto the choice vine; he washed his garments in wine, and his clothes in the blood of grapes." This verse is extremely difficult to understand. In the Bible an ass, or donkey, signifies one who labors very hard, especially laboring in the matter of transportation. Even the Lord Jesus rode upon an ass into the city of Jerusalem (Matt. 21:5, 7). Although an ass is usually used for labor in travel, in verse 11 the ass is not laboring; it is bound to the vine. This signifies that labor was over, that the destination has been reached, and that the rest has begun. Do not think that the word "binding" in this verse is negative. No, it is very positive. Any ass used for long journeys would certainly enjoy being bound to a vine. Whenever a rider binds an ass to something, even to a stake, the ass will be happy. In the poetic language of verse 11, the binding of the ass depicts rest. According to this verse, even the donkey has stopped his work. The ass here is not bound to a stake, but to a fruitful vine full of vegetation.

If we consider this picture, we shall see that it signifies that labor is over and that the harvest has come. We know that this verse refers to the harvest because it speaks of wine, the produce of the vine. This implies the riches of the harvest. The latter part of verse 11 says, "He washed his garments in wine, and his clothes in the blood of grapes." This indicates that there is an abundance of wine. The supply of wine is so bountiful that people not only drink it, but even wash their clothes in it. Revelation 6:6, speaking of famine, says, "Do not harm the oil and the wine." This warning indicates the scarceness of wine during famine. However, in Genesis 49:11 there is an abundance of wine. The words "the blood of grapes" refer to grape juice. Have you ever seen a country with such riches that its inhabitants even washed their clothes in grape juice? Although America is a rich land, it is not that rich. What a picture we have in verse 11! This picture shows that labor is over and that rest in the enjoyment of the riches has begun, even for the donkeys. Now is not the time for sowing the seed; it is the time of harvest. Verse 11 is a poetic description of the millennium, the coming age of the thousand years. In that age, labor will cease, and instead of labor, there will be rest. If you still choose to labor, you should bind your ass. Do not loose it. According to Leviticus 23, on the day of the feast of Tabernacles, no one was permitted to work. Labor was prohibited because everything had been accomplished. All that remained was to enjoy the produce of the rich harvest. The feast of Tabernacles typifies the millennium. During the millennium there will be no labor because all the labor will have been completed in the preceding dispensations. The asses, the laboring ones, will be bound. Instead of labor, there will be the rich enjoyment of an abundant harvest. There will be so much wine that we shall wash our clothes in it.

Verse 12 says, "His eyes shall be red with wine, and his teeth white with milk." In the Bible wine symbolizes the joy of God's salvation of life. The first miracle the Lord Jesus performed was that of changing water into wine (John 2:1-11). This wine signifies not only redemption, but also the salvation of life and the salvation in life. When we have the salvation of life, this salvation becomes the wine that constantly stirs us to rejoice. Along with the wine, we have milk. Just as the source of the wine is the vineyards, the source of the milk is the sheepfolds spoken of in verse 14 (Heb.). Milk signifies the nourishment of life that satisfies us.

When someone is dying of starvation, the area around his eyes becomes greenish grey. But in this verse the eyes are not greenish grey; they are "red with wine." Furthermore, the teeth are "white with milk." The calcium contained in milk produces healthy teeth with the proper color. These figures regarding the eyes and the teeth indicate that, when the asses are bound and labor is over, the produce of the rich harvest will be more than sufficient. It will be so adequate that people will even wash their clothes in wine. Eventually they will have eyes that are red with wine. Also, their teeth will be strong and white.

This rest and enjoyment depend on Christ as the fighting, resting, and producing lion. As such a lion, He has brought forth us, His baby lions. Because the work has been accomplished, there is no need for us to labor. Instead, we should simply rest and enjoy the rich produce of the good land. Today we are enjoying the wine and the milk. Whenever people look at us, our eyes should be red and our teeth white. This is a picture of the church life today and of the millennium in the coming age.

Even in today's church life, all the asses should be bound. Often the brothers and sisters bring a laboring ass with them to the meeting. This indicates that they are still laboring and journeying and that they have not yet come to their goal, their destination. But all these asses must be bound. Because we have already entered into rest and have come to our destination, there should be no laboring or journeying. We have reached our destination, our goal, the place where we can enjoy the boundless supply of wine and milk. Do you still need a laboring donkey? Some of the older ones always have a donkey with them. It seems they are still journeying, still laboring. After hearing one of my messages, they expect to labor and journey even more. But verse 11 says that we must bind our ass to the rich vine. This means that we must cease our laboring and our journeying. Today, in the church life, we are in the goal, the destination. Here there is no labor, only rest and enjoyment. I expect to see all the asses bound. Instead of laboring, go home to wash your clothes in wine. Then come to the next meeting with red eyes and white teeth. Come full of milk, full of joy and nourishment.

(8) Concerning Zebulun and Issachar

(a) Zebulun Being at the Haven of the Sea

After Judah, Zebulun comes in. Verse 13 says, "Zebulun shall dwell at the haven of the sea; and he shall be for a haven of ships; and his border shall be unto Zidon." This verse says Zebulun is a haven for ships. The method of transportation here has been changed from asses to ships. We cannot understand the poetry in this verse without referring to the New Testament. The fulfillment of this verse is in Matthew 4:15, which says, "Land of Zebulun and land of Naphtali, way of the sea beyond the Jordan, Galilee of the nations." Christ began His ministry from Zebulun in Galilee, and it was the Galileans who brought the glad tidings of Christ to all the earth. The Galilean disciples were a haven of ships. They brought forth the good news of Christ as the fighting, resting, and producing lion to every part of the world represented by Zidon.

(b) Zebulun Rejoicing in Going Out

Deuteronomy 33:18 says, "Rejoice, Zebulun, in thy going out." According to this verse, Zebulun had to go out. And Zebulun did go out. All the Galileans went out with the glad tidings of the victory of Christ, bearing the word of the victorious, restful, and productive Christ. These Galileans went forth with Christ's victory, Christ's satisfaction, and Christ's productiveness. This is the glad tidings.

Although Zebulun went out, Issachar stayed in the tents (Deut. 33:18). Thus, Zebulun rejoiced in going out, and Issachar rejoiced in his tents. One had to go out, and the other had to stay.

(c) Issachar Being a Strong Ass Couching between the Sheepfolds

Genesis 49:14 says, "Issachar is a strong ass couching down between the sheepfolds." In interpretation, this is linked to the foal and the colt, the young ass, in verse 11. The young ass there is tied to the rich harvest; hence, the strong ass is couching, resting, here. Issachar is not working; he is couching, that is, he is lying down and resting between the sheepfolds. Are you today's Issachar? Are you couching or laboring? Some think I am always working. But they are wrong. They do not realize that my working is my couching. There is a hymn which says that as we work, we rest. If I do not work, I have no rest. The more I work, the more I rest. As I am working, I am couching. In the Lord's recovery there is no need for laboring asses. Although we need strong asses, they should couch, not work. According to the picture portrayed in this verse, Issachar is couching between the sheepfolds. Although the strong ass does nothing, the sheep produce the milk. I can testify that I am a strong ass couching down and watching the sheep produce milk. While you are producing the milk, I am resting.

(d) Issachar Enjoying Rest in the Rich Land and Becoming a Servant under Taskwork

Verse 15 says, "And he saw that rest was good, and the land that it was pleasant; and bowed his shoulder to bear, and became a servant under taskwork" (Heb.). Issachar saw that the rest was good and that the land was pleasant. Issachar, the strong ass, is resting and enjoying the pleasant, rich land, which is Christ. At such a time, he bows his shoulder to bear burdens and thus he becomes a servant under taskwork. This means that he serves in order to have something to offer to the Lord. Instead of "under taskwork," the King James Version says "unto tribute," which is a payment given as an offering. Without experience, we cannot understand this matter. According to Christian experience, proper Christians do not labor as hard-working asses. Rather, they rest as strong asses. While they are resting, they enjoy the riches of Christ. Through the enjoyment of these riches, they become willing to bow their shoulder, take up a burden and serve for tribute rendered to the King. In the proper church life, we do not labor as common asses. Instead we lie down to rest and enjoy both the finished work of Christ and the riches of Christ. By this enjoyment we are willing to bow our shoulder and lift up a heavy burden, serving to gain tribute to render to our Master, our King. Although this will be completely fulfilled in the millennium, we have a foretaste of it in the church life today.

In the church life we experience our Christ as the fighting, resting, and producing lion. Due to His victorious work, there is a rich produce, a rich harvest. Thus, there is no need for our labor. But there is the preaching of the glad tidings concerning Christ; for Zebulun, the haven of ships, sends out the good news of the Lion of the tribe of Judah. We also have the experience of Issachar. We are not laboring; rather, we are resting and enjoying the riches of Christ. As we rest and enjoy Christ in such a way, we are willing to bow our shoulder to bear a heavy burden to do the taskwork, the work assigned by our King-Master, so that we may be able to render tribute to our King. Thus, today's church life is a miniature of the coming millennium. If you pray over all the points covered in this message and digest them, you will see that in this portion of the Word we have a portrait of the coming millennium. This portrait reveals that we may now participate in a miniature of the millennium. By considering this picture, we shall know where we must be today.

LIFE-STUDY OF GENESIS

MESSAGE ONE HUNDRED

THE SPIRITUAL SIGNIFICANCE OF THE BLESSING PROPHESIED CONCERNING JUDAH, ZEBULUN, AND ISSACHAR

(1)

In this message I am burdened to give a further word on 49:8-15. The language used to describe the group composed of Judah, Zebulun, and Issachar is strange, new, and foreign to our understanding. In these verses a number of figures are used in relation to Judah: a young lion, a couching lion, a lioness, the scepter, the ruler's staff, the foal bound to the vine, the ass's colt bound to the choice vine, the garments washed in wine, and the clothes washed in grape juice. Have you ever heard of someone washing his garments in wine or his clothes in grape juice? Verse 12 speaks of eyes that are red with wine and teeth that are white with milk. With respect to Zebulun we have the figure of a "haven of ships" (v. 13), and Issachar is likened to a "strong ass couching down between the sheepfolds" who sees that the rest is good and that the land is pleasant and who bows his shoulder to become a servant under taskwork (vv. 14-15, Heb.). All these points are rich, and we need to be impressed with them.

None of these points could be covered in Genesis 1, an account of God's creation. According to the record of Genesis 1, on the sixth day God made man in His own image. At the time of Genesis 1 it was impossible to have a word about Judah being a young lion, a couching lion, and a lioness, or a word about tying our donkey to the vine. Neither was it possible to hear of garments washed in wine. Although in Genesis 2 we have a garden and the two trees, we find none of the points mentioned in 49:8-15. Because these matters are part of the prophecy with blessing uttered by a man who was both transformed and mature in the divine life, they can only be found in chapter forty-nine.

In Genesis 2 Adam was wonderful, for he was able to give names to all the animals. This indicates that he was very capable. However, although he could name the animals, he could not utter a prophecy with blessing. Adam was merely a created being. He did not have the divine life wrought into him. In Genesis 1 and 2 he had not yet fallen. In a sense, we need to appreciate the fall of man. The children who fall the most are the strongest. A child who has never fallen is surely very weak. Adam, the man in Genesis 1, was perfect, but he was not very strong. However, Jacob, the man in Genesis 49, was not only perfect, but also strong. If this transformed Jacob had been surrounded by serpents, he still would not have fallen. Instead, he would have crushed the head of those serpents and cut off their tails. Which do you prefer to be—Adam in chapter one or Jacob in chapter forty-nine? I prefer to be Jacob.

In chapter forty-nine Jacob uttered a prophetic blessing which Adam could never have spoken. Only Jacob was qualified to utter such a blessing. Adam, however, was altogether unqualified for this because he did not have the divine life wrought into him and he was never transformed or matured in the life of God. But Jacob was not only created and fallen; he was regenerated, and the divine life had been wrought into him. Although there is no record that Adam's name was changed, we are told that Jacob's name was changed to Israel. Adam means "red earth," but Israel means "the prince of God." Do you prefer to be red earth or the prince of God? Red earth can never prophesy such a word as Jacob spoke in chapter forty-nine.

Jacob passed through the full experience of man's fall. I doubt that anyone else has ever fallen as low as Jacob. Although Jacob's story is our biography, we cannot compare with him as far as the fall is concerned. Jacob was the expert in being fallen. No one can surpass him in this matter. Jacob cheated, robbed, and supplanted everyone, including his mother. The fact that he utilized his mother proves that he supplanted her. (To supplant a person is simply to utilize him, to usurp him.) On one occasion Jacob even did his best to supplant God. That night at Peniel Jacob exercised all his energy to grasp God, to supplant Him, and to compel Him to do something for him (32:24-31). Jacob, of course, could not defeat God. Eventually, God touched his thigh, and Jacob became lame. Because Jacob supplanted everyone, he fell all the way to the bottom. Nevertheless, eventually he was transformed and matured and reached the peak of the experience of the divine life. Therefore, in chapter forty-nine he was able to speak a rich word of prophecy with blessing.

Prior to this chapter it was impossible for such a word to be spoken, for there was no one transformed and mature enough to do it. Furthermore, before chapter forty-nine the proper environment had not been created. The imparting of a heavenly vision always requires a suitable environment. In order for Jacob to speak the word recorded in 49:8-15, he had to be transformed and matured, and he had to have the sons over whom to prophesy. Let us now consider the spiritual significance of the blessing prophesied in these verses, a portion of the Word that requires the entire Bible for its development.

I. CONCERNING JUDAH—
THE GLAD TIDINGS OF CHRIST

Verses 8 through 12 concern Judah. Verse 9 says that Judah is a lion. In Revelation 5:5 Christ is called the Lion of the tribe of Judah. This proves that Genesis 49 needs Revelation 5 for its development. It also proves that these verses of Jacob's prophetic blessing require the whole Bible for their development. My burden in this message is to impress you with the spiritual interpretation of these verses.

We have seen that Genesis is a book of seeds. Nearly all the truths in the Bible are sown as seeds in Genesis. In the New Testament there are three main truths concerning Christ.

The first is the truth of the victory of Christ. The fact that Christ is victorious means that He has accomplished everything God required of Him. In this accomplished work He took care of sin, solved the problem of the world, defeated Satan, abolished death, and eliminated every negative thing.

He has gained the full victory for the accomplishment of God's purpose. This is the victory of Christ, the first basic truth in the New Testament regarding Christ.

The second main truth is the truth of the authority of Christ, the kingdom of Christ. Because Christ has won the victory, He has been made Lord of all. All authority in heaven and on earth has been given to Him (Matt. 28:18). Furthermore, He has received the universal and eternal kingdom of His Father. Thus, He has the authority, the kingship, and the kingdom.

The third main truth in the New Testament concerning Christ is the truth of the enjoyment and rest in Christ. Christ has accomplished everything in His victory and He has received the authority and the kingdom so that we may have enjoyment and find rest in Him. What enjoyment and rest we have in Christ! These three truths are a summary of the New Testament.

Because the New Testament is the harvest of the seeds sown in Genesis, we must now locate the seeds of Christ's victory, of Christ's kingdom, and of the enjoyment and rest in Christ. They are found in Genesis 49:8-12. These five verses contain three wonderful seeds: the seed of Christ's victory, the seed of Christ's kingdom, and the seed of the enjoyment and rest in Christ. How I thank the Lord and worship Him that, at this end time, He has opened this portion of the Word to us!

A. The Victory of Christ

1. Christ as the Young Lion Overcoming the Enemies

In 49:8 and 9 we see the victory of Christ. Genesis, a marvelous book, is a book of pictures. In his prophecy Jacob likened Judah to a lion in three aspects: a young lion, a couching lion, and a lioness. The young lion is for fighting, for seizing the prey. Verse 9 says, "Judah is a young lion: from the prey, my son, thou art gone up" (Heb.). The words "thou art gone up" imply that the young lion first had to come down. He came down from the mountain to the plain to capture his prey. After the young lion seized his prey, he went up to the mountaintop again to enjoy it. When Christ was on earth and was crucified on the cross, He was a young lion seizing the prey. And what a prey He captured! It included the whole world, all the sinners, and even Satan, the serpent. From seizing His prey Christ has gone up to the mountaintop, that is, to the third heaven. This means that from His victory, He has ascended to the heavens. Ephesians 4:8 says that when Christ ascended to the height, He led captive those taken captive. Christ gained the victory; He put His hand upon Satan's neck. Hallelujah, He has put His hand upon the neck of His enemies! As the young lion, He has overcome all His enemies. Many chapters in the New Testament reveal how Christ came as a young lion, how He went to the cross to seize His prey, and how He ascended to the mountaintop in the third heaven.

2. Christ as the Lion Couching in Satisfaction after Enjoying the Prey

Genesis 49:9 also says, "He couches, he lies down as a lion" (Heb.). Christ is also a couching lion, the lion couching in satisfaction after enjoying His prey. After a lion has enjoyed his prey and has been satisfied, he couches; he lies down to rest in satisfaction. The figure of the couching lion in verse 9 describes Christ as the One enjoying His rest in the heavens. After gaining the victory and enjoying the prey, He was satisfied. Thus, He is now resting in the heavens in His satisfaction. This rest and satisfaction are the issue of Christ's victory. Christ is no longer fighting; rather, He is couching.

3. Christ as the Lioness Producing Cubs

In verse 9 (Heb.) Christ is also likened to a lioness. As a lioness, He has produced many cubs. We all are Christ's cubs. In a very real sense, the church is lion country, and everyone in the church is a baby lion. Have you ever realized that you are a lion cub? If we saw the situation from God's viewpoint, we would realize that in the eyes of God the church is a country of lions. Toward men we are lambs following the Lamb; but toward Satan we are lion cubs. Although you may not have such a realization, Satan recognizes this fact. He knows that all the believers in the Lord's recovery are lion cubs. Frequently we need to tell Satan, "Satan, don't touch me. Don't you know that my family is the lion family?" Christ is the young lion, the couching lion, and the reproducing lioness, and we are His lion cubs. This is the full victory of Christ. This is why verse 8 says that Christ, typified by Judah, is to be praised and worshipped.

B. The Kingdom of Christ

1. The Authority and Kingship of Christ

Christ's victory brings in the kingdom (v. 10). Even on earth today, wherever there is a victory, there is also a kingdom. Christ ascended to the heavens, and there He was given all authority. There He also received the kingdom. If we have the divine sight, we shall see that the entire earth is the kingdom of Christ. The nations today use Christ's calendar. According to history, the kingdom belongs to the one whose calendar is used. The fact that the nations use Christ's calendar indicates that they are His kingdom. Even the nations who oppose Christ follow His calendar. For this reason, Christ may laugh at them and say, "Although you oppose Me, you are using My calendar. In this way you are recognizing Me as your King." Christ is the King, and everyone is under His rule. If you do not believe this, I would ask you to wait for a period of time. Eventually you will see that the whole earth will be the kingdom of Christ.

Christ has been commissioned with all the authority in heaven and on earth. This should not be merely a doctrine to us. We must realize that we are under His authority. Verse 10 says, "The sceptre shall not depart from Judah, nor the ruler's staff from between his feet" (Heb.). It is correct to translate the Hebrew word rendered "scepter" as "authority." To say that the scepter will not depart from Judah means that the authority will not depart from Judah. The scepter here signifies royal, kingly authority. Christ has this authority, and we all must come under it. We, the kingdom people, are under the heavenly ruling of Christ.

We Christians also need to learn how to exercise the authority of Christ. As we face certain hardships and difficulties, there is no need to pray in a begging way. Instead, we should pray with the exercise of authority. When the children of Israel were pursued by the Egyptians, the Lord told Moses to lift up his rod and stretch out his hand over the sea (Exo. 14:15-16). Moses did so. That was an exercise of divine authority. Likewise, instead of begging, we should exercise the authority of our King and command the difficulties to flee. Because we are under the heavenly ruling, we have the position and the right to speak to difficulties, hardships, and attacks. We may say to them, "You must flee. I do not allow you to remain." We all must learn to exercise such authority.

In order to exercise this authority we must first be under the ruling of Christ. If we are rebellious and command Satan to flee, he will say, "Who are you? I will not obey you because you don't obey Christ. As one who does not obey his King, you have no position to command me." Therefore, we must be the obedient kingdom people. Our obedience gives us the position to exercise the King's authority. This is the kingdom. In the kingdom everything has been accomplished, every enemy has been defeated, and every problem has been solved.

2. *Christ Coming as the Peace-bringer*

Verse 10 says that the scepter will not depart from Judah nor the ruler's staff from between his feet until Shiloh comes. Shiloh means Peace-bringer. The proper kingdom is a realm of peace. If you do not have peace, you are not actually in the kingdom. The King must be the Peace-giver, the Peace-bringer. When our King comes back, He will come as the great Shiloh who brings peace to the whole earth. But there is no need for us to wait until that day to enjoy Him as our Shiloh. We may enjoy Christ as Shiloh today.

Consider the example of family life. In a sense, family life is a stormy sea full of turmoil. We never know when a storm will come. I have been sailing on the family-life sea for many years, and I can testify that it is often very stormy. In Matthew 14 we read of the disciples' experience on a stormy sea (Matt. 14:22-33). When Jesus was about to go up into a mountain to pray, He charged His disciples "to step into the boat and to go before Him to the other side" (Matt. 14:22). When evening had come, the boat was being tossed by the waves. Eventually, after praying there on the mountaintop, the Lord came to the disciples in the boat, walking on the sea (Matt. 14:25). When He entered the boat, the wind ceased (Matt. 14:32). This is very meaningful. The storm ceased because there can be no storm where Jesus is. The storm is not afraid of us, but it is afraid of the heavenly King. Although the storm may trouble us, it cannot trouble Him, for He walks upon the waves. In the midst of the stormy family-life sea we should not pray in a begging way. Instead, we should exercise the authority and say, "Lord, You are walking upon the sea. You are the King and You have the authority. Now I exercise Your authority over this stormy situation." Try to pray like this.

In the eyes of God the victory has been won, the kingdom is here, and peace is present. Everything has been accomplished. Therefore, we should not look at our environment. In Matthew 14:28 Peter said, "Lord if it is You, command me to come to You on the waters." Peter seemed to be saying, "Lord, if it is You, give me the word and I'll come to You. You are walking on the sea, and I'll walk on the sea also." The Lord said, "Come," and Peter came out of the boat and walked on the water to go to Jesus (Matt. 14:29). Peter had the faith to jump out of the boat and to walk on the waves. But when he began to look at the environment, his faith disappeared, and he began to sink. Peter's experience is a lesson to us not to look at our environment, but to stand on the Lord's word. Faith is a matter of standing on His word. Faith is not based on the environment; it is based on the word of the Lord. If you jump out of the boat and stand on the Lord's word, many problems will be solved. You have prayed too many begging prayers. Instead of begging, issue a command to the environment and say, "I will not allow you to disturb me. Jesus is King. The kingdom is His, and He is Shiloh. Therefore, I must have peace in my surroundings."

Often before troubles come our way, we have accepted them already. This is entirely a matter of psychology. Before

Satan, the subtle one, attacks you, he first takes you over in a psychological way. Job said, "For the thing which I greatly feared is come upon me, and that which I was afraid of is come unto me" (Job 3:25). Before Job's difficulties came upon him, he thought about those difficulties and became afraid of them. To be afraid of something means that you have already received it. Whenever you are fearful, you must immediately say, "Satan, get away from me. I am not afraid of anything. I do not accept this fear." Fear is Satan's calling card. If you accept his calling card, Satan himself will come. Every fear is a calling card. Before Satan sends you the actual difficulty, he first sends the fear of that difficulty. Do not accept Satan's calling card of fear—throw it away. This is a matter related to spiritual warfare. Some brothers have been afraid of being laid off from their jobs. A few days after they accepted this fear, they were laid off. Do not receive the thought of being laid off, but say, "Satan, I will never be laid off. Although everyone else may be laid off, I will still be employed. Because I am in the kingdom, I don't accept this fear." Christ has won the victory, and the issue of His victory is the kingdom.

3. *The Submission and Obedience of the Nations*

Genesis 49:10 says that unto Shiloh "shall the obedience of the peoples be" (Heb.). This word refers to the millennial kingdom. When Christ will come the second time as Shiloh, all the peoples will submit themselves to Him and obey Him. In principle, it is the same today. Where the authority and kingdom of Christ hold sway, there will be the submission and obedience of the peoples.

C. Rest in the Enjoyment of Christ's Riches in Life

1. *Ceasing from Labor and Resting in the Enjoyment of Christ's Life*

Now we come to the heart of my burden in this message. Verse 11 says, "Binding his foal unto the vine, and his ass's colt unto the choice vine." We all must bind our donkey to the vine. I hope that this saying will become a proverb among us.

In the Bible a donkey is an animal used for transportation. The prophet Balaam traveled by means of a donkey (Num. 22:22). When the Lord Jesus entered Jerusalem shortly before His crucifixion, He also rode upon a donkey (Matt. 21:5). According to the Bible, a donkey is always used for traveling toward a goal. To tie a donkey to something indicates that the journey is over, that you have arrived at your destination, and that you have reached your goal. To bind a donkey is not a negative thing. Any donkey would be happy to be bound to a vine. A donkey's labor is to travel to a certain destination with a certain goal. What a meaningful picture we have in 49:11! All the worldly people today are donkeys traveling, striving, laboring, and journeying to reach their goal. Without one exception, all Christians are also journeying, striving, and laboring donkeys. I certainly used to be like this when I was young. I was striving to overcome sin with the goal of one day becoming an overcomer. That was my destination, my goal. I continued my striving until the day I saw the vision of binding my donkey to the vine. I saw that there was no need for me to labor or travel to reach my destination because I had already come to my destination and I had already reached my goal. Our destination is the vine, the living Christ who is full of life. We must bind our donkey to this vine. This means that we must cease our labor and our striving and rest in Christ, the living One.

Suppose a brother tells you of his desire to be holy. Holiness is his goal, and the holy country is his destination. He tells you that he is striving and endeavoring to reach this goal; he is laboring to be filled with holiness and to dwell in the holy country. What would you say to this brother? You should say, "Brother, bind your donkey to the vine. There is no need for you to labor and strive to reach the goal of holiness. Christ is here. He is the vine, the source of life. Christ is so rich in life. Bind your donkey to Him. This means that you must cease your striving and rest in the rich, living Christ."

Suppose another brother, recently married, says to you, "Brother, as one in the Lord's recovery, I want to live a victorious life. My wife is a great test to me. Day and night I am striving to keep from being angry with her. My goal is never to lose my temper with my wife." What would you say to this brother? Firstly, you must be one who has had the experience of binding your donkey to the vine. After you have experienced this yourself, others may come to you with their problems. When they do, you should say, "You need to bind your donkey to the vine. Cease from your labor and your striving. There is no need for you to strive, because Christ has won the victory. The scepter, the kingship, and the kingdom all belong to Him. You simply need to rest in Him as the vine." How often have you heard that you must cease from your striving and simply rest in Christ, the source of life? I believe that many of us have done this. But I hope that in the recovery we shall have a new proverb to help us in this matter: Bind your donkey to the vine. This proverb is a proverb of rest. Sisters, why are you still striving? You need to bind your donkey to the vine. People used to bind their donkeys to stakes. But we do not bind our donkey to a lifeless stake; we bind it to a vine that is full of life. Just recently I have seen a clear vision concerning this matter. However, hundreds of times in the past I bound my donkey to the vine. I stopped my journeying, ceased my striving, gave up my goal, and forgot my destination. I could give up my goal because I had already reached it, and I could forget my destination because I had already arrived at it. Holiness is Christ. The power to overcome our problems with our wives is also Christ. We are already in Christ. How foolish it is to continue journeying, striving, and endeavoring! All such labor is vain. When I saw this vision, I bound my donkey to the vine.

When many young brothers first come into the church life, they are striving donkeys. In the meetings they even compete with the others. But whenever you strive, endeavor, and compete, you are not at rest. Instead of striving and competing, you should tie your donkey to the vine, which is Christ, the source of life, the One who is full of life. Christ is not only the vine, but even the choice vine, the very choice source of life. We must stop our labor and rest in Him.

Now we must see how to bind our donkey to the vine. In gaining the victory over the enemy, Christ is the lion. But to us He is the vine for our satisfaction and rest. It is through

His victory that He can be the vine. If Christ had never won the victory, He could never be the vine to us. But because the victory is Christ's, He is our vine full of life. Thus, we must cease our labor and be tied to Him and rest in Him.

As some read this message, they may think that I have gone too far in interpreting these figures to apply to Christ. But if you do not interpret verse 11 in this way, how do you interpret it? What does it mean to bind your donkey to the vine? Some may say that this is a reference to the riches of the tribe of Judah, that it is a figure showing that the tribe of Judah was so full of wine that even the laboring donkeys could be bound to the vine. This is correct. But remember that verse 11 is also a picture and an illustration. We have seen that according to Revelation 5:5 Christ is the Lion of the tribe of Judah. Based upon the principle of interpreting the lion in verse 9 as the victorious Christ, we may say that the significance of binding our donkey to the vine is that we cease our labor at Christ who is the source of life. This is not an imaginative interpretation. It is a proper, genuine, and sound interpretation according to the principle of the Bible. We thank the Lord for giving us this proper interpretation. Hallelujah, we have the vine to which we can bind our donkey! Are you still laboring? Are you still striving and journeying to reach your goal? Even the young ones among us must say, "Praise the Lord! I don't need to labor, strive, or journey. I simply need to bind my donkey to the vine."

2. Soaking Our Behavior in the Enjoyment of the Riches of Christ's Life

Verse 11 also says, "He washed his garments in wine, and his clothes in the blood of grapes." Years ago, I could not understand what it meant to wash our garments in wine and our clothes in the blood of grapes. In the Bible our behavior in our daily living is likened to garments. Figuratively speaking, garments or clothes signify our behavior. They represent our walk and acts. Hence, to wash our garments in wine and our clothes in grape juice signifies that we soak our behavior, our daily walk, in the enjoyment of the riches of Christ's life.

Both grape wine and grape juice are for nourishment.

Grape juice is mainly for quenching our thirst, whereas grape wine is mainly for stirring up our excitement. Our thirst needs to be quenched, but our excitement needs to be stirred up. Every Christian must be "crazy," beside himself, in a proper sense. Every Christian who binds his donkey to the vine will be happy and excited. This is the function of grape wine. The grape juice that we drink is for quenching our thirst. On the one hand, the rich Christ stirs up our excitement; on the other hand, He quenches our thirst. We need to soak our behavior, our daily walk and actions, in the rich enjoyment of Christ's life. Then our behavior will be permeated and saturated with the full enjoyment of the riches of Christ's life. Then others will say, "Look at these Christians. Look at how they live and conduct themselves. Surely there must be something to what they are." This something is the rich life of Christ as the cheering wine to stir us up and as quenching juice to satisfy us. Such Christians are happy, satisfied, excited, and even beside themselves with joy. Because they are so excited, they become exciting. Their behavior, their daily walk, and all their actions are full of Christ's life as wine and as juice.

Are you the kind of Christian who is always dissatisfied? Are you a Christian who does not know how to be happy, who always has a wrinkled brow and a long face, who always looks sad? All those in the kingdom of Christ must be smiling, happy, pleasant, excited, cheerful, and satisfied. This indicates that we are soaking our behavior in the rich enjoyment of the life of Christ.

3. Being Transformed with the Rich Enjoyment and Rich Nourishment of Christ's Life

Through resting in the enjoyment of Christ's riches in life, we are transformed. Verse 12 says, "His eyes shall be red with wine, and his teeth white with milk." This signifies transformation by the rich life of Christ. When we are transformed in this way, our appearance is changed. Those who suffer from famine have a gray color around their eyes. Because they lack adequate nourishment, they are short of the blood supply to their eyes. But we, the kingdom people who enjoy Christ, are never undernourished. On the contrary, we are so fully nourished that our eyes become red. This indicates that we have been transformed from death to life. If my face were gray, you would be very concerned about my health, probably expecting that I would not live very long. But my face is not gray. My complexion is very healthy because I eat nourishing meals. Hallelujah, I have been transformed from death to life! According to verse 12, the eyes are red with wine. This redness does not come from outward coloring or painting, but from the inward, energizing wine.

Verse 12 also speaks of teeth that are white with milk. Our teeth have two functions. The first is to eat, to receive food into the mouth; the second is to help our utterance. The whiteness of the teeth here indicates the sound, healthy function of the teeth. Because I have received the proper nourishment, I have healthy, white teeth to take in God's Word as food and to utter His Word that others may be nourished. In order to take in the Word of God as our nourishment and to utter it for others' nourishment, we must have healthy teeth. Not many Christians are able to take in God's Word in a proper way or utter it in a strong way. But every sound, healthy Christian must be one who receives God's Word properly and who utters it richly.

We in the church life are ceasing from our labor, resting in Christ, and enjoying the riches of Christ's life as grape wine and as grape juice. We are also soaking our behavior in this rich enjoyment. Eventually, we shall have the fragrance of Christ. Then our entire being will be fully transformed and full of life, and we shall be able to take in God's Word as our nourishment and to speak it to others for their nourishment. This is the enjoyment and rest in the victorious Christ. Therefore, in verses 8 through 12 three significant seeds are sown: the seed of Christ's victory, the seed of Christ's kingdom, and the seed of our enjoyment and rest in Christ. These seeds, requiring the Old and the New Testaments for their development, are the real glad tidings, the true gospel. These glad tidings were proclaimed by Jacob in his prophecy with blessing concerning Judah.

LIFE-STUDY OF GENESIS

MESSAGE ONE HUNDRED ONE

THE SPIRITUAL SIGNIFICANCE OF THE BLESSING PROPHESIED CONCERNING JUDAH, ZEBULUN, AND ISSACHAR

(2)

According to the Old Testament, the twelve sons of Jacob are arranged in four groups of three. Jacob's prophetic word of blessing in chapter forty-nine is based upon these groups. We have already covered the first group, the group of Reuben, Simeon, and Levi. That group was utterly evil in the eyes of God. Reuben was defiled, and Simeon and Levi were cruel. The record of the first group is the beginning of the record of the twelve sons of Jacob. What a poor beginning it was! However, this should be an encouragement to us because our beginning was also very poor.

The second group is composed of Judah, Zebulun, and Issachar. Because Christ comes in with this group, it is the group of victory. In this group we have the gospel, the preaching of the gospel, and the church life.

Some may think that it is too much to say that in Genesis 49 we find the preaching of the gospel and the church life as the issue of that preaching. Remember, the first tribe in the second group is Judah, and the most significant aspect of the record concerning Judah is the lion. Verse 9 says, "Judah is a young lion: from the prey, my son, thou art gone up: he couches, he lies down as a lion, and as a lioness" (Heb.). This verse is interpreted by Revelation 5:5, where Christ is called the Lion of the tribe of Judah. Without Revelation 5:5, it would be difficult to interpret Genesis 49:9. But with Revelation 5:5 before us, no one can deny that Judah signifies Christ.

Although the New Testament often interprets the signs

and symbols in the Old Testament, it does not always give every detail of these interpretations. Regarding Judah as a lion, Genesis 49 has three aspects: the young lion, the couching lion, and the lioness. Revelation, however, simply speaks of the Lion of the tribe of Judah in a general way, saying nothing of these detailed aspects. Those who are legal would say, "Now don't go too far. We can only say what the New Testament says. We must not say any more." This is legality. Genesis 49 reveals that Judah is a lion in three aspects, but the New Testament only gives us an interpretation in a general way. Why then should we not continue on to supply the interpretations of the details?

There are at least two or three places where the New Testament indicates that it did not tell us everything (Heb. 5:11; 9:5; 11:32). Consider Hebrews 11:32: "And what more shall I say? For time would fail me to tell of Gideon, Barak, Samson, Jephthah, and both David and Samuel, and the prophets." Here the writer of Hebrews seems to be saying, "I do not have time to tell you everything. I have only included part of what the Old Testament says. I have left a great deal untouched." What then should we do about this? We must go to the Lord ourselves and inquire of Him. The writer of Hebrews took the lead to give us a way to interpret the Old Testament. He did not have the time to interpret everything for us. He left something for us to work out by going directly to the Lord ourselves. No one can disagree with this principle. Nevertheless, some Christian teachers argue that if the New Testament does not speak about a certain thing, we should not say anything about it either.

Although there is a very clear interpretation of Judah in Revelation 5, what is spoken in the New Testament concerning Zebulun and Issachar? There is a partial interpretation of Zebulun in Matthew 4:15, but there is no interpretation whatever of Issachar. According to those who insist that we should be silent when the New Testament is silent, we should not say anything about Issachar. But we do not agree with such a short-sighted concept. The fact that the tribe of Judah has a spiritual significance is fully proved by Revelation 5. Should not the tribes of Zebulun and Issachar have a spiritual significance as well? Would there be a spiritual significance to Judah, but no spiritual significance to the other tribes in the same group? To say this is not logical; it is absurd.

As we pointed out in the foregoing message, with Judah there are three main points: the victory of Christ, the kingdom of Christ, and the rest in the enjoyment of Christ's riches in life. We see the victory of Christ in verses 8 and 9, the kingdom of Christ in verse 10, and the rest and enjoyment of Christ's riches in life in verses 11 and 12. These three points are not an arbitrary interpretation of these verses. If you think my interpretation is arbitrary, I would ask you why in verse 9 the young lion is mentioned before the couching lion and the lioness. Why is there this sequence? Why is the lioness not put first? Following the threefold mention of the lion, we have in verse 10 the scepter and the ruler's staff, denoting the kingship and the kingdom. Why does the kingdom follow the lion? Why is it not mentioned first? After the kingship, we have, as the third item, the rest in the enjoyment of Christ's riches in life. If you do not follow the interpretation put forth in the previous message regarding binding the donkey to the vine, how do you interpret these words? What do they mean? Furthermore, what does it mean to wash your garments in the wine? Also, what is the meaning of eyes that are red with wine and teeth that are white with milk? As the New Testament only gives us the interpretation for verse 9 in Revelation 5:5, there should be some interpretations for verses 11 and 12. What are these interpretations? Concerning all the points in verses 9 through 12, we need to spend much time quietly in the presence of the Lord, saying, "Lord, what would You say about this? What does it mean to bind the donkey to the vine?" The Lord would say, "If you look into the Bible, you would see that a donkey is used for journeying toward a goal. This journeying donkey is always laboring." Then you would say, "Surely I am such a donkey. I need to bind this donkey to the vine." The vine spoken of in verse 11 is Christ. In John 15:1 Christ said, "I am the true vine." Thus, to bind the donkey to the vine means to bind our donkey to Christ. This is just one illustration of the correct way to understand this portion of the Word.

II. CONCERNING ZEBULUN—
THE PREACHING OF CHRIST'S GLAD TIDINGS

A. Shipping Out the Riches of Christ

Verse 13 says, "Zebulun shall dwell at the haven of the sea; and he shall be for a haven of ships." This verse does not say, "Zebulun shall dwell at the stable full of horses and donkeys." Furthermore, it does not say that Zebulun would dwell on the mountain. The tribe of Judah dwelt in hilly country, in the region around Mount Zion, where the capital of the nation was located. Zebulun, however, dwelt at the haven of the sea. This is very meaningful.

Judah signifies the victorious Christ, the One who gained the victory for the kingdom so that His people may rest in Him. Surely Judah must dwell on the mountain. But Zebulun dwelt at the haven of the sea, at a seaport. A port is for exporting goods, for sending out ships. Thus far in this portion of the Word, we have seen two methods of transportation: donkeys and ships. Pictures like these are often used in the Bible. For example, John 1:29 says, "Behold, the Lamb of God!" This simple picture of the Lamb of God depicts a great deal. Likewise, much is portrayed by the pictures of the donkey and the ships in chapter forty-nine. A donkey is an animal that transports things by its own labor. But in the ancient times the ships sailed by the power of the heavenly wind. No doubt this refers to the shipping out of the gospel of Christ. Judah was the factory producing the gospel, and Zebulun was the haven exporting the gospel produced by Judah.

Matthew 4:15 indicates that Zebulun was part of Galilee. The Lord Jesus began His ministry of the preaching of the gospel of the kingdom from Galilee. After His resurrection, the angel charged the women to tell the disciples, "Behold, He goes before you into Galilee; there you shall see Him" (Matt. 28:7). There in Galilee the resurrected Christ met with the disciples and charged them to preach the gospel. The disciples "went into Galilee, to the mountain where Jesus appointed them," and it was there He said to them, "Go therefore and disciple all the nations" (Matt. 28:16, 19). Zebulun was part of the region of Galilee. Acts 1:11 reveals that the first preachers of the gospel were men of Galilee. In Acts 1:8 the Lord had said to these Galileans, "But you shall receive power when the Holy Spirit has come upon you, and you shall be My witnesses both in Jerusalem, and in all Judea and Samaria, and unto the remotest part of the earth." By all this we see that Zebulun signifies the preaching of the gospel. Judah signifies the gospel composed of the victorious Christ, the kingdom of Christ, and the rest in the enjoyment of the riches of Christ. This is the gospel represented by Judah. Thus, Judah is the tribe producing the gospel. After the gospel is produced, there is the need for the preaching of the gospel. Therefore, Zebulun comes in to carry out this mission, to discharge the burden of sending forth the gospel.

The proper way to send out the gospel is not by donkeys journeying by their own hard labor. The proper way is to export the gospel by sailing ships empowered by the heavenly wind. In Acts 1:8 the Lord told the Galilean preachers to wait until they had received the power from on high, and Acts 2:2 says, "And suddenly there came a noise out of heaven like a rushing violent wind." From that time onward, the ships began to sail. One of these living ships was named Peter. On the day of Pentecost, Peter was not a donkey journeying and laboring, telling others that Jesus was the Savior and they had to believe in Him or else they would perish. He was a ship sailing by the power of a rushing mighty wind. The preaching of the gospel in today's Christianity is carried out mainly by laboring donkeys. But as you read Peter's message in Acts chapter two, you see that on the day of Pentecost he was sailing like a ship, not plodding along like a donkey.

I would also point out that the gospel goes out by sailing ships, not by steam ships powered by man-made engines. Do not use any gimmicks in the preaching of the gospel. To preach the gospel by means of gimmicks is to change the sailing ship into a steamer. History proves that the gospel has never been exported by either donkeys or steamers. According to church history, whenever the gospel has been carried out, it has been carried out by sailing boats, by saints who sailed like ships under the power of the heavenly wind.

If you do not interpret verse 13 in this way, then how do you interpret it? Was Zebulun a haven of ships for shipping out potatoes, oranges, or olives? Do not neglect the context of the whole Bible. The interpretation of the second group of three tribes is governed by Judah. The significance of Judah controls the interpretation. Judah signifies Christ as the gospel. According to spiritual history, the book of Acts follows the four Gospels, and the Acts is the book of the Galilean preachers. These Galilean preachers were ships sailing by the power of the heavenly wind. Since Judah has produced the riches of Christ, Zebulun is needed to export these riches to the nations.

B. Reaching the Gentile World

Verse 13 also says, "And his border shall be unto Zidon." It does not say that his border shall be unto Jerusalem. Zidon was a heathen city outside the holy land. It was located on the sea, and from it the sea traffic went to the uttermost parts of the earth. Because verse 13 is poetry, it must be interpreted in an allegorical way. In this verse we have the haven of ships and the border of the Gentile world. The history of the preaching of the gospel in Acts corresponds to this. In Acts the early preachers sailed from the holy land to Asia Minor and then across the Aegean Sea to Greece, Rome, and Spain. The Apostle Paul took a ship from the holy land and sailed firstly to Sidon (Zidon) and eventually to Rome (Acts 27:3; 28:14). Therefore, verse 13 was fulfilled in the history of the gospel preaching recorded in Acts.

One day I looked into Darby's Synopsis to see what he had to say about Zebulun. He said that the border being unto Zidon indicates mixture with the Gentile world. Even such a great biblical scholar as Darby was mistaken in his interpretation of Zebulun. As he sought to interpret the significance of Zebulun, he must have forgotten Judah, the first tribe in this group. Moreover, he must not have considered the significance of Zebulun as revealed in the New Testament. In the New Testament, we see that Zebulun was in Galilee of the nations, whence the Galilean preachers were sent forth. Thus, we must be careful in accepting the opinions of others.

Although we have followed some scriptural teachers, we do not follow anyone blindly. Rather, we check every point thoroughly and carefully with the Bible. According to history, after the gospel was produced in Judah, the preaching of the gospel was carried out by Zebulun.

In the record of Judah the significant word is lion, and in the record of Zebulun the significant word is ships. The lion is singular, whereas the ships are plural. There is just one Christ, but many Galilean preachers. There is one gospel, but many ships. The church in Anaheim is a haven of ships. We are ships in the haven being prepared to sail out with Christ as the gospel. Young people, are you not Galilean ships ready to sail out? As ships, you must be ready to sail. But do not sail forth to start a movement.

C. Rejoicing in Going Out

Hundreds of years after Jacob uttered the prophetic blessing recorded in Genesis 49, Moses, an old lawgiver, said, "Rejoice, Zebulun, in thy going out" (Deut. 33:18). The going out mentioned in this verse refers to the shipping out. Thus, the word of Moses corresponds to the word of Jacob. Jacob likened Zebulun to ships, which, of course, are for going out, and Moses told Zebulun to rejoice in his going out. If we go out for the preaching of the gospel, we shall rejoice. The person most full of rejoicing and happiness is the gospel preacher. If you are a ship sailing by the power of the heavenly wind, you will be happy, rejoicing, and beside yourself with joy. Following Judah, Zebulun comes in as the preaching of the gospel. Hallelujah, we have Judah as the four Gospels and Zebulun as the book of Acts!

III. CONCERNING ISSACHAR—THE CHURCH LIFE

Now we come to Issachar. It is important that Issachar does not precede Zebulun. What is the spiritual significance of Issachar? Verses 14 and 15 say, "Issachar is a strong ass couching down between the sheepfolds: and he saw that rest was good, and the land that it was pleasant" (Heb.). After the four Gospels and the Acts, we have the Epistles, which cover the matter of the church life. Therefore, Issachar signifies and represents the church life.

A. Resting in the Church

Issachar is likened to a strong donkey couching between the sheepfolds (v. 14). The mention of the donkey in verse 14 connects this verse with verse 11, which speaks of binding the young donkey to the vine. Thus, the donkey links Issachar to Judah. In Judah, in the gospel, we have the young donkey bound to Christ the vine. In Issachar, in the church life, we have the strong donkey couching between the sheepfolds. In Genesis 49 couching means resting in satisfaction. After Christ, the young lion, seized His prey and enjoyed it, He couched, rested in His satisfaction. Here in verse 14 we have a strong donkey couching down between the sheepfolds. In Judah we are young donkeys, but here in Issachar we are strong donkeys. These strong donkeys are neither laboring nor journeying, but couching. When you first came into the church life, you were probably a young donkey. But now, after a number of years in the church, you may be a strong couching donkey.

Notice that this couching donkey is not resting in the sheepfolds; rather, he is resting between the sheepfolds. Every denomination and religion is a fold. Today, we are not resting in any denominational fold. Instead, we are resting outside the folds. In chapter ten of John the Lord made it clear that Judaism was a fold holding God's flock and that He came into this fold for the purpose of leading the flock out of it. In John 10:16 the Lord said, "I have other sheep which are not of this fold; I must bring them also, and they shall hear My voice, and there shall be one flock, one shepherd." Hallelujah, this couching donkey is not resting in any fold; he is couching between the folds. Although he is not very far from the folds, he is not in any of them. This is exactly our situation today. We are not very far from the denominational folds; we are among them.

You may be wondering how a donkey could be among the sheepfolds. In a sense, we all are sheep of the flock. But according to our natural man, we all are donkeys. Many times

I have been rather happy with myself before the Lord and I praised Him, saying, "O Lord, thank You that I am in Your church. I am one of the many sheep in Your flock." However, at other times I looked at myself and said, "You don't look like a sheep. Probably you are a donkey, a horse, or a cow. Sometimes you even look like a buffalo." At night when all your work is over and you are sitting quietly in the presence of the Lord, you may say, "Lord, how I praise and thank You that I am in Your flock." But at the same time you may look at yourself and say, "Poor me, I don't look like a sheep. I look like a horse or a cow." According to our nature, none of us is a sheep. Instead, we are either donkeys or horses, cows or buffaloes. Nevertheless, we are also the transformed ones. Although I was a typical Chinese, I have been transformed. I was born Chinese, but I have become a Christian through regeneration. By origin, I was a donkey. But by regeneration I am now a sheep resting among the denominations. Thus, we are a flock of transformed donkeys resting between the sheepfolds. We admit that we were not born sheep. Nevertheless, today we are the flock couching between the sheepfolds.

As Issachar couched down between the sheepfolds, "he saw that rest was good" (v. 15). We all have seen this good rest. What good rest there is between the folds! This is the rest in the church life, which is to cease from our labor and rest in Christ (Matt. 11:28). As we are couching here, we see that this rest is good.

B. Enjoying the Pleasant Christ

Verse 15 also says that Issachar saw "the land that it was pleasant." As we are resting in the church life among the denominational folds, we enjoy the good rest and the rich pleasant land. This land is Christ. If you consider your experience, you will realize that this is true. As we are resting in the church life among the denominations, we see the good rest and the pleasant land, which is Christ as our green pasture. If you do not interpret these verses in this way, they have no meaning. But in this interpretation these verses are full of meaning and they strengthen our experience.

C. Issuing in Taskwork as a Tribute to the Master

Verse 15 also says, "And bowed his shoulder to bear, and became a servant under taskwork" (Heb.). This is true to our experience. As we rest in the church life, couching between the denominations, realizing the rest, and enjoying the pleasant land, we are willing to lower our shoulder to serve and to bear some responsibility. We become a servant under taskwork. Taskwork does not refer to the work of our choice, but to some assigned work. It is not our chosen work, but the work assigned by the Lord. It is the task assigned by the Head to us as members of the Body. Whatever we do as an assigned portion of the Body service is taskwork. Eventually this taskwork becomes a tribute offered to our Master. After the producing of the gospel, we have the preaching of the gospel. As the issue of the preaching of the gospel, we have the church life. In the church life we all are donkeys couching down among the divisions, seeing the good rest, and enjoying Christ as the pleasant land. As we are couching, spontaneously we say, "Lord Jesus, I love You. I would like to bear the burden of the work You have assigned to me. I am willing to bear such a burden under Your taskwork so that I may have something to offer You for Your satisfaction." This is the tribute we offer to our King. How marvelous!

D. Rejoicing in the Church Life

Deuteronomy 33:18 says, "Rejoice, Zebulun, in thy going out; and, Issachar, in thy tents." We have seen that Moses told Zebulun to rejoice in his going out. Now we see that Issachar is to rejoice in his tents. Undoubtedly, the tents here refer to the church life. For the preaching of the gospel, we must be joyful in our going out. But for the church life, we must be joyful in remaining in the local churches.

IV. THE CONSUMMATION

A. The Peoples Invited to the Mountain of God

After the producing of the gospel, the preaching of the gospel, and the issue of the preaching of the gospel, the church life, we come to the consummation, which is found in

Deuteronomy 33:19. This verse says, "They shall invite the peoples unto the mountain; there they shall offer sacrifices of righteousness: for they shall suck of the abundance of the seas, and of treasures hid in the sand" (Heb.). Firstly, in the consummation the peoples are invited to the mountain of God. In the church life today we are inviting others to the mountain of God, that is, to the kingdom of God. Of course, this invitation will be completely fulfilled during the time of the millennial kingdom. In the millennial kingdom all the peoples, the nations, will be invited through preaching to God's kingdom in Mount Zion. But we have a miniature of this in the church life today. Due to the preaching and the church life, that is, due to Zebulun and Issachar, the peoples are invited to God's kingdom, to the mountain of God. This verse with "the peoples" invited links Issachar to Judah, to whom "shall the obedience of the peoples be" (v. 10, Heb.).

B. Sacrifices of Righteousness Offered to God

Secondly, on the mountain the peoples will offer sacrifices of righteousness to God. In God's kingdom in the church life today such righteous offerings are being presented to Him (1 Pet. 2:5; Heb. 13:15-16; Phil. 4:18). All the sacrifices we offer to God in the church life are of righteousness, according to the righteous requirement of God. It will also be so in the coming kingdom (Mal. 3:3).

C. The Church and the Kingdom Becoming Our Enjoyment

Thirdly, the church and the kingdom become our enjoyment. This is signified by the words, "They shall suck of the abundance of the seas, and of treasures hid in the sand." In order to interpret this portion of the verse, we must consider the parables of the treasure and the pearl in Matthew 13:44-46. In Matthew 13, the treasure refers to the kingdom, and the pearl refers to the church. I believe the abundance of the seas in verse 19 is the church. Undoubtedly, the seas signify the nations, the Gentile world. Out of the Gentile world the church is brought forth as the abundance. All the Gentile believers are the abundance of the seas, the abundance of the nations. This is the church. The kingdom is the treasure hid in the sand, or hid in the earth. If we would apply the proper interpretation of these two parables in Matthew 13 to Deuteronomy 33:19, we would see that the result of the gospel, of the preaching of the gospel, and of the church life as the issue of the gospel is the enjoyment of the church life and the kingdom. Even today we are sucking of the abundance of the seas and of the treasures hid in the sand. We are sucking of the church life and of the kingdom life. The church life is the abundance out of the nations, and the kingdom life is the treasure hidden in the earth. Even today it is still hidden. The outsiders do not understand what we are doing in the church. They may say, "I can't understand those people. It seems they go to meetings almost every night. What are they doing?" We are sucking of the abundance of the seas and of the treasures hidden in the sand.

In this second group of Jacob's sons we have the gospel signified by Judah and fully recorded in the four Gospels; the preaching of the gospel signified by Zebulun and fully recorded in the book of Acts; and the church life signified by Issachar and fully recorded in the remaining books of the New Testament beginning with Romans. The result is the enjoyment of the church life and the kingdom life. It takes the whole Bible to understand Genesis 49. It takes the entire New Testament to interpret even the second group alone. In the four Gospels we see Judah as the gospel, in Acts we see Zebulun as the preaching of the gospel, and in the Epistles and Revelation we see Issachar as the church life. The consummation of all this is our enjoyment, our sucking, of the rich church life and of the kingdom. Hallelujah, today we have Judah, Zebulun, Issachar, and the consummation! With Judah we have the lion, the one Christ, and the one gospel; with Zebulun we have the many ships and the many Galileans; and with Issachar we have the tents, the many local churches. We have Christ as the gospel, we have the preaching of the gospel, and we have the church life. Now we are the flock couching between the sheepfolds enjoying the church life and the kingdom life.

Some Christians today only care for Judah, only care for

the victorious life in Christ, and others care for Zebulun, for the preaching of the gospel. But very few care for Issachar, for the church life. In the Lord's recovery, however, we must care for all three of this group: for Judah, the victorious life; for Zebulun, the preaching of the gospel; and for Issachar, the church life, so that we may have the full enjoyment in Christ.

LIFE-STUDY OF GENESIS

MESSAGE ONE HUNDRED TWO

BEING MATURED
THE MANIFESTATION OF MATURITY

(5)

In this message we come to the third group of Jacob's twelve sons. As we have seen clearly, the prophecy with blessing in Genesis 49 portrays not only the lives of the twelve tribes of Israel in the Old Testament, but also the spiritual life of Christians in the New Testament. This is based on the principle that the twelve tribes of Israel are a type of the church with all the believers. Thus, everything in chapter forty-nine is a type, a shadow, a picture, and our experience today is the reality, the fulfillment, of Jacob's prophecy with blessing.

The prophecy with blessing uttered by Jacob is poetry. It is difficult to understand the language of poetry. Poetic language is meaningful and descriptive, but it is not easy to probe the depths of its meaning. If you are able to probe into the depths of the poetic language in this chapter, you will realize how meaningful, rich, and profound it is.

There is another reason many readers of chapter forty-nine have difficulty understanding it, and that reason is the shortage in their Christian experience. Even if we are able to understand the poetic language in this chapter, we may lack the experience necessary to know how to make the application. In order to understand such a prophetic record, we must know the language in black and white, we must know the history of the twelve tribes of Israel, we must know the significance of the poetic figures, and we must have experience. Jacob used many poetic figures in this chapter: a young lion, a couching lion, a lioness, a foal, a young donkey, wine, the vine, garments, the haven, ships, the serpent, and the horned snake. In order to know the significance of these figures and to know how to interpret all these types and apply them to our situation, we need experience. The reason this chapter has been closed for centuries is this lack of experience.

More than fifty years ago, I sat at the feet of a great Brethren teacher. He gave a number of messages expounding Genesis 49, showing us how these prophecies were fulfilled in the following books of the Bible. However, he had a great shortage in the matter of experience. All he had was the knowledge of the language in black and white. But because he did not know the spiritual significance of the figures, he did not apply any of them to today's Christian experience. Therefore, I did not receive from him any help in life or spiritual experiences. Nevertheless, I still thank God that I heard from him the interpretation and exposition of this chapter in a historical and scriptural way. Later, by putting this chapter together with my spiritual experience, I was able to get into the depths of the significance of this prophecy with blessing.

This record concerning Jacob's twelve sons begins with Reuben, a sinner. No one has been more sinful than Reuben. Although Paul said that he was the chief of sinners, I would say that Reuben was actually the foremost sinner, more sinful than Saul of Tarsus. What a terrible sin he committed! At the beginning of our Christian experience we also were sinners. How we thank the Lord for His mercy! Although I was once a Reuben, now I have been saved. Although this prophecy with blessing begins with a sinner, it ends with the two beloved sons of Jacob, Joseph and Benjamin. It begins with a sinner and ends with a king, a reigning one, one in power and authority. Between Reuben and Joseph we have Simeon, Levi, Judah, Zebulun, Issachar, Dan, Gad, Asher, and Naphtali.

We have seen that this prophetic record begins with a group of sinners, Reuben, Simeon, and Levi. Reuben's sin was lust, and the sin of Simeon and Levi was the anger that issued from their disposition. Matthew chapter five also speaks of the sins of lust and anger. After this group of sinners, who were filled with lust and anger, Christ came in as the lion. Judah is Christ as our glad tidings. Following him is

Zebulun, the haven for shipping out the gospel, and Issachar, the enjoyment of the church life. How wonderful! Are there still some Reubens among us today? We have to declare that in the church there are no Reubens and no Simeons and that all the Levis have become priests. Thus, there are no more sinners. Christ is here and He is everything. Because Christ is here, we have the glad tidings that are shipped out through the preaching of the gospel, and we have the church life. Hallelujah, we are no longer sinners! We are in the church life. On the one hand, we are the haven to ship out Christ; on the other hand, we are the tents to stay with Christ in the full enjoyment of Him.

(9) Concerning Dan

(a) A Young Lion Fighting for More Land

Deuteronomy 33:22 says, "And of Dan he said, Dan is a young lion: he shall leap from Bashan" (Heb.). The mention of the young lion in this verse links the second and third groups of the twelve sons, showing that the third group is the continuation of the second. The crucial figure in the second group is the lion; and Dan, the first of the third group, is also called a lion. As a young lion, Dan is not fighting for the prey, but for more land (Josh. 19:47; Judg. 18:27-29). By this we see that the young lion has progressed from fighting for the prey to fighting for the land. In typology, to fight for more land means to fight for more Christ. The young lion in Judah was for seizing the prey. But the young lion here is fighting for more land, fighting to gain more Christ. In Judges 18 we see Dan as a young lion, fighting for more land.

(b) A Serpent, a Horned Snake on the Way, Biting the Horse's Heels and Causing the Rider to Fall Backward

After Dan obtained the city of Dan in Judges 18, an idol, made by Micah, was set up in it (Judg. 17:4-5; 18:30-31). At that time God's tabernacle was in Shiloh. But in the city of Dan there was an idol. Today we have the light to understand the spiritual significance of this. It means that some Christians have been able to gain more of Christ. But after gaining more of Christ, they set up another center of worship. According to the book of Deuteronomy, in the good land there should have been only one center of worship for God's people (Deut. 12:11, 13-14, 21; 14:23-26). At that unique center there were God's name and God's habitation. During the time of the book of Judges, the center of worship was in Shiloh, where God's tabernacle and priests were. Although Dan gained the victory, this victory made him independent. All independence comes from pride. Do not think that spiritual gain cannot make you proud. Even the gain of Christ can make us proud. This is what is called spiritual pride. Those who are spiritually proud will not be subject to others. Rather, they say, "Why must we go to Shiloh? We can set up something ourselves." Immediately after Dan's victory, another center of worship, with the idol made by Micah, was established in the city of Dan.

If you consider the history of Christianity, you will see that this kind of thing has happened again and again. A certain individual or group of believers has been victorious in gaining more of Christ. But this gain of Christ made them proud and independent. Because they were not willing to submit to others, they set up another center of worship. They should have gone to the worship center in Shiloh, for the priests ordained by God were in Shiloh. But they set up something man-made and man-ordained. This is the creeping in of the serpent, the subtle one.

The serpent of Genesis 3 appears again in Judges 18. In this way Dan, the young lion, became a serpent. Genesis 49:17 says, "Dan shall be a serpent on the way, a horned snake on the path, that biteth the horse's heels, so that his rider shall fall backward" (Heb.). The serpent here is worse than the serpent in Genesis 3, for here it is a horned snake. Without knowing the history in the Old Testament, the spiritual significance, and how to make the practical application, it is difficult to understand this verse. However, if we know all these things, we shall see that there have been many Dans in Christian history. First these Dans were young lions gaining more of Christ, but they eventually became serpents, even horned snakes, setting up other centers of worship. Even today, many spiritual ones who have gained something of Christ have set up another center of worship in addition to the unique center ordained by God and established by Him. We must apply this to ourselves and ask if we are setting up other centers of worship. It is a shame and a sorrow to say that during the past fifteen years at least two or three who were once among us have done this very thing. They gained something, but that gain made them proud and independent, unwilling to submit to what the Lord has ordained. As a result, other centers were set up. These have caused some to fall backward.

In Genesis 49 this was prophecy. But today we see the fulfillment of this prophecy in past history and in the present situation. Once again, this convinces us that the Bible is truly inspired by God. How impressive is the picture given here of Dan! Today we see centers of worship with spiritual idols, with so-called spiritual images. The idol and the separate center of worship became the greatest stumbling block to the nation of Israel. By reading the historical books in the Old Testament, we see that by taking in this idol Dan truly became a horned snake. This snake bit the horse's heel and caused the rider to fall backward. This means that the snake became a great frustration and held the people back. As they were riding on, Dan bit the heels of the horse and caused them to fall backward; that is, he frustrated them from going on.

(c) Jacob Waiting for the Lord's Salvation

At this point Jacob said, "I have waited for thy salvation, O Lord" (v. 18). After speaking about Dan as a serpent by the way and a horned snake on the path that bites the horse's heels, Jacob cried to the Lord for salvation. If we see the situation of today's Dans, we also will cry "O Lord, save us. Lord, save us from the Dans, from the idols, and from the other centers of worship. Lord, save us from the serpent and from the horned snake. O Lord, save us from the biting of the serpent." Jacob not only prayed; he also called on the name of the Lord. This verse does not say, "I am waiting for thy salvation," or, "I will wait for thy salvation." It says, "I have waited for thy salvation." Jacob seemed to be saying, "Lord, with this situation with Dan, nothing can help except Your salvation.

Only Your salvation can save us from this harm, this damage. Lord, I have already waited for Your salvation. Lord, I have cried to You. I have called on You. Lord, we need Your salvation."

Throughout history, many Dans have become serpents setting up idols to frustrate others. Our heart has been deeply hurt by this. In 1969 another center of worship was set up, and many young people have been frustrated by it. The heels of many horses were bitten, and many young riders fell backward. The only thing we can do about such a situation is to call on the Lord and say, "Lord, I have waited for Your salvation." In the past we have seen the Lord's salvation and we are still seeing it today. I can testify that many have been saved from the bite of the serpent.

We have seen that Dan is firstly the continuation of Judah, the continuation of the victory of Christ. Then Dan fell into the worship of idols. Whenever the worship of idols is introduced, the serpent is there. Behind every image there is an evil spirit. Behind every idol is the subtle one seeking the worship of people. Thus, when the image was set up, Dan became a serpent. In other words, because Dan was one with the idol, he became Satan. After this terrible fall, God's salvation came. Praise the Lord for His salvation! History testifies of this, and our present surroundings and environment confirm it. We have seen the fall, and we have seen a situation where the serpent has come in. But we have also seen the salvation of the Lord. Hallelujah, a great many have been saved! O Lord, we have waited for Your salvation.

(d) Still Being One of the Tribes (Scepters) Judging His People

Jacob prophesied that Dan would judge his people as one of the tribes of Israel (v. 16). This prophecy with blessing indicates that Jacob was concerned that Dan would be cut off. According to the Mosaic law, anyone who set up an idol or worshipped an idol had to be cut off from the people (Deut. 13:5-18). Among the twelve tribes, the tribe of Dan brought in an idol. Thus, according to the law, Dan should have been terminated as a tribe. Therefore, Jacob, not wanting to see one of his sons cut off, blessed him prophetically out of a loving heart. This is the reason Jacob said that Dan would still be a tribe judging his people. This word was particularly fulfilled in Samson, who was of the tribe of Dan (Judg. 13:2, 24; 15:20).

Jacob said that Dan would judge his people as one of the tribes of Israel. The Hebrew word for tribe firstly has the meaning of branch, then stick, staff, and scepter. A scepter signifies authority. Therefore, the Hebrew word for tribe actually means scepter. Every tribe has a scepter, an authority. The twelve tribes were twelve scepters, twelve powers, twelve authorities. During the time of Samson, the tribe of Dan certainly became a scepter. With Samson, the tribe of Dan was a power, a real authority. This is the meaning of Jacob's prophetic blessing concerning Dan in verse 16. Jacob's word meant not only that Dan would remain as a tribe, but also that Dan would be a scepter, an authority. This prophecy has been fulfilled.

(e) His Tribe Omitted in First Chronicles and Revelation,
but Included as a Tribe in the Millennium

In 1 Chronicles 2—9 the tribe of Dan was omitted in the record of the holy people of God. In 1 Chronicles 2:2 Dan's name is mentioned, but in the following record his tribe was omitted. Furthermore, the tribe of Dan is also not mentioned in the record in Revelation 7. It is a serious matter to be omitted from God's record of His people. We find this warning in the New Testament in Revelation 3:5, where we are told that he who overcomes will not have his name erased out of the book of life. This implies that the names of the defeated believers will be erased from the book of life during the coming age of the kingdom. This does not mean that the defeated believers will perish. The tribe of Dan did not perish. But because Dan fell and became one with God's enemy, becoming the serpent and bringing in a stumbling block to God's people, his name was omitted in the record in 1 Chronicles and Revelation.

Many Christians today have become Dans. Although they have become one with Satan in bringing in stumbling blocks to frustrate God's people, they seem not to care about what they have done, or to have any feeling concerning it. Yes, God will forgive them, but their names will not be found in the record during the time of the coming kingdom. There will be a certain situation in which their names will be omitted. Although Dan was omitted in the record in 1 Chronicles and Revelation because of his evil, he will still be a tribe in the millennium because of his father's blessing (Ezek. 48:1). This is a picture of God's mercy.

We should not read the record of Dan merely as history. We must see it as a shadow, a figure, of our experience as Christians. Although we may be the continuation of Judah, of Christ's victory, we must be careful. Often, after a time of victory there is the danger that our gain of Christ may immediately cause us to be proud and independent, making us unwilling to submit to others. At such a time we may set up another center of worship and thus become one with God's enemy, Satan. This will cause us a great loss. We shall not perish, because once we are saved, we are saved forever. But there is the definite possibility that in a certain period of time and in a certain situation we may be omitted in the record of God's people.

(10) Concerning Gad

(a) Raided by a Raiding Band and Raiding Their Heels

Because of the failure of Dan, Jacob called on the Lord for His salvation. The Lord has answered this call. Thus, after Dan we have Gad as his continuation. Verse 19 says, "Gad, a raiding band shall raid him: but he shall raid their heels" (Heb.). With Dan we see the defeat, but with Gad we see the victory brought back. Do not consider Dan separate from Gad or Gad separate from Dan. They are part of a whole. Dan ends with failure, but Gad, who shall raid the heels of the raiding band, comes in with the recovered victory.

(b) Enlarged by God

Deuteronomy 33:20 says, "Blessed be he that enlargeth Gad." By this victory Gad was enlarged by God. It is exactly the same in our spiritual experience. Some time ago we may have been defeated, but by means of God's mercy through the prayer of some saints, the salvation of the Lord has come to us. Thereby, we regain the victory. Now we are no longer Dan—we are Gad, the one who raids the heels of the enemy. Through this victory, we are enlarged by God. Many of us can testify that God has enlarged us.

(c) Dwelling as a Lioness, Tearing the Arm,
Even the Crown of the Head of the Prey

Deuteronomy 33:20 also says, "He dwelleth as a lioness, and teareth the arm, even the crown of the head" (Heb.). Here we see that Gad is a lioness. Gad is not couching: rather, he is dwelling. This is an improvement over Judah as a couching lion. The Gad who is dwelling as a lioness tears the arms and even the crown of the head of the prey. In Moses' poetic language here, the top of the head, the crown, refers to the skull. This prey, of course, is not an animal, but a person. Gad tears the arm of his prey, even the head, the skull of his prey. This means that Gad is so strong that he not only defeats his enemy, but also tears him to pieces. He even tears his skull into pieces. The poetry here describes the tearing of the enemy to the uttermost. As Gad, we smash Satan into pieces. In Deuteronomy 33 the lioness is not couching for enjoyment; she is dwelling, settling down, and tearing the enemy to pieces. It seems that Gad could say, "Enemy, don't bother me. I want to dwell here peacefully. But if you trouble me, I will not only tear your arm, but I will also tear your skull into pieces. After that, no one will see your figure again."

(d) Providing the First Part of the Good Land for Himself

Deuteronomy 33:21 says of Gad, "He provided the first part for himself, for there a portion of the lawgiver was reserved" (Heb.). Victory always gives us enlargement, which is the expansion of space. Therefore, this verse says that Gad provided the first part for himself. For years I was not able to understand this. According to the history in the Old Testament, the first part refers to the first part of the good land east of the Jordan River. In their journeys, the twelve tribes firstly entered this part, which was on the east side of Jordan. Desiring this rich, fertile land, Reuben, Gad, and half of Manasseh begged Moses to give it to them. Although Moses agreed, he charged them not to stay there, enjoying their good land, while their brothers had not yet obtained their portion of the land. Thus, Moses charged them to fight the battle for the rest of the land (Num. 32:1-32). After that, they would divide the land justly. If the two and a half tribes had stayed there and had not gone on to fight for the rest of the land, they would not have been just. Thus, Gad provided the first part for himself. There a portion was reserved for the lawgiver. This points to the fact that Moses, the lawgiver, was buried there (Deut. 32:48-52; 34:1-6).

(e) Coming with the Heads of the People to Execute the Justice of the Lord and His Ordinances with Israel

Verse 21 also says, "And he came with the heads of the people, he executed the justice of the Lord, and his ordinances with Israel" (Heb.). Gad came with the heads of the people, the leaders, to take the rest of the good land to execute the justice of the Lord in dividing the land and His ordinances with Israel (Josh. 22:1-5). Dan's failure was his pride. When he gained more land, he became proud and set up another center of worship. He did not care for his brothers. In your spiritual experience, you must beware of pride when you gain more land, more of Christ. Never set up another center of worship. On the contrary, you must take care of your brothers. Do not say, "I have won the victory. I have more land, more Christ. I don't care about the others. I will stay here to enjoy my victory." If you do this, you will be defeated. Even though you have gained the land, you must press on to take care of the need of your brothers. You have obtained your portion, but what about the portion of your brothers? You must fight the battle to get the rest of the land so that all your brothers may have their share. To enjoy your portion of the land without helping your brothers obtain their portion would not be just. It would not be the execution of God's justice. You must go on with the other leaders to fight the battle for the rest of the land. Then all your brothers will have a portion. To do this is to execute the justice of the Lord and to keep His ordinances with Israel.

Gad had a number of good points. He recovered the victory, he was enlarged, and he tore the enemy to pieces. Furthermore, although he provided a place for himself, he did not enjoy it until he helped his brothers gain their portion. He went on with them to fight until everyone had a portion. This was the execution of the justice of the Lord and of His ordinances with Israel. Again I say, Dan warns us not to be proud, to be independent, or to set up another center of worship. Gad helps us to know that even after we have gained the victory and have been enlarged, we should not forget our brothers. We should not rest in our portion until we have helped our brothers gain their portion. To win a spiritual victory and to gain Christ is truly wonderful. But beware of pride. You may set up a separate worship center, neglecting your brothers. Never do this. Do not enjoy the portion you have gained until you have helped your brothers win theirs. Do not be proud and do not forget your brothers. Hearing this should be a help to us all. Now we know what we should do after gaining the victory of Christ. We should not establish another center, but we should take care of our brothers, fighting for the sake of their portion.

(11) Concerning Asher

(a) Rich Food and Royal Dainties

After Gad comes Asher. The sequence here is certainly under God's inspiration. Verse 20 says, "Out of Asher his bread shall be fat, and he shall yield royal dainties." Asher's bread is fat; that is, his food is rich. When we have the victory of Christ and help our brothers gain their portion before we enjoy our own, we have rich food. This rich food even becomes royal dainties, the royal food. It is not food for the common people, but food for kings, for the royal family. What we enjoy in the victorious life is not only regular food, but also royal dainties. No one can deny that the food in the church life is rich. In fact it is so rich that it becomes the royal dainties. We are not only a lion family, but also a royal family. We are a kingly family, and our dining is royal. Whatever we feed on in these life-study messages is royal dainties.

(b) More Blessed Than the Sons and Most Favored among His Brothers

Deuteronomy 33:24 says, "Asher shall be blessed more than [the] sons; let him be favored among his brethren" (Heb.). You may wonder how Asher could be more blessed than Judah or Joseph. For Asher to be more blessed than the sons means to be more blessed in the riches of food and minerals.

(c) Dipping His Foot in Oil

Deuteronomy 33:24 also says, "Let him dip his foot in oil." Judah was to wash his garments in wine, but here Asher is to dip his foot in oil. Revelation 6:6 speaks of not harming oil and wine. In times of famine oil and wine become scarce. Undoubtedly the oil here is olive oil. According to both history and geography, there is an abundance of olive trees in this part of the good land. For this reason, it is rich in oil. The fact that Asher will dip his foot in oil indicates that, as far as food is concerned, he is richer than all the other tribes.

(d) Iron and Copper under His Sandals

Deuteronomy 33:25 says, "Under thy sandals shall be iron and copper" (Heb.). Iron and copper are for fighting the battle and for building. Oil is food for nourishment, but iron and copper are materials for fighting and for building up the kingdom. Because Asher is so rich, the most favored in food and minerals, he is more blessed than the other tribes. He has the food for nourishment and the minerals for weapons and building materials.

(e) His Rest Being as His Days

Deuteronomy 33:25 also says, "And as thy days, so shall thy rest be" (Heb.). The Hebrew word rendered "rest" here is not the common word for rest. This word is very difficult to translate. It means safety, security, strength, peace, and quietness. It denotes a leisurely life, a life in which there is sufficiency, with no need to worry or rush. Thus, Asher was to have a leisurely life, a life that was safe and secure, with sufficiency guaranteed. This means that throughout life he would not lack anything. He would have the rich food for nourishment, the weapons for defense, and the materials for building. Instead of scarcity, there would be sufficiency, rest, peace, and leisure. He would constantly enjoy life.

Unless you have come into this stage of the spiritual life, you may not understand what I am talking about. But there is such a stage. If you have not yet arrived at it, I encourage you to go on. One day you will come to such a country. In this realm there is no need to hurry or rush. Here there is safety, security, and peace. Here we are short of nothing. We have food, weapons, and materials. When you have arrived at this stage, there is no need to worry or care about tomorrow, and there is no anxiety. Rather, there is continual rest in the riches of food and in the strong iron and copper. At least some of us have come to this point. This is the maturity of life.

(12) Concerning Naphtali

(a) A Hind Let Loose

Genesis 49:21 says, "Naphtali is a hind let loose." Immediately after Asher comes Naphtali, who is neither a young lion nor a lioness, but a hind. According to the Hebrew text, the title of Psalm 22 speaks of the hind of the morning, indicating that the resurrected Christ in Psalm 22 is a hind let loose. With Naphtali we have not only the victorious Christ as a lion, but the resurrected Christ as a released hind skipping on the mountaintops. Nothing can frustrate Him, and no one needs to pave the way for Him. He is the resurrected hind. Because He is in resurrection, He can leap upon the high mountains.

(b) Giving Beautiful Words

Verse 21 also says, "He giveth beautiful words" (Heb.). The resurrected hind in Genesis 49 corresponds to the resurrected Lord in Matthew 28. Matthew 28 firstly reveals that

Christ has risen and then it tells us that when the disciples were gathered together to Him, He charged them, saying, "Go therefore and disciple all the nations...teaching them to observe all things, whatever I commanded you" (Matt. 28:19-20). This is to give beautiful words. In resurrection we can utter beautiful words. This is the maturity of life in resurrection. In order to say something beautiful for Christ, we must be in resurrection. When we are in resurrection, it is easy to speak beautiful words for the Lord.

(c) Satisfied with Favor
and Full with the Blessing of the Lord

Deuteronomy 33:23 says, "O Naphtali, satisfied with favor, and full with the blessing of the Lord." Here we see that Naphtali is satisfied with favor. Favor in the Old Testament is the equivalent of grace in the New Testament. Thus, Naphtali is satisfied with grace. When we are in resurrection speaking beautiful words, we also are satisfied with grace. Often as I am speaking, I am satisfied with favor, with grace. This verse also says that Naphtali is filled with the blessing of the Lord. He is satisfied with grace and full of blessing. This is the victorious and matured life in resurrection. As we speak for Christ to nourish others, we ourselves are satisfied with grace and filled with blessing.

(d) Possessing the Sea and the South

Deuteronomy 33:23 also says, "Possess thou the sea and the south." The result of speaking beautiful words in resurrection and of being satisfied with favor and full of blessing is the possessing of the west and the south. For Naphtali to possess the west is to possess the Mediterranean Sea, which was on the west of Naphtali's portion of the good land. Therefore, some versions render the Hebrew word in this verse as "west." Actually, it denotes the sea, because the sea was to the west of the good land. The word "south" signifies the land. The sea, the west, signifies the Gentile world, and the south, the land, signifies the Jewish world. Therefore, to possess the sea and the land signifies possessing the Gentile world and the Jewish world. In other words, Naphtali is to possess the whole earth.

In order to take the earth, we must begin from Reuben and continue through Simeon, Levi, Judah, Zebulun, Issachar, Dan, Gad, and Asher until we come to Naphtali. When we have become Naphtali, we shall possess the west and the south, the sea and the land. We shall be qualified and empowered to take the earth. How wonderful! When we are Naphtali, it is easy to take the earth because we are in resurrection speaking beautiful words, and we are satisfied with favor and full of blessing. Thus, we are ready to possess the sea and the land, the Gentile world and the Jewish world. We are ready to take the earth.

LIFE-STUDY OF GENESIS

MESSAGE ONE HUNDRED THREE

THE SPIRITUAL SIGNIFICANCE OF DAN, GAD, ASHER, AND NAPHTALI

In this message I am burdened to give an additional word concerning the spiritual significance of Dan, Gad, Asher, and Naphtali. In a sense, I love this group more than the group that includes Judah. Judah's group is the second, and this group is the third, which, of course, is more advanced. We have seen that there is a link in this third group connecting it with the second. Judah is a young lion and a lioness (49:9, Heb.), Dan is a young lion, and Gad is a lioness (Deut. 33:22, 20, Heb.). Thus, these two figures, the young lion and the lioness, link the third group to the second.

When I was young, I often studied Genesis 49. Many times I felt that these words were not very meaningful. For example, verse 21 says that Naphtali is a hind let loose and that he gives beautiful words (Heb.). I could not understand how a hind could give beautiful words. It seemed to me that the hind and the beautiful words were not related to each other. Furthermore, I wondered how a hind could speak. Consequently, for quite a long period of time, I did not care for Genesis 49. However, when we probe into the spiritual significance of this chapter, we see how meaningful all of it is. In message one hundred we considered the rest in the enjoyment of Christ's riches in life (pp. 1279-1284). We saw that we need to bind our donkey to the vine and soak our garments in wine. If we do this, our eyes will be red with wine and our teeth white with milk (vv. 11-12). One brother may ask another, "Have you bound your donkey to the vine?" The other may reply, "Brother, have you soaked your garments in wine?" Then the first brother may ask, "Are your eyes red with wine?" The second may respond, "Are your teeth white with milk?" The outsiders may think that this is the secret, mysterious language of the church people. No matter what others may say, how meaningful these new proverbs are to us! "Bind your donkey to the vine!" "Soak your garments in wine!" I want my eyes to be red with wine and my teeth to be white with milk. In order for this to take place, we must first rest in Christ and then soak our being, our behavior, in the riches of the life of Christ. Then we shall experience transformation, and our appearance will be changed. Our eyes will be red with wine, and our teeth will be white with milk, indicating that they are strong to take in the Word and to utter it to others.

The sequence in these four groups in chapter forty-nine is marvelous. It corresponds both to the history of the church and our spiritual experience. Firstly, we have Reuben, signifying that we all began as sinners. After Reuben, Simeon, and Levi, Judah comes. This means that Christ has come as the victorious lion. Following Judah, Zebulun, and Issachar, we have the fall of Dan. Dan's fall, however, was not only a failure and a defeat; it was apostasy. After the apostasy of Dan, we have the recovery with Gad, the sufficiency in Asher, and the consummation with Naphtali. In church history we also see the apostasy, the recovery, the sufficiency, and the consummation. If we cannot see the consummation today, we shall surely see it in the next age and especially in the new heaven and new earth with the New Jerusalem. Naphtali will be completely fulfilled when New Jerusalem is manifested in the new heaven and new earth. The New Jerusalem will be the eternal Naphtali. These four items—apostasy, recovery, sufficiency, and consummation—also match our Christian experience. After a downfall, the apostasy, we have the recovery. Then come sufficiency and consummation. We have seen these things in the Lord's recovery. Throughout the years in the recovery we have been with Judah, binding our donkey to the vine and soaking our garments in wine. Our eyes have become red with wine and our teeth white with milk. But suddenly the apostasy of Dan came in. Nevertheless, following Dan there was the recovery with Gad.

I. THE APOSTASY OF DAN

A. Gaining More Christ by His Victorious Life

Dan was the continuation of Judah, for Judah was a lion and Dan was a young lion. As the continuation of Judah, Dan was successful in gaining more Christ by his victorious life (Deut. 33:22; Josh. 19:47; Judg. 18:27-29).

B. Being Individualistic and Independent

Because Dan was successful and victorious, he became proud, individualistic, and independent. He cared only for himself, not for others. As Judges 18:30 says, "The children of Dan set up for themselves the graven image" (Heb.).

C. Setting Up a Divisive Center of Worship and Ordaining a Hired "Priest"

Dan's apostasy was the setting up of a divisive center of worship (Judg. 18:30-31; 17:9-10; 1 Kings 12:26-31; 2 Kings 10:29). In a divisive way Dan set up a center apparently for the worship of God. Many use the matter of the worship of God as a cloak for setting up a divisive center. Some would say, "What could be wrong with doing such a thing for the worship of God? Isn't it better to set up a center of worship than to go to a movie theater?" According to the history in the Old Testament, nothing throughout the generations was more sinful or more damaging to God's people than Dan's act of setting up a divisive center of worship. In Deuteronomy 12, 14, 15, and 16 the Lord through Moses charged the children of Israel at least fifteen times not to offer their burnt offerings in the place of their choice. They were commanded to go to the unique place the Lord had chosen for His name and for His habitation. Deuteronomy 12:13 and 14 say, "Take heed to thyself that thou offer not thy burnt offerings in every place that thou seest: but in the place which the Lord shall choose in one of thy tribes, there thou shalt offer thy burnt offerings, and there thou shalt do all that I command thee." The Lord seemed to be saying, "When you enter into the good land, you must not offer your burnt offerings in any of the places you see. You must go to the unique place, the place I have chosen for My name and My habitation. You have no right to choose any other place. You must go to this unique center. It is this center that keeps My people in oneness." Again and again Moses, the elderly, loving lawgiver, charged the children of Israel concerning this matter. If you read these chapters, you will see that Moses charged the people concerning the unique place, the place the Lord had chosen for His name and for His habitation. The reason the Lord commanded Moses to issue this charge repeatedly was that He was concerned about maintaining the unity of His people.

After the children of Israel entered the good land, the tabernacle, the house of God, was in Shiloh (Judg. 18:31). As long as the tabernacle was in Shiloh, Shiloh was the unique center for the worship of God. As the unique center, it should have maintained the unity of God's people. However, Dan set up another center in the north, which caused the first division among the children of Israel. In this way God's people were divided, not by a movie theater, but by a worship center. Today Christians excuse themselves by saying, "We are doing something here for the worship of God. What is wrong with this? God is not narrow; He is omnipresent. You have Him with you in your place. Is He not also here with us in our place? Certainly God is not as narrow as you are. He is everywhere. How can you limit Him to a particular place?" Nevertheless, God enjoys being limited for the purpose of keeping the unity of His people. Most Christians today are too free. Like the Danites, they feel free to set up another center of worship.

Judges 18:30 says, "The children of Dan set up for themselves the graven image" (Heb.). Here we see that the Danites did something for themselves. They did not care for the other tribes. Thus, the source of their apostasy was not caring for their brothers. Not caring for the other parts of the Body is the source of apostasy. This apostasy crept in under the guise of the worship of God. The principle is the same today. Many Christians set up other centers, not for gambling or dancing, but for worshipping God. Although this seems so positive, it is actually done by the self and for the self. Every divisive center is established for someone's self-interest. Such a practice causes not only division, but also competition.

If Dan had not set up another center of worship, there would have been only the unique center of worship in Shiloh. There would have been no competition. No matter how far the Israelites were from Shiloh, they had to go there to worship. But after Dan set up his center of worship in the north, he used the matter of convenience as a good selling point for his cargo. He could say, "You don't need to travel to Shiloh. Look, we are worshipping God right here in your own neighborhood." A divisive group in New York has done something very similar. A member of this group called an elderly sister and said, "Come meet with us. We meet in Chinese and have a Chinese flavor. In America it is difficult to have some Chinese flavor. Come meet with us and enjoy this Chinese flavor." This was their method of salesmanship for their cheap, divisive cargo.

Like the children of Israel, all Christians should be one, and the worship of God should have only one center. But the Danites could use the convenient location of their worship center to persuade their neighbors to meet with them for the worship of God. Suppose you were a neighbor of the Danites and one of them said to you, "Brother, why are you so foolish as to travel all the way to Shiloh? We are worshipping God right here in Dan. Why don't you meet with us?" This is competition. Today there is much competition in Christian salesmanship, with every Christian group trying to sell its cargo. This is sinful. What a shame to see this competition among today's Christians!

Some argue with us, asking, "Why are you separate from others?" Certainly Shiloh is separate from all other places. Shiloh is only one with Shiloh. Today some say, "Why do you call yourselves the church and say that the others are not the church?" We would answer, "Shiloh is Shiloh. No other place is Shiloh. On this earth, there is just one Shiloh. These other groups do not call themselves the church. Instead, they have taken other names. As long as they keep these names, this is an indication that they are not Shiloh. Rather, they are divisive places of worship."

Judges 18:31 says, "And they set them up Micah's graven image, which he made, all the time that the house of God was in Shiloh." The words, "all the time the house of God was in Shiloh," indicate competition. After Dan had set up a divisive center in competition with Shiloh, it was never taken away. For the whole time the tabernacle was in Shiloh the graven image was in Dan. This indicates that there was competition. Later, the temple was built in Jerusalem as the continuation of the tabernacle. After the temple had been built by Solomon, Jeroboam, in the next generation, set up a more solidly established idol in Dan to compete with the temple in Jerusalem (1 Kings 12:26-31). Jeroboam feared that if the people went to worship at Jerusalem, they would return to Rehoboam, the king of Judah (1 Kings 12:27). "Whereupon the king took counsel, and made two calves of gold, and said unto them, It is too much for you to go up to Jerusalem: behold thy gods, O Israel, which brought thee up out of the land of Egypt. And he set the one in Bethel, and the other put he in Dan" (1 Kings 12:28-29). Jeroboam seemed to be telling the people, "You don't need to go to Jerusalem. We have a worship center right here." But what he did came out of the fear that his kingdom would be lost. Thus, the competition between Dan and Jerusalem was intensified. Firstly Dan competed with the tabernacle at Shiloh. Later he competed with the temple in Jerusalem.

In the Old Testament we firstly see the competition of the graven image in Dan with the tabernacle at Shiloh. Then we see the competition of the golden calf in Dan with the temple in Jerusalem. After the temple of God was solidly built, the idol in Dan also became more solid. Both the tabernacle in Shiloh and the divisive worship center in Dan were set up by the common people. However, the temple in Jerusalem was built by a king, Solomon, and the divisive center was also strengthened by a king, Jeroboam. This is a very clear picture of the competition. The situation is the same today. When the church is solidly built, the denominations will also become more solid. The strengthening of the denominations comes from their competition with the church. Sooner or later, other groups will compete with the Lord's recovery. They may oppose and criticize us at first, but later they will imitate us and compete with us. Fifteen years ago terms such as the life-giving Spirit and the human spirit could not be heard among Christians in the United States. But recently even a paper put out by some Catholic charismatics used many of the terms of the Lord's recovery.

We need to understand the proper meaning of apostasy. Apostasy means to be distracted from the right track in following God. Apostasy is worshipping God in a devilish way. Whenever someone uses the worship of God as a cloak to take a devilish way, he has fallen into apostasy. The Roman Catholic Church is a total apostasy. No wonder it is called the apostate church. The Roman Catholic Church worships God, but it worships Him in a devilish way. Although those in Catholicism worship God in name, they are actually worshipping idols. The Roman Catholic Church does exactly the same thing Jeroboam did when he set up the idols and said, "Behold thy gods, O Israel." Jeroboam seemed to be saying, "This is the God you must worship." In reality that was not God; it was a golden calf. Hence, apostasy is worshipping God in a way that is false and devilish.

Today's Christianity is filled with apostasy. Apostasy is universal. Many who claim to be worshipping God are in fact worshipping idols. If you visit a Catholic cathedral, you will see people worshipping the idols that are along the walls and burning candles to the so-called saints. In name they worship God and Jesus; in actuality, they worship idols. According to G. H. Pember, one of the idols in the Roman Catholic Church is Buddha, who was assimilated into Catholicism under the name of St. Josaphat. What apostasy!

The words "for themselves" in Judges 18:30 are very significant. Many who claim to be worshipping God are really doing something for themselves. Apostasy is doing something for the self under the cloak of worshipping God. Jeroboam had no heart for God. Rather, his heart was for his own little empire. In his heart he feared that the kingdom would return to the house of David (1 Kings 12:26). Using the name of God as a cloak, he did everything possible to preserve his empire. This is apostasy. The whole of Christendom today is an apostasy. So many are doing things for themselves under the name of Jesus Christ and under the cloak of the worship of God. This is the reason the Lord needs a recovery. The Lord's recovery will always offend others. As long as the recovery is here, the divisive groups will stand condemned. As long as the temple was in Jerusalem, the golden calf was under condemnation. Was it possible for Dan to love Jerusalem? No, there could be no reconciliation between Dan and Jerusalem. Often others have come to me and said, "Brother Lee, please don't be so bold. Why not be a little nice?" I replied, "To whom should I be nice? To the serpent? To the horned snake? To the graven image? To the golden calf? I hate the golden calf, and I would like to burn the graven image and crush the head of the horned snake." How can we be kind to today's apostasy? There can be no compromise. Do not try to compromise with the serpent, the horned snake. If you are kind to the snake, you will be poisoned by it. If you try to be nice to today's apostasy, you will be damaged. The testimony is the testimony, and apostasy is apostasy. In Jerusalem there was God's temple as His testimony, but in Dan there was apostasy. Both in church history and in our own Christian experience we have seen this very thing. There may have been times when we were distracted from the right way in following God and fell into a type of apostasy. We might have said that we were working for the Lord when we were actually working for something else. This is apostasy.

Dan did not care for the other tribes; he cared only for his own tribe. After he won the victory and gained the expansion, the enlargement, he did something for himself. This was the source of his apostasy. According to the Old Testament, the Lord never forgot Dan's apostasy. In the eyes of God it was the worst sin in His economy. Nothing is more damaging than divisiveness. Nothing is more destructive than division among God's people. Divisive worship centers are often related to idols. Because the Devil lurks behind idols, by setting up an idol Dan became a serpent. Whenever you become divisive, no matter how good your reason may be, there will be something behind you—the serpent, the subtle one. The whole history of the church testifies of this and our experience confirms it. Whenever you do not care for others, but only for your interests, doing something merely for yourself, the serpent is at hand. The best way to be safeguarded from falling into apostasy is taking care of others. Suppose Dan had contacted the other tribes and said, "Brothers, do you agree that I set up another worship center in the city of Dan?" Had he done this, the others would have said, "Brother, don't do this. Deuteronomy 12, 14, 15, and 16 forbid us to have any other center of worship that we may come to the unique center." If Dan had consulted the other tribes, he would have been kept from apostasy. But being individualistic, he set up another worship center and fell into apostasy.

Dan fell into apostasy because he cared only for his own interests. In principle, every divisive center of worship is the same. Those who establish them care only for their interests, their desires, and they neglect all the other saints. They are like Dan, who cared only for his tribe, not for the others.

Dan not only set up a divisive center, but also ordained the hired "priests" (Judg. 18:30; 1 Kings 12:31). To hire the common people to be priests was profane because it destroyed God's holy ordination. In the downfall of the church, many unsaved ones have been hired to do the service of God. This is apostasy. In God's New Testament economy, all true believers are made priests of God (1 Pet. 2:9; Rev. 1:6; 5:10). But degraded Christianity has built up a system to ordain some of the believers to do the service of God, making them a clerical hierarchy and leaving the rest of the believers as laymen. This also is a form of apostasy. To have the clergy and the laity is an apostate practice which we must abhor and abandon.

II. THE RECOVERY WITH GAD

A. Coming Back to the Victory of Christ

Praise the Lord that, under the inspiration of God, after Dan, Jacob spoke of Gad! With Gad we see recovery. After the apostasy of Dan, Gad came in to recover the lost victory (49:19). The victory of Judah, the lion, had been lost by Dan's apostasy, but Gad regained it and even enlarged it. Gad is not a young lion, but a lioness producing cubs. He is the continuation of the victorious Judah and Dan.

B. Enlarged by God

God was so happy about Gad's recovery of the victory that He enlarged him. Deuteronomy 33:20 says, "Blessed be he that enlargeth Gad." Gad was enlarged not only by God, but also for God. He was enlarged for the executing of God's justice among God's people.

C. Crushing the Enemy by the Productive Life of Christ

Gad crushed the enemy by the productive life of Christ. Deuteronomy 33:20 says, "He dwelleth as a lioness and teareth the arm, even the crown of the head" (Heb.). Gad crushed the enemy not as a lion, but as a lioness producing young lions. This implies that his destruction of the enemy is a corporate matter. It is the same with us today in the Lord's recovery. We are the young lions destroying the enemy in a corporate way.

D. Taking Care of the Brothers

The best aspect of Gad is not merely that he crushed the enemy's head, but that he would not enjoy his victory by himself. Although he gained land on the east of the Jordan, he would not enjoy it until the other tribes had won their portion of the land. Gad went with the other tribes to fight the battle to gain more land so that all the tribes might be able to have their share. The New Testament interpretation of this Old Testament figure is that we must always take care of the brothers, the members of the Body.

For many years I could not understand Moses' word in Deuteronomy 33:21. This verse says, "And he provided the first part for himself, for there a portion of the lawgiver was reserved; and he came with the heads of the people, he executed the justice of the Lord, and his ordinances with Israel" (Heb.). Although I studied this verse again and again, especially the last part about the heads of the people, I simply could not understand it. But today I understand this verse. The "first part" refers to the land east of the Jordan. Gad provided that part for himself; yet he would not remain there to enjoy it. Instead, he came with the heads of the people, the princes of the other tribes, to fight the battle for the rest of the land. Here we see the action, the move, of the Body. Dan took care of himself individualistically, but Gad took care of the Body corporately. In the church today we would say that Gad was filled with the sense of the Body.

The reason for Gad's success was that he let go of his own enjoyment in order to take care of the Body. This is justice in the eyes of God. It is the executing of the justice of the Lord. In New Testament terms, it is the accomplishment of God's will. When the children of Israel entered the good land, it was God's will in His justice that His people be settled. God did not want only Gad; He wanted all the twelve tribes to be settled to become His kingdom that His ordinances may be observed. This is to accomplish the will of God. Romans 12:1 and 2 say that if we present our bodies a living sacrifice, we shall be able to prove what the will of God is. According to Romans 12, the will of God is simply to have the Body life. Thus, to have the Body life, to take care of the needs of others, is to execute God's justice for observing His ordinances. Nothing is so just as caring for the members of the Body. No ordinances can be observed without the execution of God's justice. God's New Testament ordinances can only be observed in the Body of Christ, which is built up by the mutual care of its members in justice.

Dan's failure was that he was individualistic. Gad's success was that he was corporate, moving with the brothers. Dan was for himself, but Gad was for all the tribes. Whenever you are concerned only for your own spiritual interests, you are a Dan. But when you forget your own spiritual interests and care for all the other brothers, that is, care for the Body, you are a Gad. We must care for the Body and move with the Body. Are you a Dan or a Gad? Are you taking care only of your locality or of the whole Body? As long as we do not care for the Body, we are today's Dan, and we have fallen into a form of apostasy.

III. THE SUFFICIENCY OF ASHER

A. The Exceeding Blessing and Surpassing Grace

After the recovery with Gad, we have the sufficiency of Asher. The account of Asher begins with the exceeding blessing and the surpassing grace. Deuteronomy 33:24 says, "Asher shall be blessed more than [the] sons; let him be favored among his brethren" (Heb.). Asher received the exceeding blessing and the foremost grace. Many of us are able to understand this language. In Dan's apostasy we lost all the blessing and the grace, but in Gad's victory the blessing was recovered and the grace was returned. Now in Asher we are enjoying the exceeding blessing and the surpassing grace.

B. The Rich Provision of Life

In Asher we also see the rich provision of life. Firstly, Asher has the rich provision for living and growing. Genesis 49:20 says, "Out of Asher his bread shall be fat, and he shall yield royal dainties." Deuteronomy 33:25 indicates that Asher also has the rich provision of life for fighting and building. The first part of this verse says, "Under thy sandals shall be iron and copper" (Heb.). The fat bread and royal dainties are for Asher's living and growing, and the iron and copper are minerals for fighting and building. Asher certainly received the richest provision.

C. The Bountiful Supply of the Spirit for Our Daily Walk

Asher also has the bountiful supply of the Spirit for his daily walk (Gal. 5:25). Deuteronomy 33:24 says, "Let him dip his foot in oil." This certainly is figurative speech. The spiritual significance of dipping the foot in oil is being full of the Spirit. In typology oil refers to the Spirit of God. Asher does not have a mere trickle of oil, but enough to dip his feet in. This means that in Asher we have the rich, bountiful supply of the Spirit (Phil. 1:19). Oh, we can walk in oil! A number of times in the Lord's recovery I have had the sense that we are walking in oil. I worship, thank, and praise the Lord, saying,

"Lord, this is too rich! The supply of the Spirit here is too rich! Our oil is so bountiful!" Do you have oil in which to dip your feet? We do. We have the fat bread, the royal dainties, and the rich, bountiful oil in which to dip our feet.

D. The Absolute Rest with Peace, Strength, Security, and Sufficiency

Deuteronomy 33:25 says of Asher, "And as thy days, so shall thy rest be" (Heb.). When we have the exceeding blessing and surpassing grace, the rich provision of life, and the bountiful supply of the Spirit, we have absolute rest with peace, strength, security, and sufficiency. This was the experience of the Apostle Paul in Philippians 4:11-13. He was content in any situation. I can testify that this week I have had the deep sense that I am walking in oil and that I have satisfaction, peace, and rest. I have also been full of strength. Thus, I have security and sufficiency. The Lord is my Shepherd, and I have no want, shortage, or lack (Psa. 23:1). Instead of want, I am full of sufficiency. I have fat bread, royal dainties, deep oil, and iron and copper under my sandals. Everywhere there is provision. Hence, I am safe and secure, and I have rest and strength. Do you have the boldness to say that you have this security and sufficiency? Or would you say that this morning your wife gave you a difficult time and that you barely endured it? You need to be able to say, "This morning my wife gave me a difficult time. But praise the Lord that I walked in deep oil! Now I have rest, peace, security, strength, and sufficiency. My strength is as lasting as my days. As my days, so shall my rest, my security, and my sufficiency be." This is the experience of Asher.

IV. THE CONSUMMATION WITH NAPHTALI

Although Asher is wonderful, he is still not the end of Jacob's poetic prophecy with blessing. After Asher comes Naphtali (49:21). How good it is that Jacob had twelve sons! This number is truly sufficient, even eternally sufficient. When Jacob needed someone to represent sinners, he had Reuben. When he needed someone to expose the evil, cruel disposition, he had Simeon. When he needed someone to express the victory of Christ, he had Judah. He also had Dan to represent apostasy, Gad to signify recovery, and Asher to portray sufficiency. Now we come to Naphtali.

A. Experiencing the Resurrected Christ and Uttering the Beautiful and Pleasant Words of Life

Genesis 49:21 says, "Naphtali is a hind let loose: he giveth beautiful words" (Heb.). In his prophetic blessing Jacob used many animals as figures: a lion, a lioness, a donkey, a foal of a donkey, a serpent, a horned snake, and a hind. Naphtali is neither a lion nor a donkey, but a hind. We thank God both for His creation and for Jacob's poetry. A hind is a lovely animal, so living and active. Although a hind is not proud or especially large, it is quite strong, able to skip upon the mountaintops. According to the Hebrew text, the title of Psalm 22 speaks of the hind of the morning. Years ago I heard a message by Brother Nee in which he said that the hind of the morning signifies the resurrected Christ. Psalm 22 firstly speaks of Christ's death on the cross. Then, beginning with verse 22, it proceeds to His resurrection. Psalm 22:22 says, "I will declare thy name unto my brethren: in the midst of the assembly will I praise thee" (Heb.). This indicates that in His resurrection Christ declared the name of the Father to His brothers and praised Him in the midst of the assembly, the church. Thus, this psalm eventually issues in the resurrection of Christ as the hind of the morning. Resurrection surely is a morning, and Christ in His resurrection is the hind of the morning.

Genesis 49:21 says that as a hind Naphtali gives beautiful words. When I was young, I could not understand the relationship between the hind and the beautiful words. It seemed that these things were absolutely unrelated. But now we can see the significance of this in our spiritual experience. When you experience Christ as the resurrected One, you will be filled and bubbling over with pleasant words. Instead of gossip, out of your innermost being will flow living waters through the words you speak. This means that all your words will be rivers uttered out of the resurrected Christ. In Matthew 28 and Acts 2 we see that the speaking of the pleasant words is intimately related to the resurrected Christ. After Christ was resurrected, He told His disciples to come to Him on a certain mountain, and there He charged them to go forth to speak not with their natural words, but with the resurrected Christ as their words (Matt. 28:16, 18-20). Thus, on the day of Pentecost Peter stood up to speak beautiful words (Acts 2:32-36). Peter's message that day was a proof that he had been experiencing the resurrected Christ. Because he had been experiencing this resurrected Christ, his teeth were white.

Rich words, pleasant words, beautiful words, words of joy and life—all these come out of the experience of the resurrected Christ. The more we experience Christ as the resurrected One, the more we have something to say. We could never be silent. Everyone who experiences Christ as the resurrected One will be bubbling over with beautiful words. This does not mean that we shall be talkative. No, it means that because we are filled with Christ, we are bubbling over and always have something to say. Christ is the word of God, the word of life, and the word that is spirit. I am filled with this resurrected Christ; thus, I have many words to utter. The principle here is that we always utter what is filling us within. The word we speak comes out of the abundance of our inner being. When our inner being is filled with Christ, we must speak lest we burst. Now we can understand why Naphtali, a hind let loose, gives beautiful words. Because he has experienced Christ, he is filled with beautiful words.

B. Satisfied with God's Grace and Full with God's Blessing

Deuteronomy 33:23 says, "O Naphtali, satisfied with favor, and full with the blessing of the Lord." The favor and blessing here link Naphtali with Asher, who is more blessed than the sons and favored among his brothers. In the Lord's recovery we are daily satisfied with rich grace and full of God's blessing. This blessing does not refer to the material blessing, but to the blessing in the spirit, the blessing in life, the blessing in the heavenlies. What grace we have tasted and what blessing we have enjoyed since coming into the church life! We all can testify that in the Lord's recovery we are satisfied with the rich grace and full of the rich blessing (1 Cor. 15:10; 2 Cor. 13:14).

C. Taking the Earth for the Lord

Deuteronomy 33:23 also says of Naphtali, "Possess thou the sea and the south" (Heb.). Naphtali will possess the west, the sea, the Gentile world, and the south, the land, the nation of Israel. This means that Naphtali will take the earth. It is the resurrected Christ experienced by us who will take the earth. At the end of Psalm 22 we see that the resurrected Christ will gain the nations. Psalm 22:27 says, "All the ends of the earth shall remember and turn unto the Lord: and all the kindreds of the nations shall worship before thee" (Heb.). All the nations will submit to Him, obey Him, and worship Him. Naphtali, the one who experiences the resurrected Christ, will possess the sea and the land. When we truly experience Christ in resurrection, we become those who will take the earth by preaching Christ (Matt. 28:19; Acts 1:8; Rom. 15:19).

LIFE-STUDY OF GENESIS

MESSAGE ONE HUNDRED FOUR

BEING MATURED
THE MANIFESTATION OF MATURITY

(6)

In this message we come to the last group of Jacob's twelve sons mentioned in his prophecy with blessing, the group composed of Joseph and Benjamin (49:22-27). The twelve tribes of the sons of Jacob in the Old Testament are always grouped together. In Numbers 2 we see the arrangement of the twelve tribes around the tabernacle: Judah, Issachar, and Zebulun on the east; Reuben, Simeon, and Gad on the south; Ephraim, Manasseh, and Benjamin on the west; and Dan, Asher, and Naphtali on the north.

Among the twelve sons of Jacob, only three were types of Christ: Judah, Joseph, and Benjamin. Judah was a type of Christ as the overcoming victorious Lion. Joseph was a type of Christ as the beloved Son of the Father bringing all the riches to feed the world. Benjamin was a type of the ascended, exalted Christ. When he was born, his mother called him Benoni, which means "son of sorrow," but his father changed his name to Benjamin, which means "son of the right hand." Therefore, Judah, Joseph, and Benjamin typify Christ in a full way. Although Reuben was the firstborn, he lost the birthright because of his defilement. Hence, in God's administration, Judah took the lead. However, without Joseph and Benjamin, the history and significance of the twelve tribes of Jacob would have no conclusion. Joseph and Benjamin provide an adequate, full conclusion of the history of the twelve sons of Jacob.

The twelve sons of Jacob are a complete type of God's people, including all of us. We have seen that the history of God's people begins with sinners, for we were all sinners like

Reuben, Simeon, and Levi. Reuben was full of lust, and Simeon and Levi were full of anger. Thus, the history of God's people began with sinners who were full of lust and anger. Then came Christ, typified by Judah. Later Naphtali appeared as a hind set loose and giving beautiful words. If the history of God's people ended with Naphtali, it would be good, but not adequate. For an adequate conclusion both Joseph and Benjamin are needed.

This history of God's people begins with sinners. Eventually these sinners are transformed into Levis with the priesthood and even into Judahs with the kingship. Then Naphtali, the resurrected Christ, brings forth beautiful words. This means that we once were Reubens and Simeons, but we need to be transformed into Levis, Judahs, and Naphtalis. Furthermore, we must go on to become Josephs and Benjamins.

Before we consider the significant aspects of Joseph and Benjamin, I wish to point out that Joseph and Benjamin, two sons born of one mother, Rachel, are two aspects of one person. When Jacob saw Rachel, he fell in love with her, and his heart was set on her. However, he did not firstly marry Rachel, but Leah, who brought forth six sons. Although children had also been born to the maids of Rachel and Leah, Rachel herself did not bear any children until ten sons had been born. Only then did Rachel give birth to Joseph, whose very name indicated that another was to be added. This signifies that in himself there was no completion with Joseph; there was the need of another part. Benjamin, therefore, was Joseph's completion. Thus, Joseph and Benjamin are one. If you read the Old Testament, you will see that it places Joseph and Benjamin together as a unit. Eventually, Joseph received the birthright and through his two sons, Ephraim and Manasseh, inherited the double portion of the land. In this way Joseph became two tribes, the tribe of Ephraim and the tribe of Manasseh. Furthermore, the tribe of Manasseh received two portions of the land: one half of this tribe received land on the east of the Jordan River, and the other half received land on the west. Joseph and Benjamin are one. The fact that Joseph was the eleventh son and Benjamin, the twelfth indicates that they were close to each other in sequence. Thus, among the twelve sons, Joseph and Benjamin were the last pair. Later they became the three tribes of Ephraim, Manasseh, and Benjamin, which were encamped at the rear of God's dwelling place. Judah was the leading tribe in the front of the tabernacle, but Joseph was at the rear.

Let us now consider the significant aspects of this group. Joseph was very faithful, and he was absolutely victorious. According to the record of the Old Testament, Joseph was the first perfect person. No one who preceded him, including Noah, was perfect. But in Joseph we can find no fault; he was utterly perfect in his behavior. Joseph was perfect because he was altogether victorious. Furthermore, the Old Testament likens Joseph to an ox full of strength (Deut. 33:17, Heb.). He was not a fierce lion or a threatening wolf, but an ox full of strength. As an ox, Joseph had two horns: Ephraim and Manasseh. With these two horns Joseph will push the peoples together to the ends of the earth. This indicates that Joseph is strong in victory.

Joseph also trusted in God and believed in Him. Because Joseph was perfect and victorious, and because he trusted in God, God blessed him. No one in the Bible received a blessing greater than that given to Joseph. As we shall see, he was blessed with ten items in time and in space, with everything from eternity past to eternity future and from heaven to earth. Joseph received everything. The entire universe became a blessing to him.

Benjamin is described as a tearing wolf (49:27, Heb.). Also, God's dwelling place is with Benjamin (Deut. 33:12). Thus, Jacob's prophecy with blessing ends with the fullness of the universal blessing and with God's dwelling place. The end of Genesis 49 requires Revelation 21 and 22 for its complete development.

(13) Concerning Joseph

(a) A Son of a Fruitful Tree by a Fountain

Genesis 49:22 says, "A son of a fruitful tree is Joseph, a son of a fruitful tree by a fountain; whose branches run over the wall" (Heb.). Firstly, Joseph is a son of a fruitful tree. This son is, of course, the bough of a tree. If Joseph is the bough, the son, then the fruitful tree must be Jacob. According to the record of the Bible, no one prior to Jacob had twelve sons. (Twelve is the number of eternal completion.) The fact that Jacob had twelve sons means that he was very fruitful. Jacob was the son of Isaac, and Isaac was the son of Abraham, the father of the called race. In the Bible God is called the God of Abraham, the God of Isaac, and the God of Jacob (Exo. 3:6; Matt. 22:32). This title is also the title of the Triune God. The God of Abraham refers to God the Father, the God of Isaac refers to God the Son, and the God of Jacob refers to God the Spirit. As we have pointed out, we should not consider Abraham, Isaac, and Jacob as three persons, but as three aspects of one person. In like manner, the three of the Triune God are three in one. Jacob signifies the coming of the Spirit, the third of the Triune God. The Father was in the Son, and the Son became the Spirit. Thus, the Spirit is the issue of our God.

If we touch the spirit of the Bible, we shall see that, as a fruitful person, Jacob signifies the producing God. God is the fruitful tree. This is proved by the fifteenth chapter of John, where Christ says that He is the vine tree. Christ as the embodiment of God is the producing tree. Christ truly is fruitful. Here in Genesis 49 we see a son of this tree. The Son of God is the branching out of God. For this reason, in the Old Testament Christ is called the Branch (Jer. 23:5; Zech. 6:12). The Bible is deep, profound, and far beyond our understanding. On the one hand, the Bible says that Christ is a tree and, on the other hand, it says that He is the branch. Is He then the tree or the branch? He is both. As the embodiment of God, He is the tree, but as the branching out of God, He is the branch. Joseph, a type of Christ, was also the son of a fruitful tree, the branching out of God. Joseph was God's branching out. As we all know, the branch of a tree is part of the tree. Thus, Joseph, the son of Jacob, was part of Jacob, the fruitful father. Speaking typically, Joseph was Christ as the Son of God who was the branching out of the fruitful God.

Verse 22 says that Joseph is a son of a fruitful tree by a

fountain. The fountain is God. The tree is God; the fountain is also God; everything is God. Jacob, a type of the fruitful tree, lived by God as the fountain. A tree requires water. If it has water, it will grow fruitfully. Jacob realized that all his fruitfulness came from God as the fountain. Here we are told that Joseph, as the son of Jacob, branches out all the riches of this tree that come from the fountain.

(b) His Branches Running over the Wall

The son, the bough, of this fruitful tree has branches that run over the wall. Chapter forty-nine is filled with figurative speech. In verse 22 we have a garden, a wall, and a tree inside the wall. The bough of this tree has many branches, and these branches run over the wall. According to the figure, this means that Jacob was moving out beyond the wall. He was not limited to the good land, but he ran out over the wall to Egypt, spreading beyond the limits of the good land into another region. Today, Christ as the very Joseph within us is spreading over the restricting wall. The wall cannot restrict Joseph's spreading; it cannot limit the branching out of this bough. We have this Joseph within us. This means that we have Christ within us as today's Joseph. Our Joseph has many branches which are running over the wall. These branches run over all limitations, for example, the limitations of family, school, or the restrictions of the opposition. No matter how high the wall may be, Joseph's branches will run over it. No matter how high the opposing wall may be, the very Christ within us will run over the wall by means of the many branches.

(c) Having Been Harassed by the Archers

Verse 23 says, "The archers have bitterly harassed him, and shot at him, and lay in wait for him" (Heb.). This refers to Joseph's suffering. His brothers were like archers who attacked him and shot arrows at him. When they were shepherding the flock of their father, Joseph was sent by their father to visit them, and they were actually lying in wait for him. When he came, they seized him.

(d) His Bow Remaining Firm and the Arms of His Hands Being Made Strong and Agile

However, Joseph's brothers did not gain the victory over him. Verse 24 says, "But his bow remained firm, and the arms of his hands were made strong and agile by the hands of the mighty one of Jacob; (from thence is the shepherd, the stone of Israel)" (Heb.). Joseph's brothers were not victorious because Joseph's bow remained firm and the arms of his hands were made strong and agile by the mighty One of Jacob. This mighty One of Jacob was Jacob's shepherd and his stone. Jacob had a shepherd who took care of him, and he had a stone on which to stand. Both this Shepherd and this rock were the mighty One of Jacob. Joseph was made strong through this mighty One of his father.

(e) Helped by the God of His Father and Blessed by the All-sufficient

The God of Joseph's father helped him and the all-sufficient One blessed him. Verse 25 says, "Even by the God of thy father, who helpeth thee; and by the All-sufficient, who blesseth thee" (Heb.). When we combine the blessings mentioned in 49:25-26 with those in Deuteronomy 33:13-16, we see that the blessings bestowed upon Joseph were of ten aspects. First, he was blessed with the precious things of heaven (Deut. 33:13). Certainly some of the blessings of the precious things of heaven should include rain and snow. Second, he was blessed with the dew. Third, he was blessed with the blessing of the deep that lies beneath. This refers to the springs, fountains, and waters underneath the earth. Fourth, he was blessed by the precious fruits brought forth by the sun (Deut. 33:14). After that, as the fifth blessing, he had the blessing of the precious things put forth by the moon. We need both the sun, which typifies Christ, and the moon, which typifies the church. Some fruits are brought forth by Christ, and some precious things are put forth by the church. All these were among the blessings bestowed upon Joseph. The sixth blessing Joseph received was the blessing of the best things of the ancient mountains, and the seventh was the precious things of the eternal hills (Deut. 33:15, Heb.). In all these blessings all of time and space is included. From ancient times to eternity, all of time is included, and from heaven to earth, including the deep under the earth, all of space is included. This indicates that all the good things in the universe have become blessings to Joseph. The eighth blessing includes the precious things of the earth and its fullness (Deut. 33:16). Certainly this must include minerals such as gold and silver. The ninth blessing is seen in Genesis 49:25: "Blessings of the breasts, and of the womb." The blessings of the womb are for begetting, and the blessings of the breasts are for nourishing. These refer to the producing of life. This is the only blessing that is of life. The tenth blessing is "the good will of him that dwelt in the bush" (Deut. 33:16). Later we shall see that the One who dwelt in the bush (Exo. 3:4) will dwell in the temple, in the church, and then in the New Jerusalem. All the bushes will be transformed into precious stones. Formerly, God dwelt among the bushes, but eventually He will dwell among the precious stones in the New Jerusalem. This is the very desire of God's heart, His good will. All these things are included in the universal blessing bestowed upon Joseph.

The greatest blessing is the dwelling of the One who dwelt in the bush. God's dwelling among us is the foremost blessing. Suppose your father gives you many things and then leaves you and goes away. This would not be very good. The Father has given us so much, but eventually He gives us His ultimate blessing—His dwelling. As we read the Bible from Genesis to Revelation, we see that God has given us many good things. But what God finally gives us is His dwelling.

All these blessings are Christ's inheritance. Hebrews 1:2 says that God has appointed Christ Heir of all things. All the good things throughout time and space are the inheritance of Christ. This is God's blessing to Christ. And we are Christ's partners participating in His inheritance. Joseph here represents Christ. All the blessings of the Father go to Him. In the New Testament we are told that all things have been given to the Son. These are the blessings in space, in time, and in life. All this is Christ's inheritance, and we, His partners, join Him to inherit all these blessings. It is not simply a matter of salvation or of the kingdom. All the things in time from ancient times to eternity, everything in space from heaven to underneath the earth, and all the producing and nourishing aspects of life are the blessings bestowed upon Christ.

This Christ was the One separate from His brothers (49:26). The Hebrew word rendered "separate" is also the word for Nazarite. According to Numbers 6, certain Israelite males were separated from the others to live absolutely for God. Joseph was such a one. He was the first Nazarite in the Bible, separate from his brothers, and Christ became the real Nazarite, separate from all the people. Thus, Joseph typified Christ as the Nazarite, the One who was separated from the common people to live wholly for God. This separated One has received the blessing of the whole universe. The universal blessing is bestowed upon the crown of the head of such a Nazarite.

(f) His Majesty Being like the Firstborn of His Ox, and His Horns Being like the Horns of the Wild Ox

Deuteronomy 33:17 says, "His majesty is like the firstborn of his ox, and his horns are like the horns of a wild ox: with them he shall push the peoples together to the ends of the earth: and these are the ten thousands of Ephraim, and these are the thousands of Manasseh" (Heb.). Joseph was strong, like the firstborn of the ox. This ox has two horns. One was Ephraim, and the other was Manasseh. With these two horns the ox pushes together the peoples to the ends of the earth. This also is a picture of Christ. Christ is a strong ox with two horns, pushing the peoples together as He desires. This will take place at the Lord's coming back. Today the peoples are scattered and spreading. But the day will come when Christ as the strong ox will push the peoples together. He may say, "Russians and other nations, don't spread yourselves out. I shall push you together to the ends of the earth." Remember, Genesis 49 is a prophetic record of the entire history of God's people, beginning with sinners and ending with the Christ who inherits all things and takes over the whole earth. Christ is not only fruitful, victorious, and blessed to the uttermost;

He is also full of strength to push the peoples on earth according to His purpose.

For centuries, the Russians, inhabitants of a cold region, have been trying to spread to the south, to the Mediterranean Sea. When they tried to reach the Persian Gulf, the British fought them back. Then they built the Siberian railroad to the Far East in order to reach the sea, and after that they constructed the Manchurian railroad to the Pacific. But the British helped the Japanese to defeat them. Today the Russians are trying to penetrate the Mediterranean Sea and the Red Sea. For this reason, Egypt is very important. The hidden intention of the Russians is to take over the good land, including Jerusalem. But eventually Christ, the strong ox, will come with two horns and push the Russians back to the northern region. He may say, "Russians, your destiny is to live in a cold region. Do not try to come down to the Mediterranean Sea, which is reserved eternally for My people." This strong ox will push back the Russians and other peoples to the uttermost. If you think I am speaking nonsense, I ask you to wait and see. Sooner or later, this will happen. The crucial center of international relations today is the Middle East, and many nations want to spread into that region. But Joseph, the strong ox, will come with the ten thousands of Ephraim and the thousands of Manasseh to push the peoples back to the ends of the earth. He may say, "Get away from the Mediterranean Sea. This region is for My people. You must not come here!"

(14) Concerning Benjamin

(a) A Tearing Wolf

Now we come to the two main points concerning Benjamin. Genesis 49:27 says, "Benjamin is a tearing wolf: in the morning he shall devour the prey, and in the evening he shall divide the spoil" (Heb.). In Hebrew the word translated "tearing" means "to tear into pieces." For years I was troubled by the word "wolf" in this verse. Although a lion or a tiger seems positive, a wolf is not positive. However, Christ is not only the overcoming lion, but also the tearing wolf. Benjamin, a tearing wolf, is also a type of Christ. Therefore, the reference to a wolf here is positive, not negative. In the morning he will devour the prey, and in the evening he will divide the spoil, that is, prepare the spoil for the next morning's meal. This means that Christ is not only the overcoming One, but also the tearing One, the One who eats His enemy.

> (b) Dwelling by the Lord, and the Lord Covering Him
> All the Day Long and Dwelling between His Shoulders

Speaking of Benjamin, Deuteronomy 33:12 says, "The beloved of the Lord shall dwell in safety by him; and the Lord shall cover him all the day long, and he shall dwell between his shoulders." The words "by him" indicate that Benjamin will be the Lord's neighbor. He will dwell next door to the Lord. Because he will dwell next door to the Lord, he will dwell in safety. Certainly anyone who dwells by the Lord will dwell in safety. This verse also says that the Lord will cover, overshadow, Benjamin all day long and even dwell between his shoulders. Here we need to point out that Jerusalem was not located in the territory of Judah, but in the territory of Benjamin (Judg. 1:21). If you consult a map, you will see that the territory of Benjamin lies with two shoulders toward the south and that between these two shoulders of Benjamin was Jerusalem, where the temple, the Lord's dwelling, was located.

The Lord's dwelling was a cover that overshadowed Benjamin all the day long, as the Lord will overshadow His people in eternity with His tabernacle (Rev. 7:15). Today the church as the Lord's dwelling is also a cover that overshadows the church people.

Among the twelve sons of Jacob, the first was a sinner, and the last became the dwelling of God. In Genesis chapter three we all were sinners, but at the end of the Bible, in Revelation 21 and 22, we all become Benjamin, the dwelling of God. This is the reason I said that, without Joseph and Benjamin, there would not be an adequate conclusion of the history of God's people. But with Joseph we see that Christ receives the all-inclusive blessing of the universe, and with Benjamin we see that God is dwelling among His chosen people. This is the

New Jerusalem and the new heaven and new earth. The new heaven and new earth are the sphere in which every blessing is bestowed upon Christ. Everything in this new sphere will be part of the blessing granted to Christ, and within this sphere will be a certain place, the New Jerusalem, which will be God's eternal dwelling. All this is pictured by the lives of Joseph and Benjamin.

Today we are in the church life, and ultimately we shall be in the New Jerusalem. Do you know who will be there? Joseph and Benjamin. In the proper church life today there is no Reuben or Simeon. Eventually, in the church life there will be only Joseph and Benjamin, the blessing of the Lord and the dwelling of God. The time will come when the church will be just Joseph and Benjamin. The church will be under His blessing universally and it will be His dwelling. The conclusion of the entire Bible as the record of the history of God's people is the universal blessing and the eternal habitation of God. The new heaven and the new earth with the New Jerusalem portray the universal blessing inherited by Christ and God's habitation. We shall go all the way from Reuben to Benjamin, from sinners to God's habitation. Joseph is a sign of God's full blessing, and Benjamin is a sign of God's eternal dwelling. In the churches today we have a miniature of the things to come in the new heaven and new earth with the New Jerusalem; for we are enjoying the foretaste of the full blessing, and we are God's dwelling. In a sense, we all are Josephs and Benjamins. We are a blessed people, and we are the dwelling of God. This is Joseph and Benjamin.

LIFE-STUDY OF GENESIS

MESSAGE ONE HUNDRED FIVE

THE SPIRITUAL SIGNIFICANCE OF JOSEPH AND BENJAMIN

(1)

I became familiar with the history of Jacob's twelve sons long before I realized how sweet and wonderful their history was. The more time I spend on Genesis 49, the more I appreciate these twelve sons. It is very worthwhile to delve into their history. The first four sons—Reuben, Simeon, Levi, and Judah—were all sinful. But Joseph and Benjamin, the last two, are without fault or defect. They are perfect. Between the first four sons and the last two, we have the other six sons. With Dan we see apostasy; with Gad, recovery; with Asher, sufficiency; and with Naphtali, resurrection. If you put together the record of these twelve sons according to Genesis 49, you will have a portrait of yourself. On the one hand, when I look at these twelve sons of Jacob, I marvel at them; on the other hand, I am thankful to God, because in them I see a picture of myself. I also see the very Christ I have experienced and the salvation and transformation that are in Christ. In the past we all were Reubens, Simeons, Levis, and Judahs, but today we are Josephs and Benjamins.

Two of the sinful ones, Levi and Judah, were transferred into something positive. Levi was transferred into the priesthood, and Judah was transferred into the kingship. Thus, among the twelve sons of Jacob, we eventually have the priesthood, the kingship, and finally the ultimate consummation, which we see in Joseph and Benjamin. In the following message we shall see that the ultimate consummation is of two things: blessing and dwelling. We shall be brought fully into the universal blessing under God, and then we shall become His dwelling. Sinners become God's priests and kings, and ultimately they are under His universal blessing and become His eternal dwelling. If we saw the significance of this record, we would shout and praise the Lord. We would say, "Once I was a Reuben, but today I am a Levi, a Judah, a Joseph, and a Benjamin!" For eternity, we shall be the kings under God's blessing, and we shall be God's dwelling.

Have you ever realized that the Bible could be so wonderful? Have you ever seen that in one chapter, Genesis 49, we could have an abstract of the whole Bible and a summary of the history of the twelve sons of Jacob, of the history of the nation of Israel, of the history of the church, and of our own spiritual history? Everything is here. Although this chapter is poetic and very profound, it is nonetheless quite simple. It is all-inclusive. It includes all the Bible, it encompasses the history of the twelve tribes, it indicates the history of the church, and it portrays our personal history. How wonderful! Without doubt, this summarizes God's dealing with His chosen people. God's dealing with His people began with sinners, it proceeds to transformation, and eventually it reaches the ultimate consummation, which is the blessing and the dwelling of God.

Among Jacob's twelve sons, there are various types of persons. How I thank God for giving Jacob twelve sons. What if Jacob had had just one son? In the eyes of God, Abraham and Isaac each had just one son, for God counted only Isaac and Jacob, not Ishmael or Esau. But God's economy required twelve tribes. For this, Jacob had to have twelve sons. Not even ten tribes would have been sufficient. One day, after the death of Solomon, the kingdom of Israel was divided into two parts with ten tribes in one part and two in the other. But not even these ten tribes were sufficient; there had to be twelve. We need to remember the names of Jacob's twelve sons: Reuben, Simeon, Levi, Judah, Zebulun, Issachar, Dan, Gad, Asher, Naphtali, Joseph, and Benjamin. In this message we shall consider part of the spiritual significance of Joseph and Benjamin, covering three matters: fruitfulness, victory, and trust. In the following message we shall consider the blessing and the dwelling.

I. FRUITFUL

A. A Son of a Fruitful Tree

Genesis 49:22 says, "A son of a fruitful tree is Joseph, a son of a fruitful tree by a fountain; whose branches run over the wall" (Heb.). Joseph was very fruitful. He was fully occupied with fruitfulness, having no time for anything else. He had no time to argue with his brothers or to fight with others. People become occupied with negative things because they are not fully occupied with positive things. It is not profitable for a large number of saints to be gathered together and not be fully occupied. In such a case they will not be occupied with the positive things. Rather, spontaneously they will become occupied with negative things, just like the man in Matthew 12 who was vacant and who became possessed with seven demons (vv. 43-45). That man was like a clean, unoccupied apartment. Many saints are clean, but they are empty, unoccupied. Therefore, negative things come in. The saints need to be occupied with positive things. Then they will have no capacity, time, or energy for things such as gossip. Gossiping proves that not all our energy is being used. Joseph, however, was not an unoccupied person. As we shall see in later messages, from the time of his youth, he was occupied with positive things. He was occupied with his father's will, his father's mind, his father's interest, and his father's commission. Hence, there was no opportunity for the "gophers" or "dogs" to come in. If a room is filled with twenty people, no gopher would dare to come in. But if the room is unoccupied, gophers and dogs may try to come in. The best way to keep the saints from negative things is to fill them with positive things. Again I say that from his youth, Joseph was fully occupied with positive things, mainly with fruitfulness.

When Joseph's father and eleven brothers and their families came down to Egypt, they became the channels for the branching out of Joseph's fruitfulness. At that time in Egypt Joseph was not simply branching out personally; he was branching out God's administration with seventy people. Joseph was very fruitful. The entire world was under the branching out of Joseph. Joseph was a picture, a type. This means that the fulfillment must be with the church. The church people should be the most fruitful people. Acts chapter two reveals how fruitful Peter and the other eleven apostles were. Throughout the centuries, all who have loved the Lord and who have been occupied with Him have also been fruitful.

Verse 22 says that Joseph was a son of a fruitful tree. The word "son" here indicates a bough or a branch. Most versions translate the Hebrew word as "bough," which is a large branch. This means that Joseph was a branch of a fruitful tree. In the entire universe there is just one fruitful tree, and that tree is Christ. As the branch of God, Christ is a fruitful tree. Zechariah 6:12 says, "Behold the man whose name is The BRANCH." This branch is Christ. Christ as the branch of God has branched out God to humanity, eventually becoming a tree. In John 15, a chapter on fruitfulness, the Lord Jesus said, "I am the true vine" (v. 1). Christ is the vine tree. In John 15:5 the Lord said, "I am the vine, you are the branches; he who abides in Me and I in him, he bears much fruit." As branches of such a fruitful tree, we all need to be fruitful.

Do not consider your weaknesses, failures, or the pitiful situation around you. Church history has two sides—a dark side and a glorious side. When we look at the glorious side, we see abundant fruitfulness. Not only Peter and Paul but all those who love the Lord have been fruitful. Sometimes we may say, "We are weak, our situation is not promising, the increase is coming slowly, and the number remains small." But if you have the heavenly view, you will see that the church is very fruitful and that the history of the church is a history of fruitfulness. Again I say, do not look at the situation from the dark side, but from the glorious side. God is victorious, and the church is fruitful. The branch is branching out. Peter, Paul, and all the lovers of Christ throughout the centuries have had many branches.

B. Branching over the Wall

These branches are branching out over the wall (49:22), that is, they are spreading Christ over all restrictions, magnifying Him in all circumstances (Phil. 1:20). Genesis 49:22

says that Joseph's branches run over the wall. The wall signifies restriction. Since the day of Pentecost, wall after wall has been erected to restrict the spreading of the branches. One day Peter was even put into prison (Acts 12:3-4). But not even that stronghold could restrict the branching out. Year after year, decade after decade, and century after century, walls have been raised up by the opposers and by the enemy to restrict the church's fruitfulness. But the branches have run over the wall every time.

I can testify of this by what I have seen and experienced during the past fifty years. During these years I have seen the fruitfulness of the branches. Brother Nee, raised up by the Lord in China, was certainly a bough of a fruitful tree, a branch of the fruitful Christ. When I was with him, I became very clear that nothing could restrict his testimony. Brother Nee was burdened to bear a testimony of Jesus that was opposed to organized Christianity. As a result, even many Christians put up walls to restrict him, and they spread rumors about him. Let me give you an illustration of the evil rumors. After he was saved, Brother Nee received great help from a sister named Margaret E. Barber. Miss Barber had a co-worker named Miss Gross. Both Miss Barber and Miss Gross were missionaries who had come from Britain to China. However, by the time Brother Nee was saved, they had left their missions and were in China living by faith in God. Because Brother Nee received so much help from Miss Barber, Miss Gross also came to know him. Since Brother Nee was under the helping hand of Miss Barber, he was simultaneously also under the help of Miss Gross. In 1929 Miss Barber went to be with the Lord, and Miss Gross remained and moved to Shanghai. One day Miss Gross heard the report that a woman was living with Brother Nee, and she came to him to check with him about this. Brother Nee was still single, and, like Miss Barber, Miss Gross, as an elderly sister, loved him and was very concerned about him. Miss Gross said, "I have heard that a woman is staying with you. Is this true?" When Brother Nee answered, "Yes," Miss Gross rebuked him, asking how he, a single young man, could have a woman staying with him. Brother Nee related this incident to me himself to help me understand something about self-vindication. He told me that he was happy to be rebuked. He also told me that the woman staying with him was his mother. He said this, not to vindicate himself, but to render some help to me. When I asked Brother Nee why he did not tell Miss Gross about this, he replied, "She didn't ask me who the woman was. She only asked whether or not a woman was staying with me. When I told her that a woman was living with me, she rebuked me. I didn't say anything." This is one illustration of the rumors spread about Brother Nee.

Another illustration: Immediately after his wedding, a great turmoil was stirred up in Shanghai. This was another wall raised up by the enemy. Brother Nee showed me a newspaper, the leading newspaper in Shanghai and perhaps in all of China. In huge Chinese characters there was a negative article regarding his marriage. Brother Nee said to me, "Witness, in my whole life I never heard about such a thing happening after a wedding."

Today many rumors are being circulated about us, but as yet none of them are as evil as the rumors spread about Brother Nee. The fact that a rumor was circulated concerning a woman staying with Brother Nee indicates that the enemy was constantly trying to raise up walls to restrict his fruitfulness. But Brother Nee's fruitfulness has run over the wall. Today his fruit can be found throughout the earth. No one can wall it in. Even if some raise up a wall one hundred forty-four cubits high, the branches will still run over it.

As the years went by, I saw all the things that happened to Brother Nee. I thank the Lord that I was allowed to see those things and experience them with him. Thus, when I hear the rumors spread about me, I can laugh and say, "I am prepared for this. In the past I saw a wall one thousand feet high. But your wall is a mere fifteen feet." I would like to tell all the opposers throughout the United States, "I don't think you can build a wall one thousand feet high. Probably the highest wall you can build is five hundred feet. However, I have already experienced branching over a wall one thousand feet high." The Lord knows that I am not boasting. At least two elderly brothers from China among us here can testify that in the past I suffered together with Brother Nee. Having rumors spread about us is nothing new. If possible, we should tell the opposers they are wasting their time, for they cannot suppress this testimony. The higher the walls are built to restrict us, the faster the branches will spread over them.

In Acts 5 Gamaliel spoke a good word: "Stay away from these men and leave them alone; for if this counsel or this work is of men, it will be overthrown; but if it is of God, you will not be able to overthrow them, lest perhaps you even be found fighters against God" (vv. 38-39). If this is not the Lord's recovery, it should be overthrown. If it is not the recovery, let it sink to the bottom of the Pacific Ocean. But if it is the Lord's recovery, the opposers should be careful, for they will suffer shame. They will never be able to defeat this testimony. The more they try to hold it down, the higher it will rise up. Church history testifies of this.

Let me share a little of my personal experience. After I was saved, by the mercy of the Lord I became a seeking Christian, one who sought the Lord. The Christians in my home town loved me. One day, however, I was caught by the Lord for His recovery, and a church was raised up in my home town. According to the outsiders, I was the one doing the preaching and teaching there. Before the church was raised up, some of the Christians invited me to speak at their meetings. They even provided transportation to and from the meeting. In China, that was considered an expression of love and respect. But after the church was raised up there, those very ones who invited me to the meetings and even provided transportation for me completely ignored me when they saw me on the street. Then rumors were spread about me. Some of those rumors said that I was teaching heresy. I have been condemned as heretical from the time I first came into the church life. This is nothing new to me.

Fifty years ago, my home town was the most famous city in North China for Bible knowledge. Hearing the rumors that my teaching was heretical, certain young men, sons of fundamental Christian preachers, came to the meetings to find out for themselves what was going on. Prior to this, instead of attending services of their fathers' denominations, they went to operas, theaters, and gambling places. When these young men were engaging in such sinful activities, their parents were not very concerned. However, when some of them were attracted to the church life and caught by it, the pastors began to warn them not to attend the meetings. One of these young men said to a certain pastor, "When I was going to the gambling places and to the theaters, you did not come to warn me about what I was doing. But now that I am going to a place where I can listen to the Word of God and where I am receiving much help in spiritual life, you come to warn me not to go there. Do not come to me again. I have been helped by attending these meetings, and I intend to keep on receiving this help." This shows that the branches were running over the wall.

Throughout the years, the opposers have followed me from my home town to many other places, including Taiwan. A certain preacher purposely went to Taiwan from my home town to try to destroy my ministry. When I was bothered by the opposition, the Lord said, "Look at Paul, and read the book of Acts again. Wherever the apostles went, the opposing Jews followed and caused trouble."

Recently, one of the brothers received a letter from Australia, written by a traveling preacher, filled with negative statements about me. In the whole letter there was nothing positive concerning me. However, several years ago the same man who wrote this letter had written another letter in which he praised me very highly. In the letter written several years ago, this traveling preacher said, "To me, Witness Lee has always been a great man of God in his personal life, and a most fruitful servant of God in his ministry. I'm sure I cannot lace his shoes. I would be a happy man if I thought the Lord would give me half the reward, or even one tenth, He has for His eminent servant." But recently the same person has written a letter filled with slanderous lies about me. It is difficult to believe that both were written by the same person. This second letter was written because the fruitful branch has spread to Sydney. Some, seeing the branching out in Australia, were stirred up and wondered what they could do about it. Hence, this letter was written in an attempt to restrict the branching out of the Lord's recovery in Australia. When I consider things such as this in the light of 49:22, I am happy, for the branches are still running over the wall. What is happening today exactly corresponds to what is written in this verse. The opposers are wasting their time. The more walls they raise up, the more branching out there will be.

How can a traveling preacher, one who preaches the gospel in the name of the Lord Jesus and teaches the Bible, speak lies, even slander a brother? This is the poor situation of today's Christianity. There is no conscience and no moral standard. As long as some can frustrate the Lord's recovery, they are happy. But no wall can frustrate the spread of the branches. In fact, the opposition actually helps the Lord's spreading. This is the experience of Joseph.

In 1958 I was invited to England. From that time onward, some have tried to restrict the Lord's recovery from spreading to Europe. But when the Lord's Recovery began to spread there, they were not able to do anything. The branches are spreading over the wall in Germany, Switzerland, and even in Denmark and Sweden. No one can restrict the spreading of Joseph. If we are today's Joseph, who can restrict us?

Rumors about us have also been spread in Central America and in South America. But praise the Lord that His recovery in Brazil is spreading like wild fire! None of the "firemen" know what to do about it. Before this wild fire began to spread, the opposers in Christianity circulated rumors concerning me and the churches. I ask you to wait for another period of time and see what will happen. Everything depends on whether or not we are today's Joseph. If we are, no one and nothing will be able to restrict the spreading of the branches over the wall.

II. VICTORIOUS

A. Overcoming the Archers' Attack

Genesis 49:23 and 24 say, "The archers have bitterly harassed him, and shot at him, and lay in wait for him: but his bow remained firm" (Heb.). Joseph overcame the archers' attack. The spiritual significance of this is that in all suffering we more than conquer (Rom. 8:36-37). The sufferings cannot suppress us; rather, we subdue the sufferings.

B. Being Made Strong by the Mighty One

Although Joseph was persecuted, harassed, and attacked, he remained strong. He was not only strong, but also agile. Verse 24 says, "The arms of his hands were made strong and agile by the hands of the mighty One of Jacob" (Heb.). The more Joseph suffered and the more he was attacked, the more he became strong. His suffering also trained him to be agile. In order for our arms and legs to be agile, we need to be trained by suffering. Joseph was a trained person; he was trained through his sufferings. It is the same with us today. All the opposition and the rumors only help us to be agile.

Joseph, of course, was made strong and agile by the mighty One of Jacob. The source of his strength and agility was God. If you read Joseph's history, you will see that God was always with him. When he was tempted by Potiphar's wife, he said, "How then can I do this great wickedness, and sin against God?" (39:9). This indicates that God was with him. His strength and his agility came from God.

Today in the Lord's recovery we are empowered in the grace of Christ to withstand all opposition for the Lord's testimony (2 Tim. 2:1). Our strength is not of ourselves, but of the Lord. As long as we have Him as the source of our strength, no opposition can suppress us.

C. Tearing like a Wolf

In 49:27 Benjamin is likened to a tearing wolf: "Benjamin is a tearing wolf: in the morning he shall devour the prey, and in the evening he shall divide the spoil" (Heb.). The term "wolf" is not a pleasant term. However, whenever you tear anything, you cannot be nice; rather, you must be like a wolf. When we had to tear down some things in order to complete the building of the meeting hall in Anaheim, I observed the expressions of those who were doing this work. The expression on every face was fierce. A gentleman cannot tear down anything. Whenever you are about to tear something down, you must be a wolf. Benjamin was a wolf.

In 2 Corinthians 10:5 Paul says, "Overthrowing reasonings and every high thing rising up against the knowledge of God, and taking captive every thought unto the obedience of Christ." When I was young, I thought that Paul was proud in saying this. Speaking about overthrowing reasonings and every high thing and about capturing thoughts is not nice, humble, gentle, mild, or kind. When Paul wrote those words, he was a tearing wolf. Many times when I contact others I am humble and nice. But at certain times I am like a wolf tearing things into pieces. In ordinary talk, I am a gentleman, but there are times when I show no mercy. Sometimes my co-workers and even my dear wife have asked me to be merciful toward others. But can you ask a tearing wolf to be merciful? If a wolf could speak, he would say, "In my language there is no such word as mercy." A tearing wolf shows no mercy. We are not tearing people into pieces; we are tearing Satan. We are also tearing into pieces the dissenting thoughts and reasonings. All these high things must be torn to shreds.

D. Pushing like an Ox

Deuteronomy 33:17 says, "His majesty is like the firstborn of his ox, and his horns are like the horns of a wild ox: with them he shall push the peoples together to the ends of the earth: and these are the ten thousands of Ephraim, and these are the thousands of Manasseh" (Heb.). Joseph is likened to a pushing ox. In the previous message I pointed out that when Christ comes back, He will push the Russians away from the good land. I definitely believe this. But we also may experience Joseph as a pushing ox today. As I have considered my past experiences and the experiences of Brother Nee, I realize that I have certainly seen the pushing victory. The opposers joined forces to squeeze us, but there was the pushing victory, the pushing strength, and the pushing horns. Wait for a while, and you will see Joseph's pushing strength. Joseph is fruitful, and he is victorious in tearing and in pushing. We in the Lord's recovery today are all Josephs strong in tearing the opposition and in pushing the opposition away.

Many of you have read the booklet entitled, *What a Heresy—Two Divine Fathers, Two Life-giving Spirits, and*

Three Gods! Although this booklet has been out for several months, no one has written a booklet in reply to it. The mouths of the opposers have been shut, and their writing hands have been amputated, for they have no way to take care of Isaiah 9:6 and 1 Corinthians 15:45. No matter how some may twist Isaiah 9:6, they cannot eliminate the title Father found here. This verse says that a Son is given to us and that His name is called the everlasting Father, or the Father of eternity. This Father certainly is the Father of the Godhead. If you say that the Father in Isaiah 9:6 is not the Father of the Godhead, then you hold the heresy of believing in two divine Fathers. But in the whole universe there is only one source, the Father in the Godhead. There cannot be another Father as another source. Do not tell me about history or about the Nicene Creed or any other creed. I do not care for the creeds—I only care for the pure word in Isaiah 9:6.

First Corinthians 15:45 says, "The last Adam became a life-giving Spirit." Some, opposing us, have twisted this verse and said, "It says 'a spirit,' not 'the Spirit.'" But do not forget the modifier "life-giving." This verse speaks of the life-giving Spirit. Do you believe that this Spirit is different from the Holy Spirit of the Godhead? If so, then you believe in two life-giving Spirits. That is heresy! In fighting this battle, I am a wolf tearing the enemy to pieces.

Some of the opposers appeal to the Nicene Creed. The Nicene Creed is like a pair of shoes two inches long, but our feet are twelve inches long. Do you intend to cut your feet to fit into your little shoes, or will you get a pair of shoes to fit your feet? The book of Revelation speaks of the seven Spirits, but are the seven Spirits covered by the Nicene Creed? No! The New Testament also speaks of the life-giving Spirit, but does the Nicene Creed contain any reference to the life-giving Spirit? No! Thus, that pair of shoes is too short. The vision we have is much greater than what is contained in that creed. We must not reduce the vision to match the shoes; rather, we must throw away those old shoes and take the pure word of the Bible. Let all of Christianity oppose us. Eventually, we shall see what the outcome will be. In the Lord's recovery we have both the tearing strength and the pushing strength. Sooner or later, the enemy will not only be defeated and subdued; he will unconditionally surrender. God is leading us in triumph (2 Cor. 2:14). The truth is the truth, Joseph is Joseph, and Benjamin is Benjamin.

III. TRUSTING

Genesis 49:24 also speaks of the Shepherd, the stone of Israel, and verse 25 says, "Even by the God of thy father, who helpeth thee; and by the All-sufficient, who blesseth thee" (Heb.). These verses indicate why Joseph and Benjamin became the ultimate consummation: they trusted in the mighty One of Jacob. They trusted in the Shepherd of Israel, and they stood upon the stone of Israel. They trusted in the all-sufficient One. The New Testament equivalent for trusting in the All-sufficient is Philippians 4:13, which says, "I can do all things in Him who empowers me." The equivalent of the Shepherd of Israel is seen in 1 Peter 5:4, which says that Christ, the Chief Shepherd, will appear. Finally, the New Testament equivalent of the stone of Israel is seen in Christ, the rock of the church. First Corinthians 10:4 says, "For they drank of a spiritual rock which followed them, and the rock was Christ."

In Jacob's prophetic blessing of Joseph we see that Joseph's fruitfulness and victory came out of his trust in the Lord. If we would be today's Joseph and Benjamin, we must be those who trust in the mighty One, in the Shepherd of Israel, in the rock of the church, and in the all-sufficient One. My conscience testifies that without trusting in the Lord, I can do nothing. If I do not pray about everything I do in the Lord's recovery, I would have no peace. I pray about everything I do in the Lord's recovery, praying until I have the peace and the assurance. Before I deliver a message, I pray about it until I am fully inspired and empowered. The life of Joseph is a trusting life, a life that trusts in God for its living. This is the secret of Joseph's fruitfulness and victory.

Although the language of poetry is economical, Jacob nonetheless used different titles of the God who is worthy of our trust: the mighty One, the Shepherd, the stone, the

All-sufficient, and the God of thy father. We are not the first generation to trust in God. Rather, we are one of the later generations. We see the testimony of our forefathers' trust in their God, and now their God has become our God. Hence, we follow in their footsteps to trust in their God, who is the mighty One, the all-sufficient One, the Shepherd, the rock, and the foundation. Hallelujah, we are standing on Him and trusting in Him! Therefore, we are fruitful and victorious.

LIFE-STUDY OF GENESIS

MESSAGE ONE HUNDRED SIX

THE SPIRITUAL SIGNIFICANCE OF JOSEPH AND BENJAMIN

(2)

Jacob's prophecy regarding his twelve sons ends with a blessing that includes ten items. The history of these twelve sons begins with a sinner, that is, it begins with sin, even with a gross sin, not a refined sin. At the beginning we have a person who is full of sin, and at the end we have a person who receives the universal blessing. Thus, the prophecy ends with the full blessing. With Joseph, everything is a blessing, and the blessing is everywhere. There is blessing upon blessing.

The Bible is a wonderful book; no human mind can fully understand it. The more we study the Bible, the more we realize how little we really know it. The Bible is too profound. The ten blessings related to Joseph, for example, require the whole Bible for their development.

IV. BLESSED

A. With the Precious Things of Heaven

First are the blessings with the precious things of heaven above (49:25). The precious things of heaven above certainly include rain and snow. These precious things must also include the angels, for the angels certainly are a blessing to us. They are our servants and even camp around us (Heb. 1:13-14; Psa. 34:7). Every believer has at least one angel. For example, Acts 12 speaks of Peter's angel (v. 15), and in the Gospel of Matthew the Lord Jesus indicates that we have angels (18:10).

The material things in the Old Testament are shadows of the reality in the New Testament. In the New Testament the blessings are spiritual blessings. Ephesians 1:3 says, "Blessed be the God and Father of our Lord Jesus Christ, who has blessed us with every spiritual blessing in the heavenlies in Christ." In this verse we have the words blessed and blessing. We are blessed with all spiritual blessings in the heavenlies. The word "places" is not found in the original text. It is difficult to say what the words "the heavenlies" definitely refer to. Certainly this includes the heavenly nature, the heavenly position, the heavenly condition, the heavenly situation, the heavenly atmosphere, and the heavenly capacity. The spiritual blessings are of a heavenly nature, in a heavenly situation and atmosphere, and under a heavenly condition. In other words, every aspect of these spiritual blessings is heavenly. Today we are enjoying these heavenly blessings. According to the New Testament reality and fulfillment, the precious things of heaven above are the blessings in the heavenlies.

Ephesians chapter one reveals that one of these heavenly blessings is God's selection. God did not select us on earth, but in the heavens. Thus, our selection is heavenly, with the heavenly nature, under a heavenly condition, and in a heavenly atmosphere. A second spiritual blessing is predestination. Predestination is nothing earthly; rather it is heavenly. After God selected us, He predestinated us, marked us out, in the heavenlies. This marking out is heavenly in nature, in atmosphere, and in condition. Although the worldly people know nothing of the heavenly blessings, we are enjoying them, for we have been selected and predestinated by God from heaven. We all have been marked out, and wherever we go we bear this heavenly mark. This mark was made in the heavenlies before the foundation of the world. Therefore, it is not anything earthly, but heavenly. The adoption to be the sons of God is another heavenly blessing mentioned in Ephesians 1. Redemption and forgiveness are also included among these heavenly blessings. Although we are on earth, we are nonetheless enjoying the heavenly redemption and the heavenly forgiveness. The One who redeemed us and who has forgiven us is the very God in heaven. Our redemption and forgiveness come from the heavens. Besides all these, in

Ephesians 1 there are also other items listed among the spiritual blessings.

The heavenly rain and snow also come down upon us. There are many who do not like snow. However, those who live where there is snow are often healthier than those who live in a warm climate. Whether we like it or not, in our spiritual life our heavenly Father sometimes sends snow upon us. It is healthy to be outside in the snow; it is a marvelous enjoyment as well. Rain is good, and snow is enjoyable. These are some of the precious things of heaven above. We need to constantly remind ourselves that we are under God's blessing of the precious things of heaven.

B. With the Dew

Joseph was also blessed with the dew (Deut. 33:13). Dew is a finer blessing than either rain or snow. The Bible uses dew to describe God's merciful favor (Lam. 3:22-23). This indicates that something from the heavens is always descending upon us. This something is not very strong and bold; it is fine and gentle, seeming to come quietly, a little at a time. This is the dew. Psalm 133 says that the blessing upon the unity of the brothers is like the dew of Hermon that descends upon the mountains of Zion. Mount Hermon, to the north of Mount Zion, is much higher than Mount Zion. The dew of Hermon must descend upon Zion by means of a strong north wind. The dew comes from the north. Do not think that only the snow comes from the north, for dew also comes from that direction. Sometimes the Father sends us the rain and at other times He sends the snow, but more often He sends the dew. Every morning the Lord's mercy is like the dew. This is the reason we must keep morning watch. If you do not attend morning watch, you will miss the dew. After the sun rises, the dew will disappear. If you would enjoy the dew, you must rise up early in the morning. This dew is not as cold, sharp, or troublesome as the snow. It comes from the heavens by the blowing of the north wind. But when it comes, it comes gently and quietly, a little at a time. If you consider your experience, you will realize that you have had some experience of the dew. This dew that comes upon us waters us a little at a time. How gentle and fine it is!

C. With the Deep, the Springs, Lying Beneath

Both Genesis 49 and Deuteronomy 33 say that Joseph was blessed "with the deep that lieth beneath" (Heb.). This must refer to the deep springs underneath the earth. The blessings upon Joseph begin with heaven above, proceed to the snow and the dew in the air, and then go on to the springs in the earth. By the mention of the dew and the deep, the springs, we realize that the precious things of heaven above should no doubt refer to rain and snow. According to the New Testament, the real spring is not underneath the earth; it is within us. John 4:14 says, "But whoever drinks of the water that I shall give him shall by no means thirst forever; but the water that I shall give him shall become in him a spring of water welling up into eternal life." We have a spring of divine life welling up from within us. What a blessing! Therefore, we are constantly receiving and enjoying the blessings that come from above, from within, and from the air. Some of the blessings from above are like rain and snow, some of the blessings from within are like springs, and some of the blessings in the air are like the dew. We Christians, today's Josephs, are fully under these blessings.

D. With the Precious Fruits Brought Forth by the Sun

Deuteronomy 33:14 speaks of the blessing "with the precious fruits brought forth by the sun" (Heb.). The fruits of plants are produced by sunshine. Without sunshine, no fruit tree could grow very well. Many fruits are actually formed and even constituted with sunshine. Since the sun is a type of Christ, the spiritual fruits brought forth by the sun signify all the riches of Christ. In the universe, and especially to us, Christ is the real sun. In Ephesians 3:8 Paul speaks of the unsearchable riches of Christ. Nearly all the riches of Christ are items that have been processed. For example, Christ is our life. But this life is not a "raw" life; it is a processed life. The life which we have received of Christ and by which we are living is a processed life. Christ has many precious fruits, and life is one of them. Patience is another. This patience, however, is a processed patience. Christ is also our submission, but this submission is a processed submission. It is easy to say that Christ is everything to us; however, it is not so easy to itemize all the aspects of what He is to us. We need to come together for the purpose of fellowshipping regarding the riches of Christ and itemizing them. But do not speak about things in an objective way. Instead, itemize all the subjective aspects of Christ.

Fruit is what comes into being after passing through a particular process. All the riches of Christ are fruits, and every fruit has passed through a process. All the riches of Christ are blessings, and we are under these blessings today. Here I am not merely speaking about the riches of Christ, but about the riches of Christ as blessings to us. Every item of the riches of Christ is a blessing. What a blessing it is to be under the patience of Christ! And what a blessing to be under Christ's encouragement! I am encouraged by Christ, and Christ is my encouragement. This encouragement is a processed fruit that I enjoy today. The Bible also says that Christ is our way (John 14:6). Often we feel that we do not have a way to handle a certain situation. But our experience proves that Christ is our way. We need to trust in Him, live by Him, and take Him as our everything. When we need a way out of a difficulty, Christ is the way. He is also the way for us to handle our situations. Is this not a blessing to us? Whatever Christ is, is a blessing. His riches are the precious fruits brought forth by the sun.

E. With the Precious Things Put Forth by the Moon

Deuteronomy 33:14 also speaks of "the precious things put forth by the moon." The Holy Spirit never uses the wrong word in the Bible. Notice that this verse says that the sun has brought forth, but that the moon has put forth. The sun produces, but the moon does not produce. Thus, fruit is brought forth by the sun, but the precious things are put forth by the moon. In reality, Christ is the sun, and the church is the moon. The fruits are brought forth by Christ, but they are put forth by the church. One of these fruits is forgiveness, and another is justification. Other fruits put forth by the church are reconciliation, redemption, and eternal life. We receive forgiveness, justification, reconciliation, redemption, and eternal life not directly from Christ, but indirectly through the churches.

First Thessalonians 2:14 says, "For you, brothers, became imitators of the churches of God which are in Judea in Christ Jesus." This verse indicates that the Gentile churches followed the churches in Judea. The churches in Judea had been established longer, and they had learned and experienced a number of things. Whatever they learned and experienced was put forth to the Gentile churches, and the Gentile churches enjoyed their fruit. Nearly all the riches of Christ we enjoy day by day do not come directly from Christ, but come indirectly through the churches. Whatever the church in Anaheim enjoys and experiences will be put forth to all the other churches, and what the other churches experience will be put forth to the church in Anaheim. Recently the churches in Taiwan helped us to eat and digest the life-study messages. This is a fruit put forth by the churches in Taiwan. The blessings upon us include all the experiences of the church.

F. and G. With the Best Things of the Ancient Mountains and with the Precious Things of the Eternal Hills

Genesis 49:26 speaks of the blessing unto the "utmost bound of the eternal hills," and Deuteronomy 33:15 says, "And with the best things of the ancient mountains, and with the precious things of the eternal hills" (Heb.). The words "ancient" and "eternal" indicate that this blessing refers to time, but the words "mountains," "hills," and "utmost bound" indicate that the blessing also refers to space. Together time and space equal the universe. Hence, this verse indicates that the blessing we are under is universal, from eternity past to eternity future and from the ancient mountains to the eternal hills, even to the utmost bound. This, of course, is poetic language. It indicates that the blessings we are under are universal, covering all of time and space. The mention of the mountains and hills implies that the plain is included, for it is impossible to be on the mountain without passing through the plain. Therefore, the mountains, the hills, and the utmost bound imply all of space, including even the meeting hall and your place of dwelling. The universal blessing is long and wide, and it reaches from eternity past to eternity future. It is so spacious that we cannot travel through it. The blessing we are under is everywhere. Every time, morning, afternoon, and evening, day and night, is a time of blessing.

When you get into the new heaven and the new earth, you will see that at every time and in every place there will be a blessing. At that time there will be no more sea, meaning that there will be no curse. The entire universe will be a blessing. In space there will be blessing, and in time there will be blessing. The new heaven and the new earth will be nothing but a blessing. At that time you will understand that our blessing is from eternity past to eternity future and from the ancient mountains to the eternal hills, even to the utmost bound. At every time and in every place we are under this blessing.

H. With the Precious Things of the Earth and Its Fullness

Deuteronomy 33:16 speaks of the "precious things of the earth and its fulness" (Heb.). In 1 Corinthians 3:21 and 22 we find a New Testament word that corresponds to this: "For all things are yours, whether Paul, or Apollos, or Cephas, or the world, or life, or death, or things present, or things to come; all are yours." According to these verses, "all things" includes death. Thus, even death, which includes all negative things, is a blessing. We, the children of God, are the blessed people. We are the Josephs under God's blessing.

When I was young, I did a great deal of selection. For instance, I told the Lord that I wanted to be healthy, not ill, and that I did not want to suffer from certain kinds of things. I wanted to have everything that was good. Eventually, however, the selection did not depend on me. Things did not turn out to be according to my choice. When I first came into the

Lord's ministry, I prayed very much and asked the Lord to give me a co-worker who was always nice, one who was neither too strong nor too weak. In my prayer I said, "Lord, You know me and You know what I need. I need a nice person, one who is neither too quick nor too slow." But today I do not like to have any selection. Sometimes the co-worker who is not so nice in my eyes is the one who becomes the greatest blessing to me.

The same is true in married life and in family life. It is difficult for me to tell anyone what kind of wife is the best wife. When I was young, I could tell you, but I cannot tell you today. Perhaps the wife who seems to be the worst will become the greatest blessing to you. You need to believe that all things, including a difficult wife, are blessings. Furthermore, whether your children are nice or naughty, they are a blessing to you. Many times naughty children are a greater blessing than nice ones. You may ask the Lord for nice children, but He may give you naughty ones. However, even those naughty ones are a blessing.

It is even a blessing to have something stolen from us. When something was stolen from me in my youth, I became angry. But today it does not matter whether you give me something or steal something from me. It does not matter whether I gain a thousand dollars or lose a thousand dollars. Perhaps losing a large amount of money will be a greater blessing than receiving the same amount. But one thing I know—everything is a blessing; everything is a gain. But when I was young, I would lose my peace for several hours even over losing a handkerchief. But if today I lost something worth a thousand dollars, I still would have the peace to sleep soundly. To suffer over the loss of something like this indicates that you are under the curse. When the worldly people lose even a small amount of money, they cannot sleep. But if we lose a large amount, we can still praise the Lord for the blessing that such a loss will bring in. As long as I am not touched by a particular loss, I am blessed. Because we are under the blessing, no loss is truly a loss to us. Although we are not yet in the new heaven and the new earth, we have a foretaste of it today. We need the vision to see that we are today's Joseph and that everything is a blessing to us.

I do not like the rumors that are being spread about us. But others can testify for me that I praise the Lord because all these rumors are blessings to us. They are a form of free advertisement. Because of these rumors, my name has become famous throughout the world. I did not have to pay anything for all this advertising. I have never gone to Central America or to Africa, but my name is known there. Thus, even the rumors are a blessing.

Whether or not all things are blessings does not depend on what happens; it depends on who we are. If we are Joseph, everything is a blessing. But if we are Reuben, everything is a curse. My burden in this message is to impress you with the fact that to us everything is a blessing. There is no need to list all the items of the universal blessing in detail. All things are blessings. This is not a mere doctrine; it is what I have experienced.

Nothing bothers me because I realize that everything is from my Father. Everything, good or bad, positive or negative, is a blessing. We all must believe this. Even if we lose something, that loss is a blessing. Paul said that all things are ours, whether Paul, Peter, Apollos, life, death, or any other thing. Formerly, we were Reubens, but now we are Josephs. As long as we are Josephs, whatever betide, everything is a blessing. If you hate me, that is a blessing. If you love me, that also is a blessing. If you rob me, that is a blessing. If you give me something, that also is a blessing. No matter how you treat me, with love or with hatred, what you do to me is a blessing. If you do not do anything, that also is a blessing. I am altogether blessed. Because I am not a Reuben, but a Joseph, I am a blessed person. Praise the Lord that in the church we are Josephs!

Consider Joseph's experience. He was hated and betrayed by his brothers, and he was placed into some difficult situations. Nevertheless, everything that happened to him was a blessing. What his brothers did to Joseph turned out to be a blessing. When Joseph made himself known to his brothers in Egypt, he said, "Now therefore be not grieved, nor angry with yourselves, that ye sold me hither: for God did send me before you to preserve life" (Gen. 45:5). Joseph also said, "Ye thought evil against me; but God meant it unto good" (50:20). Joseph seemed to be saying, "You don't need to be afraid of me or worried about what I will do to you, for everything you did to me was a blessing." Everything in the universe is a blessing to us. Time, space, the heavens, the earth, the air, the things underneath the earth, all persons, all matters, and all things—everything is a blessing to us. Oh, we must believe this! In the early days I held this as a mere belief. But now I can testify with an honest heart that in my experience it is truly so. Everything that happens to us is a blessing.

In Jacob's prophecy with blessing there is a condition for blessing the first ten sons, but not with Joseph. Joseph's blessing is unconditional. If we saw this, we would simply pray, "Lord, I don't know what is good or what is bad. Lord, I only pray that Your will be done." Everything depends upon whether you are a Reuben or a Joseph. It does not depend upon the heavens, the earth, the air, or anything else. If you are a Reuben, everything will be a curse and a loss. But if you are a Joseph, everything will be a gain. Nothing in heaven, on earth, or under the earth could be a loss to you. Rather, all things will work together for good to you as long as you love the Lord (Rom. 8:28). Even the most insignificant thing works together for your good. Your neighbors, in-laws, and friends all work together for your good because you are blessed.

All the New Testament believers are Josephs. You may not feel that you are a Joseph, but the Lord says that you are. As long as you are a believer, you are no longer a Reuben, but a Joseph. Because you are a Joseph, everything that happens to you is a blessing. Heaven, earth, the snow, the rain, the dew, and everything under the earth is a blessing to you. This is the reason the New Testament tells us to thank the Lord for all things (Eph. 5:20; 1 Thes. 5:18). I wonder whether the parents of naughty children ever thank the Lord for their naughty children. If you have a naughty child, you must thank the Lord, saying, "Lord, how I thank You for this naughty child. Lord, I thank You for this dissenting, rebellious child. What a blessing this child is to me!" If such a child remains a Reuben, everything will be a curse to him. But if he believes in the Lord, he will become another Joseph, and then whatever happens to him will be a blessing. If you read the New Testament carefully, you will see that the New Testament believers are the blessed people. We are those under the universal blessing. This is why we should not curse anyone (Rom. 12:14). Because everything is a blessing to us, we cannot help but bless others. Even if others do something bad to us, that bad thing is a blessing. Hence, there is no need for us to curse them; instead of cursing, we would bless them. We may say, "Thank you for hating me. God bless you. Your hatred is a blessing to me. I can bless you in any kind of situation. If you treat me well, I bless you. If you mistreat me, I still bless you." Praise the Lord that we are the blessed people!

If you see this, you will realize that you are under God's blessing. However, we often still speak in a natural way. When we gain something, we thank the Lord for His blessing. But when we lose something, usually we do not thank Him. We need to see the vision that we are Josephs, that we are the blessed people, that we are under God's blessing. Whatever happens to us, good or bad, we should say, "Hallelujah! Praise the Lord! This is a blessing."

We often ask people, "Are you saved?" But now we should learn to ask them, "Are you blessed?" Whenever we are asked this question, we should reply, "Yes, we are blessed." Fundamental Christians often speak of believers as being blood-redeemed and Spirit-regenerated. We need to learn to say that we are the universally blessed people. Our home, family, and all that belongs to us is a blessing, no matter how bad things may sometimes be. We never know what the result of a thing will be. Today something may seem to be good, but it may turn out to be bad. However, a certain thing may seem very bad, but turn out to be good. Only the Lord knows. Whether things are good or bad, the result is the same. It does not make any difference whether our children are nice or naughty, whether our husband or wife is easy to live with or difficult. To Joseph everything is a blessing. If you see this, you will enjoy rest and peace. You will say, "Hallelujah! We have been selected, predestinated, called, and saved, and now we are being blessed." We are the blessed people, those under God's blessing, and everything is a blessing to us. All things are ours.

LIFE-STUDY OF GENESIS

MESSAGE ONE HUNDRED SEVEN

THE SPIRITUAL SIGNIFICANCE OF JOSEPH AND BENJAMIN

(3)

As we have pointed out a number of times, the record of Jacob's blessing found in Genesis 49 begins with a sinner and ends with the universal blessing and the eternal dwelling. If we have a proper knowledge of the Bible, we shall see that the entire Bible issues in the universal blessing of God and in His eternal dwelling. For eternity, we shall be under the universal blessing to be God's eternal dwelling. This is the new heaven and the new earth with the New Jerusalem. The new heaven and new earth will be a realm of universal blessing. We shall be under this blessing in order that we may be the New Jerusalem. According to the picture in Revelation 21 and 22, in the environment of the new heaven and new earth there is nothing but blessing, blessing upon blessing. Everything in that environment will be a blessing to the New Jerusalem, God's eternal dwelling. We, God's chosen people, shall be that dwelling within and under the universal blessing. This is the ultimate consummation of the revelation of the Bible.

It is very interesting to see that the short record of Jacob's prophetic blessing issues in the same conclusion as does the entire Bible. Although there is no sin in the first two chapters of Genesis, sin enters the scene in chapter three. The sinner in Genesis chapter three was a real Reuben. However, in the last two chapters of the Bible, there will be the real Joseph and Benjamin. We may say that Joseph is the sign of the universal blessing. All the blessings are upon the head of the one who was separate from his brothers. Benjamin is the symbol of God's eternal dwelling. Hallelujah, the church in the Lord's recovery today is a miniature of the universal blessing and the eternal dwelling! In the churches we have blessing upon blessing. Under such a blessing, we are the dwelling of God.

These two matters, blessing and dwelling, are found in the New Testament Epistles. Probably not many Christians have paid attention to these matters in the Epistles. But these two words provide the outline of the Epistles, for all the Epistles are on God's blessing. Take Ephesians as a representative illustration. Ephesians 1:3 says, "Blessed be the God and Father of our Lord Jesus Christ, who has blessed us with every spiritual blessing in the heavenlies in Christ." Here we have the matter of the blessings. Ephesians 1:23 speaks of the Body, and Ephesians 2:22 speaks of the habitation, both of which are symbols of God's dwelling. In Ephesians 3:16 and 17 the Apostle Paul prayed that the Father would strengthen us through His Spirit into the inner man that Christ may make His home in our hearts. Hence, in the short book of Ephesians, both the blessings and the dwelling are covered. God has blessed us with all the spiritual blessings in the heavenlies for the purpose that we might become His dwelling.

If you would ask me to say what the Epistles reveal, I would say that they reveal the matters of blessing and dwelling. To see this, however, we need light and vision. Without light and vision, we may read the Epistles again and again and see only things such as the charge for wives to submit to their husbands and for husbands to love their wives, to redeem the time, to be diligent, and to love our neighbors. If we view the Epistles with our natural sight, without the light and the vision, we shall mainly see these minor points and miss the blessing and the dwelling in the Epistles. The New Testament is concerned with the matters of blessing and dwelling.

So many excellent and wonderful points are covered in Genesis 49. How I thank the Lord that Jacob's first son was Reuben and that the last two were Joseph and Benjamin! If Joseph and Benjamin had been the first two and Reuben the last, everything would have been upside down. Praise the Lord that once we were Reubens, but today we are Josephs and Benjamins! I can testify that I am today's Joseph and Benjamin. Day and night, I am under God's blessing, and I am God's dwelling place. Even the young people, those in junior high and high school, must be Josephs and Benjamins. Before we came into the church, we never realized the significance of Joseph and Benjamin. But if we in the Lord's recovery are not Josephs and Benjamins, then who is? Are you not a Joseph and a Benjamin? Are you not under God's universal blessing, and are you not God's eternal dwelling? As today's Benjamin, God dwells in me, and not only in me, but between my shoulders.

I. With the Blessings of the Breasts and the Womb

In the previous message we covered the first eight aspects of the universal blessing. In his blessing of Joseph, Jacob used many poetic expressions, such as ancient mountains, eternal hills, and the utmost bound of the eternal hills. These particular expressions indicate time and space, all time from the ancient times to eternity and all space from heaven to under the earth. Hence, these poetic expressions refer to the universal blessing, for time plus space equals the universe. We have a blessing that fills the entire universe. Throughout time and space, we are under this blessing. God's blessing fills the universe, from eternity past to eternity future and from the heavens above to the depths underneath the earth. Everywhere and at every time there is nothing but blessing. Oh, we all must see this vision and have this realization! There is no need to wait for the coming of the new heaven and the new earth, for in the church life today we are in the foretaste of this universal blessing.

Although the first eight items of the blessing bestowed upon Joseph are universal, they are rather common. If you examine them, you will see that nothing of life is involved; neither is there anything of dwelling. Hence, we need to consider the last two items, one of which involves life and the other, dwelling. Remember, the record in Genesis 49 is poetic and poetry often uses symbols. One picture or symbol can take the place of a thousand words. Under the inspiration of God, in 49:25 Jacob spoke of "blessings of the breasts, and of the womb." In this poetic utterance, the womb signifies the producing of life, the begetting of life, and the breasts signify the nourishment of life. In His creation, God only blessed the living creatures and man (1:22, 28). He did not bless His work accomplished on the first four days. He did not bless the sun, the moon, the stars, or the vegetation on the earth. But on the fifth day God blessed the living creatures in the waters and the fowl in the air, and on the sixth day He blessed man. Thus, among all the works of His creation, God blessed only the living creatures and man. This impresses us with the fact that God is for life. God's intention is to have the producing life. The fact that Joseph was blessed with the blessings of the womb and of the breasts indicates that he was blessed with the begetting and nourishing life. These figures should not be applied to the animal life, nor even to the human life, but to the eternal life. The eternal life is the highest life, the most productive life. In the New Testament we see that the producing life is not the animal life nor the human life, but the eternal life. Today we in the church are experiencing the eternal life as the producing life. The many items of blessing in the church include the breasts and the womb, the producing and nourishing life.

Look at the picture given in Revelation 21 and 22. In these chapters we have the new heaven, the new earth, and the New Jerusalem. In the New Jerusalem there is the river of water of life. In this river of life grows the tree of life. In the entire new heaven and new earth with the New Jerusalem, the central item is the flowing life. No doubt, all the other aspects of the universal blessing are present, such as the blessing of the heavens, the blessing of the dew, the blessing of the earth, and the blessing of the things beneath the earth. But Revelation 21 and 22 do not mention the other things. These chapters mention only the flowing of life with the tree of life, something that provides nourishment. If you simply read Genesis 49 according to the black and white, you will not see the matter of the producing and nourishing life. You must get into the spiritual significance of the poetic expressions used in this chapter. Hallelujah, in the church life we have the blessing of life, the blessing of the breasts and of the womb, the blessing of the flowing river!

If we have every blessing except the blessing of the breasts and of the womb, this signifies that we are without the producing and nourishing life. If that is the case, we are a poor church. If the producing animals and human beings were taken away from the earth, the whole meaning of the universe would be lost. The meaning of the entire universe depends upon the animal life and especially upon the human life. Suppose in Southern California there were grass, flowers, and trees, but no animals or human beings. When the angels saw such a situation, they would say that it was full of blessing, yet short of life. But the angels are happy to see so many living creatures on earth. In the church life we enjoy the womb and the breasts, the producing and the nourishing. In the church life today we certainly have a flowing life. In the New Jerusalem, we shall have it even more.

J. With the Good Pleasure of Him Who Dwelt in the Bush

Finally, Joseph was blessed with "the good will of him that dwelt in the bush" (Deut. 33:16). The last item of the universal blessing is God's dwelling. The One who dwelt in the bush has a good will, a good pleasure. Anyone who lived in a bush would expect to have a better home. If you were dwelling in a bush, your good will would be to have a better home. I would not like to live in the bush with you, but I would like to live with you in a better home. Suppose a young man who lives in a bush desires to marry a certain young lady. The good will of the one in the bush is to live with his wife in a nice house after they are married. Before the tabernacle was built, the Lord dwelt in the bush (Exo. 3:4). God delivered His people, the children of Israel, out of Egypt with the intention that they would build first the tabernacle and then a temple for Him. Moses saw a vision of God in the bush, and God spoke to Moses from the bush. But in Leviticus 1:1 God spoke to Moses out of the tabernacle. God blessed the children of Israel with this good will. This is God's best will, with which He has blessed His chosen people. God has blessed the children of

Israel with the best blessing—to have His dwelling. What blessing could be greater than this? Eventually, Aaron, a sinner, is able to enter into the presence of God in the Holy of Holies. What blessing could be greater? The highest blessing is to enter into God's dwelling and stay in His presence. Even we ourselves become this dwelling.

At this point I wish to point out that we cannot understand the Bible according to our natural concept. Although you may read the Bible and be able to recite many verses, you cannot see anything until the vision comes. If you hear this word about God's dwelling, Exodus will be a new book to you. The book of Exodus begins with the vision of God in the bush speaking to Moses with the intention that one day Moses would lead the children of Israel out of Egypt into the wilderness to build a tabernacle for God. What a blessing! In the entire Old Testament, there is no blessing higher, greater, or sweeter than the blessing of God's dwelling place. Often the psalmists expressed their desire to be in God's temple. Psalm 84:10 says, "For a day in thy courts is better than a thousand. I had rather be a doorkeeper in the house of my God, than to dwell in the tents of wickedness." No blessing is as sweet or great as the blessing of God's dwelling. This is the ultimate blessing.

The New Jerusalem is called the tabernacle of God. When the Lord Jesus became flesh, He was a tabernacle of God (John 1:1, 14). He was also God's temple (John 2:19, 21). Following Him, the church was built up to be God's temple (1 Cor. 3:16). Eventually, the entire New Jerusalem will be an eternal tabernacle, the central blessing among God's blessings. The new heaven and new earth will be a blessing, but the center of that blessing will be the New Jerusalem, God's tabernacle. In the New Jerusalem God will dwell with us, and we shall dwell by Him.

V. DWELT

A. By the Lord between Benjamin's Shoulders

Genesis 49:27 says that Benjamin is a tearing wolf (Heb.). But Deuteronomy 33:12 says of him, "The beloved of the Lord shall dwell in safety by him; and the Lord shall cover him all the day long, and he shall dwell between his shoulders." To the enemy, Benjamin is a tearing wolf. Nevertheless, according to Deuteronomy, Benjamin is the beloved of the Lord. How could a tearing wolf be the beloved of the Lord? The Lord loves Benjamin, the tearing wolf, because God's dwelling place was in the territory of Benjamin. Many Christians think that Jerusalem, where the temple was located, is in the territory of Judah. However, it is in the territory of Benjamin, very close to Judah. The kings came out of Judah, but the capital, Jerusalem, was in Benjamin. The capital was the site of God's dwelling place. According to geography, the territory of Benjamin is shaped like two shoulders, and Jerusalem is located between the two shoulders. Hence, the Lord dwelt between the shoulders of Benjamin.

It is the head, of course, that dwells between the two shoulders of our body. This indicates that the dweller in Deuteronomy 33:12 is the Head. The very God who dwells in the temple is the Head. This means that in God's dwelling there is the headship, the lordship. The language of Deuteronomy 33:12 is poetic. Years ago, this verse was altogether a puzzle to me. I did not know what it meant to say that God dwelt between the shoulders of Benjamin. But after years of studying the Bible and of experience with the Lord, I began to understand. If you consider your experience, you will realize how real it is that God dwells between our shoulders to be our Head. Whenever we have God's dwelling, we have the headship. Thus, there is the throne within the city of New Jerusalem.

Deuteronomy 33:12 also says that the Lord will cover Benjamin all the day long. How did the Lord cover Benjamin? The tabernacle was a covering, for Revelation 7:15 says, "He who sits upon the throne shall spread His tabernacle over them." God's building is a tabernacle, and a tabernacle is an overshadowing. This tabernacle is both Christ and the church. Today we are under the overshadowing of Christ and the overshadowing of the church, for both Christ and the church are the overshadowing dwelling place of God under which we are dwelling.

B. Benjamin Dwelling in Safety by the Lord

Deuteronomy 33:12 says that Benjamin will dwell in safety by the Lord. Benjamin will be a neighbor of the Lord. Because he lives next door to the Lord, he dwells in safety. Likewise, as long as we dwell by the Lord, we are safe. Although we may not have very much experience yet, we nonetheless can testify that we are today's Benjamin, that God has His dwelling place between our shoulders, and that all our being is under His overshadowing. He is the Lord, and His kingly throne is with us. We have the dwelling, He is here, and we are dwelling by Him. God and we are neighbors. What a blessing!

If you take this concept of God's dwelling found in the first book of the Bible and read the book of Psalms in the light of it, the Psalms will be new to you. The entire book of Psalms is concerned with this matter of God's dwelling. Many verses concern the city, the temple, the house, the dwelling place, or the tabernacle. If we put all these verses together, we see that the Psalms are absolutely concerned with God's dwelling. It was in one of the Psalms that Moses said, "Lord, thou hast been our dwelling place in all generations" (Psa. 90:1). If we would take the Lord as our habitation, we must firstly be His habitation. If God has no dwelling built up on earth, we could never have Him as our habitation. But when He has a dwelling on earth, He becomes our habitation and we become His habitation. This is what is called the mutual habitation, which is revealed in John 14 and 15, particularly in the words, "Abide in Me and I in you" (John 15:4). "Abide in Me"—this is our habitation; "and I in you"—this is His habitation. In John 14:23 the Lord Jesus said clearly, "If anyone loves Me, he will keep My word, and My Father will love him, and We will come to him and make an abode with him." We shall be God's dwelling, and He will be our habitation. If we all praise the Lord for this, we shall be with Him in His dwelling place.

The last of the ten aspects of the universal blessing is the matter of dwelling. Thus, eventually all the blessings consummate in the dwelling. The reason God gives us so many items of blessing is that we may be His dwelling. Why did God save you? It was for His dwelling. Why does He give you grace upon grace? For His dwelling. Why is God doing everything for you today? It is all for His dwelling. All the blessings issue in God's dwelling. This is God's good will, the desire of God's heart. What God wants is a dwelling place.

This is revealed in Isaiah 66:1 and 2. In Isaiah 66:1 we see that heaven is God's throne and the earth is His footstool, but God does not yet have a place of rest. Many Christians think of going to heaven. To them, heaven is a lovely place. But God does not love heaven as much as these Christians do. He wants a place of rest. Isaiah 66:2 reveals that God's resting place is neither heaven nor earth, but man. God is looking to a man. This verse says, "To this man will I look, to the poor and contrite in spirit, who trembleth at my word" (Heb.). This verse corresponds to Matthew 5:3: "Blessed are the poor in spirit, for theirs is the kingdom of the heavens." The kind of man who is God's rest is a man who is poor and contrite in spirit. God's good will is to have this kind of man. God's will is that we would be poor and contrite in our spirit, empty for Him. However, if our spirits are filled with things other than God, we are not poor in our spirit. If such is the case, God cannot have His dwelling with us. Many Christians today are full in their spirit. They are filled with so many things, even fundamental things, that there is no room in their spirit for the Lord. God needs a vacant spirit. His desire is that your spirit would be made vacant for Him. One who is poor in spirit is one whose spirit is vacant, unoccupied, ready for the Lord to come in.

According to Isaiah 66:1 and 2 those who are poor and contrite in spirit are the place of God's rest. No other place in the entire universe, in the heavens or on the earth, is God's rest. As those poor and contrite in spirit, we should be able to say, "Lord, come in. Lord, I'm vacant, unoccupied, ready for You. Come in, make Your dwelling in me, and settle Yourself in me." No matter how long you have been in the church life, you need to pray such a prayer, to ask the Lord to have His dwelling in you. In Ephesians 3:16 and 17 the Apostle Paul prayed that the Father would strengthen us with power through His Spirit into our inner man so that Christ may make His home in our hearts. Paul prayed that Christ would be able to dwell in us. It is not simply a matter of loving the Lord or of serving Him; it is a matter of His making His home in us. The service we render the Lord will not satisfy Him as much as our becoming His dwelling place. We all must be the Lord's dwelling. This is what He desires, and this is what He is seeking. This is God's good will. The uttermost blessing is to become God's dwelling place. His dwelling is also our dwelling. When our God is at rest, we also find rest in His dwelling.

This concept of God's dwelling and of our dwelling with Him is found throughout the Old Testament and the New. Throughout the centuries and the generations, God has been desiring a dwelling place. Sorry to say, most of God's people have not seen this. But today in His recovery He comes to us again and again regarding His dwelling. I am not speaking something that I have not experienced myself. Whenever I have opened up the Bible during the past twenty-five or thirty years, I have mainly seen one matter—God's dwelling. In many chapters of the Bible, God's desire for a dwelling place is covered. This is the desire of God's heart, His good will. If you are blessed with the good will of Him who dwelt in the bush, you are the most blessed person.

In a sense, even today the Lord is still in the bush. Look at the situation throughout the earth. What is there except bush? Where is the tabernacle? Many cannot even see the shadow, much less the reality. But how we must worship the Lord that in His recovery we not only see the shadow, but we are in the dwelling. We can say, "Lord, praise You! With us You are not in the bush. You are in Your dwelling."

We have seen that the Lord blessed Joseph with the good will of Him who dwelt in the bush. Who is this One who dwelt in the bush, and what is His good will? If we do not interpret this verse in the way we have, then how should we interpret it? By reading the entire Bible, we can discover who it is who dwelt in the bush and what His good will is. The One who dwelt in the bush is no doubt the One who called Moses to build the tabernacle for Him. He lived in a bush, but He expected to have a tabernacle built of precious materials. That was His good will. The children of Israel were blessed with this good will. Do you believe the Lord delivered the children of Israel out of Egypt simply that they might be saved? Their deliverance was not merely for their salvation, but for God's dwelling place. Everything God did to them and for them was for the purpose that the tabernacle might be erected among them. After the tabernacle was set up, the glory of God came down and filled it (Exo. 40:34). At that time, the children of Israel were the most blessed people on earth, blessed with the good will of the One who dwelt in the bush, the One who now dwelt in the tabernacle. Thus, the tabernacle became the greatest blessing to the children of Israel.

It is the same today. The Lord's good will is to have the church. Because we are in the church, we are the most blessed people. Before the church came into existence, the Lord certainly was in the bush. Practically speaking, before the church came to this locality, the Lord was in the bush. He surely was not in a tabernacle. But today the church is here, and we can say, "Praise the Lord! He is no longer in the bush. Now He is in the tabernacle, and we are here with Him. We and God are neighbors. We are today's Benjamin dwelling in safety by the Lord. Hallelujah!" What could be better than this? As long as I have the dwelling of the Lord and I am in it, that is sufficient. This is the experience of Benjamin, Joseph's younger brother.

Benjamin is a good match to Joseph. Likewise, the church is a good match to God's blessing. Throughout the years, God has blessed you. You simply cannot deny that you have been under His blessing. But the purpose of His blessing is for the good will of the One who dwelt in the bush, and this good will is to have the church life as His dwelling. Today, God can boast to the enemy, Satan, "Satan, look, today I have a place of rest. My resting place is the church. Once I said that heaven was My throne and the earth was My footstool, but I had to ask where My rest was. Satan, I tell you, the church today is My resting place. I am satisfied, and My chosen people are satisfied also."

Many of us can testify that since the day we were saved, we have never been as satisfied in our spirit as we are in the church life today. This is not to say that the church life is perfect. No, it is not perfect. But here in the church life we are satisfied. We passed through many places without being satisfied. We did not find satisfaction until we came into the church. On that day we said, "This is home. I am satisfied." The reason we sense that we are home and are satisfied is that the church is God's tabernacle, God's dwelling. The Lord is no longer in the bush, but in the tabernacle. How happy I am that we are under the universal blessing and that we are God's dwelling!

This blessing is universal, and this dwelling is eternal. The church life will last forever. The old heaven and the old earth, including the old environment, will be terminated, but the church life we are in today will last forever. This is the eternal dwelling. I assure you that when you enter into eternity, you will recall your experience in the church life. You may say, "Oh, I can never forget what I experienced in the church life." Wait, and you will discover that this is true. Deep within, we have the full assurance that the church life is eternal.

LIFE-STUDY OF GENESIS

MESSAGE ONE HUNDRED EIGHT

THE ULTIMATE CONSUMMATION OF GOD'S OPERATION IN THE BIBLE

With this message we conclude the series of messages on chapter forty-nine. Chapter forty-nine is a record of Jacob's prophetic blessing of his sons. These blessings are given in figures, signs, and symbols, all of which need to be allegorized. We have seen that in Genesis the seeds of nearly all the truths in the Bible are sown. The seeds sown in this book are developed in the following books and are harvested in the book of Revelation. Because Genesis is a book of the seeds of the truths contained in the Bible, the conclusion of chapter forty-nine must correspond to the conclusion of the whole Bible. In the last two chapters of Revelation there are two main things: the universal blessing and the eternal dwelling of God with men.

Before we consider this universal blessing and the eternal dwelling, we need to review chapter forty-nine. The first four sons of Jacob were Reuben, Simeon, Levi, and Judah. According to the record of the Old Testament, these four sons were evil. The first and the fourth, Reuben and Judah, were full of lust. The second and the third, Simeon and Levi, were full of anger. Lust and anger characterize evil people. In the constitution of the kingdom of the heavens decreed in Matthew chapters five, six, and seven, the Lord Jesus covered lust and anger in a strong way. If a man can be kept from these two things, he will not be sinful. A man becomes sinful mostly because he is full of lust and anger. We praise the Lord that in His grace He saved the first four sons of Jacob. Moreover, two of them were transformed into something marvelous. Levi was transformed to become the priests, and Judah was transformed to become the kings. Sinners have become priests and kings. This has been accomplished by a kingly salvation.

This salvation was sent out to the Gentile world by Zebulun, the fifth son of Jacob. After the gospel was shipped out by Zebulun, Issachar came in as rest, rest in the gospel accomplished by Judah and preached by Zebulun. The saved one rests in God's salvation. After Issachar came Dan and with him a form of apostasy. Although Dan deviated from God's way, Gad came in to restore the situation. Thus, with Dan we have apostasy, and with Gad we have recovery. The recovery with Gad issues in the sufficiency of the riches of Christ symbolized by Asher. Naphtali, who follows Asher, signifies resurrection in which are the riches of Christ.

After the first ten sons, we come to the last two, Joseph and Benjamin. If you read the record of these two sons carefully, you will see that there is no account of any defect or failure in them. Although there is a long record regarding Joseph in the Bible, there is no hint that he was wrong in anything or that he failed. Joseph was perfect. Although we cannot say that Benjamin was perfect, there is no record of any defect in his life either. Joseph was called the son of a fruitful tree, and Benjamin, the son at the right hand. It is very meaningful that Joseph was fruitful and that Benjamin was at the right hand of God. Both are in resurrection. These two characteristics can easily be applied to the Lord Jesus Christ. Christ is the only Son of the fruitful tree, and He is also the only Son at the right hand of God. Hence, both Joseph and Benjamin were types of Christ. Joseph was a type of Christ issuing in God's unlimited, boundless, universal blessing. The perfect Christ typified by Joseph brought in God's boundless blessing. Benjamin was a type of Christ as the One who brought in God's eternal dwelling place.

Genesis 49:22-26 and Deuteronomy 33:13-16 indicate that the blessing upon Joseph is universal and eternal. It is from the ancient mountains to the eternal hills. This indicates space and time. The blessing that Christ has brought in fills every part of the universe. When the new heaven and the new earth come, there will be nothing but blessing in the whole universe. There will be blessing upon blessing. This is the life of Joseph, the life that issues in blessing.

The record concerning Benjamin in Genesis 49 and Deuteronomy 33 is very short. But this short record gives us a clear picture of Benjamin's life. His life issues in the dwelling of God. Eventually, this dwelling becomes God's eternal dwelling. In the record of Joseph and Benjamin we find a strong indication of what the desire of God's heart is. In his word concerning Joseph, Moses spoke about "the good will of him that dwelt in the bush" (Deut. 33:16). When God called Moses, Moses saw a burning bush. Out of that burning bush God spoke to him. Moses later came to realize that the God who dwelt in the bush desired to have a dwelling place on earth. This was the reason He called the children of Israel out of Egypt, led them into the wilderness, and charged them to build Him a tabernacle. When God called Moses, He spoke to him out of the bush. But after the tabernacle was built, God spoke out of the tabernacle (Lev. 1:1). This reveals that God's intention was to have a dwelling place with man on earth.

Deuteronomy 33:12 says, "And of Benjamin he said, The beloved of the Lord shall dwell in safety by him; and the Lord shall cover him all the day long, and he shall dwell between his shoulders." This verse says that God will dwell between Benjamin's shoulders and that Benjamin will dwell in safety by the Lord. In other words, Benjamin will be the next-door neighbor of the Lord. Many think that Jerusalem was in Judah, but it was actually in Benjamin. Although the king came from Judah, the capital was in Benjamin. Jerusalem, the capital, was the dwelling place of God. Geographically speaking, it was located between Benjamin's shoulders. Because the Lord made His home there and Benjamin lived in the Lord's neighborhood, Benjamin dwelt in safety.

The concept of blessing and dwelling is very strong in Jacob's prophetic blessing of his twelve sons. These two matters issue in the universal blessing and the eternal dwelling.

As we have pointed out, the ultimate consummation of the Bible is precisely these two things. In Genesis chapter three, man became a sinner. Out from among all the sinners, a good number have been saved. Many of the saved ones have been transformed into priests and kings. The kingly salvation has been preached as the gospel of the kingdom, and the saved ones have come to rest in this gospel. After the apostasy and the restoration, we have the issue of the riches in resurrection life. Therefore, all that is covered in the Bible is represented by Jacob's prophetic blessing.

Both in the Bible and in history there have been many Reubens, Simeons, Levis, and Judahs. Moreover, many saved ones have been transformed into priests and kings. Out of the kingship has come a salvation preached as a kingly salvation. The saved ones, as symbolized by Issachar, rest in this salvation. But Dan, the fall into apostasy, has come in. Following the apostasy, there is the recovery, the restoration, with Gad, which issues in the riches of Asher and in the resurrection of Naphtali. Eventually, Joseph and Benjamin appear, both of whom typify Christ. This is a general sketch of the Bible. This sketch, however, is rather doctrinal; hence we need to come now to the matter of experience.

We were Reubens and Simeons who have been saved and transformed into Levis and Judahs. In the church life today we are priests and kings. However, Dan, the apostate church, has come in. But following Dan came Gad signifying the recovery, which issues in the sufficiency of Asher. Asher is in Naphtali, in resurrection. All this results in Joseph and Benjamin. Therefore, today we are not Reubens and Simeons, but Levis, Judahs, Josephs, and Benjamins. From my conscience, I can testify that I used to be a Reuben and a Simeon full of lust and anger. But through the years I have been transformed into a Levi, a priest, and into a Judah, a king. Furthermore, I have been transformed into a Joseph, one full of blessing, and into a Benjamin, one who has become God's dwelling place. How about you? Are you a Joseph and a Benjamin?

Let us now consider the universal blessing and the eternal dwelling in more detail.

I. THE UNIVERSAL BLESSING—
THE NEW HEAVEN AND NEW EARTH

A. All Things Made New

In Revelation 21:1 John saw a new heaven and a new earth, for the first heaven and the first earth had passed away. Revelation 21:5 says, "And He who sits upon the throne said, Behold, I make all things new." The universal blessing has a very peculiar and strange characteristic: all things are made new. God's blessing does not go with anything old. Rather, His blessing goes with things that have been renewed. If we expect to receive blessing from God with respect to our spiritual life, health, our families, or our homes, all these things must be new. We need to be renewed, and our families and our homes need to be renewed also. According to the Bible, anything that is kept away from God is old, but anything that comes back to God is new. For example, you may have a new wife. However, if your wife is away from God, she is an old wife, even if you married her just today. But if a man has been married to his wife for fifty years and his wife has come back to God, she is a new wife.

Whether a person or a thing is new or old depends upon its relationship with God. Only God is new. There is no suggestion in the Bible that our God needs to be renewed. We are the ones who need the renewing. The heavens and the earth and everything in them need to be renewed, but God is ever fresh and ever new. He is the most ancient One, yet He is the most new One, the most fresh One. Our way of reckoning oldness is different from God's. Our way is to count by the age. But God's way is to count on the relationship of someone or something to Him. If a wife is close to God, she is new. If she gets closer to God, she becomes newer. And if she is one with God and mingled with God, she is the newest wife. As strange as it may sound, even a desk, a table, or a chair, if they are consecrated to the Lord, can become new. For example, a sister may say, "Lord, this morning I consecrate to You my kitchen and all the utensils, furniture, and appliances in it." If she does this, her kitchen and everything in it will become new. You may have a brand new house. However, if this house is kept away from God, it will become an old house. You may have a poor, old car. But if you say, "Lord, this is Your car; take a ride with me," your car immediately becomes a new car. On the contrary, you may have a new car and put two movie stars in it and your car becomes very old.

The new heaven and the new earth will be filled with God's blessing because the first heaven and the first earth will have passed away. Many years ago I thought that the new heaven and the new earth were absolutely new. Later I learned that the new heaven and the new earth will be the old heaven and the old earth renewed. It is the same with us. When we were regenerated, we were renewed. To be renewed means to come back to God and to have something of God put into us. The first heaven and the first earth became old because they were kept away from God by Satan, the head of the angelic race, and then by Adam, the head of the human race, both of whom were rebellious against God. Because the angels and mankind were kept away from God, both heaven and earth became old. Praise the Lord that in Christ we have come back to God and have received something of God into us! Thus, we are renewed.

We all expect to receive some blessing from God. The secret of receiving God's blessing is to bring everything to God and to let Him get into everything. For example, bring your kitchen to God and allow God to come into your kitchen. Do the same thing with your children and even with your bank account. If you bring your children and your bank account to God, there will be blessing. Although we are not actually in the new heaven and new earth today, we may have a foretaste. Many times I have the realization that I am in the foretaste of the new heaven and the new earth because I am surrounded by blessing. Everything around me is blessing.

B. No More Sea

When the new heaven and new earth appear, there will be no more sea (Rev. 21:1). The sea is the source of the demons, which keep things away from God. Since Satan's rebellion, God has been continually working to eliminate the sea. In Genesis 1 God limited the water of the sea. Throughout the centuries, God has done much to reduce the sea. Every time a sinner is saved, the sea is limited a little more. If a hundred sinners would be saved today, the sea would be limited a great deal. Eventually, in the new heaven and new earth, the sea will be reduced to nothing. The source of the things which have kept heaven and earth away from God will be no more.

C. No More Tears, Death, Sorrow, Crying, and Pain

Revelation 21:4 says, "And He shall wipe away every tear from their eyes; and death shall be no more; nor sorrow, nor crying, nor pain—they shall be no more; for the former things have passed away." When the sea is no more, there will also be no more tears. All tears come from the sea. After the sea has been dried up, it will be impossible for us to shed tears.

Furthermore, there will be no death, which includes sickness and weakness. According to 1 Corinthians 11, we first have weakness, then sickness, and finally death. To say that there will be no more death also means that there will be no more weakness and sickness. The sea is the source of death, weakness, and sickness. When the sea has been eliminated, there will be no more tears, no more death, no more weakness, and no more sickness. Moreover, there will be no more sorrow, crying, or pain. Although you may have read the Bible for years, you have probably never realized that the source of sorrow, crying, and pain is the sea. Spiritually speaking, the sea causes all these things. When the sea is no more, these things also will be no more.

D. No More Curse

Revelation 22:3 says, "And there shall no longer be any curse." Today on earth there is a curse almost everywhere. But the day is coming when there will be no more curse, for the source of the curse—the sea—will be dried up.

E. No More Night

Revelation 22:5 says, "And night shall be no more." To say that there is no more night means that there is no more darkness. Under God's universal blessing everything will be bright and crystal clear. There will be no darkness, no opaqueness. This is the condition of the new heaven and the new earth.

We need to apply all these aspects of the universal blessing to ourselves. In your life is there still the sea? Are there still tears, death, weakness, and sickness? Are there sorrow, crying, pain, the curse, and darkness? If these things are in your life, it indicates that you are short of blessing. When we come to the life of Joseph, we shall see that in his life there was no darkness, opaqueness, or curse. Even the result of his being put into prison was not a curse, but a blessing. Although he was persecuted by his brothers, the issue of that persecution was blessing.

Today we may have a foretaste of the new heaven and the new earth in which there is no curse, only blessing. If we still quarrel with our wife or husband, we are under the sea, death, weakness, sickness, and darkness. We are in a thick night without light. But suppose in our married life there is neither quarreling nor complaining, but praises to the Lord. This indicates that the sea in our married life has been dried up.

One characteristic of Joseph is very striking. Although he suffered a great deal, he never complained. When he made himself known to his brothers, he seemed to say, "It was not you who sent me here. It was God. I don't complain against you—I praise God." With Joseph, there is no complaining, only praising, because he was under the blessing, not under the curse. If you complain, it is a sign that you are still under the curse. You may have many reasons to complain, but every reason is a curse. If you are one under God's blessing, there will be no complaining. Instead of complaining, you will say, "Praise the Lord! Everything works for good to me!"

It is easy to read the Scriptures in an objective, doctrinal way. But we need to see that the things recorded in the Bible are for us even today. Do not wait for the new heaven and new earth. Today we can live in a foretaste of the conditions of the new heaven and new earth. We can live without complaint, blame, curse, or darkness. We can have a life full of blessing. All our tears may be tears of joy, not tears of sorrow. This is a miniature of the universal blessing which we may enjoy today.

The word "universal" means that blessing is everywhere. It does not mean that I am blessed when my wife is good to me and cursed when she is not good. Whether or not something is a blessing does not depend on your wife—it depends on you. If you complain, the way your wife treats you will be a curse. If you praise the Lord, it will be a blessing.

Let me tell you a secret: Our praises turn the curse into blessing. This is the reason the New Testament tells us to thank the Lord for all things (Eph. 5:20). This includes rumors, persecution, defamation, opposition, and condemnation. We need to praise God for everything. When we praise Him for all things, even the unpleasant things become good things. When we thank the Lord for the opposition, it becomes a blessing. This is the secret of enjoying the universal blessing today. Although we are living in a dark age we may have a foretaste of life in the new heaven and new earth. It all depends upon our realization and practice. If we practice praising instead of blaming, we shall be under the blessing. Otherwise, we shall be under the curse. Hallelujah, in the church we are in a miniature of the new heaven and new earth! Everything here is a blessing.

II. THE ETERNAL DWELLING—THE NEW JERUSALEM

A. The Tabernacle of God with Men

Now we go on to consider the eternal dwelling. Revelation 21:3 says, "And I heard a loud voice out of the throne, saying, Behold, the tabernacle of God is with men, and He shall tabernacle with them, and they shall be His peoples, and God Himself shall be with them." According to the New Testament, God's people are His dwelling place. Some Christians think that God's dwelling place is among us not in an inward way, but in an outward way. If there are one thousand saints and God is dwelling among them, they will consider God to be number one thousand one. God, however, is inside of us, and His dwelling place is among us in an inward way. If one thousand saints are together and God is among them, God is not number one thousand one; rather, He is in the one thousand saints.

Some Christians do not believe in the matter of the mingling of God and man. Nevertheless, the Bible is filled with the thought that God is mingled with His people, for God's people become His dwelling place. God's dwelling is both small and large. When we come together, we all are one corporate dwelling. However, if I stay at home, I myself am God's dwelling. If I come together with others and insist that I myself am God's dwelling place and that all the others are individual dwelling places for Him, that will be erroneous. When we come together, we are not many dwellings; we are one dwelling place of God. However, when we are all at home alone, we are each God's dwelling. At such a time, God has many dwellings. When I am alone, I may say, "Lord, now You have a house. I am Your house, Your dwelling." But when I come to the meeting of the church, I should not come as an individual house of the Lord separate from the others. If I do that in the meeting, I will no longer be God's dwelling. When I am alone, I have the sense that I am God's dwelling and that God is with me. But if I still cling to this concept in the church meeting, I will sense that I am no longer the house of God. When we come together, we are just one house, one dwelling of God. This is a matter of experience, not a matter of doctrine.

When God dwells in us, we enjoy Him as our neighbor. God is the best neighbor. Therefore, we will never be alone, for He is always with us. Because God is beside us, we have safety. Everyone today, especially little children, desires safety. When my grandchildren are with their grandmother, they feel safe. But in the presence of a stranger they feel insecure. When God, the best neighbor, is with us, we are safe.

B. Constituted of God's Redeemed

The eternal dwelling of God is composed of His redeemed, both of the Old Testament represented by the names of the twelve tribes of Israel and of the New Testament represented by the names of the twelve Apostles of the Lamb. In His redemption God dwells within and in His people. Hence, we shall be His eternal dwelling.

C. God and the Lamb Being the Temple

Pay no attention to the misleading teaching that there is no mingling of God and man and that we do not have the divine nature in us. What God has bestowed upon us and imparted into us is much more than this. Eventually, we become God's house, His dwelling, and God and the Lamb become our temple (Rev. 21:22). The New Jerusalem will be the tabernacle of God, God's dwelling place, composed, on the one hand, of all the redeemed and, on the other hand, of God and the Lamb. In God's eternal dwelling there will be no temple because God and the Lamb will be the temple. In the Old Testament the temple was not only the dwelling place of God, but also the place in which the priests served God. As God's redeemed people, we shall dwell in God forever. We shall be His dwelling (John 14:23), and He will be our dwelling (Psa. 90:1). Thus, there will be a mutual dwelling. God will dwell in us, and we shall dwell in Him. He will become our enjoyment, and we shall become His enjoyment. To see His face will be our pleasure, and to see our face will be His joy.

D. God Being the Light, and the Lamb Being the Lamp

In the eternal dwelling God within us will be our light, and Christ will be our lamp to express the very God who is within us (Rev. 21:11, 23; 22:5).

E. God's Throne Being the Source of Supply

Revelation 22 says that we may enjoy God's throne. When He dwells in us, His throne is with us, right within us. Therefore, we have the throne, the authority of God, as the source of supply.

F. The River of Water of Life with the Tree of Life Being the Supply

Out of the throne of God flows the water of life with the

tree of life in it as the supply (Rev. 22:1-2). If we have God dwelling in us, we have the life supply.

G. God's Authority, Face, and Name Being the Chief Enjoyment

In the New Jerusalem we shall participate in His authority and enjoy His face and His name (Rev. 22:3-4). We shall see His face all the time, and His name will be on our forehead forever. This will be our chief enjoyment in the New Jerusalem.

These are different aspects of God's dwelling in us. We do not need to wait for the New Jerusalem to experience them. Even today we can experience all these things. However, when we enter the New Jerusalem we shall discover something new. We may say, "Oh, we have never experienced these things in such a way. Now we are discovering something that we never thought we could experience."

At the end of chapter forty-nine there are no more sinners, no more Reuben and Simeon. Instead, there is Joseph, indicating that God has become our blessing, and Benjamin, indicating that we have become God's dwelling place. Because Benjamin was the place of God's dwelling, he enjoyed God's presence. Benjamin enjoyed safety, and God enjoyed Benjamin as His dwelling place. God has become our blessing, and we have become God's dwelling place. Whatever God is, whatever God has, and whatever God can do becomes our enjoyment and blessing; and whatever we are and have becomes God's dwelling place. Eventually, God and we, we and God, become one. In the new heaven and new earth with the New Jerusalem there are no more sinners and no more sea, death, weakness, sickness, tears, sorrow, pain, or night. Everything is God. God is a blessing to us, and we are a dwelling place to God. We enjoy Him, and He enjoys us. This is the ultimate consummation of Jacob's prophetic blessing upon His twelve sons. Today we are these twelve sons enjoying God to the uttermost and becoming God's dwelling place. Therefore, we can enjoy God, and He can be in us to enjoy all that we are to Him.

LIFE-STUDY OF GENESIS

MESSAGE ONE HUNDRED NINE

BEING MATURED
THE MANIFESTATION OF MATURITY

(7)

h) Departing in an Excellent Way

In this message we come to Jacob's departure, which we shall consider in some detail.

Genesis is a long book, composed of fifty chapters. The record of Jacob's life occupies more than half of this book, about twenty-five and a half chapters. In past messages we have seen how Jacob was born, how he had been selected by God before his birth, and how he was striving, even when he was still in his mother's womb. He continued his striving throughout most of his life. Jacob lived to be one hundred forty-seven years old. In Genesis 49 we read of Jacob's departure from this life. The quality of a man's life and the outcome of his life are determined primarily by the last stage of his life, not by the first stage. It can be compared to runners in a race. It does not mean much that you run well at the beginning of the race. The final result is what counts. In this message we come to the final stage of the life of this wonderful person, Jacob. We need to see how he behaved himself at the time of his departure.

In the Bible, the best departure from this life besides that of the Lord Jesus was the Apostle Paul. When Paul was about to depart, he declared, "I have fought the good fight, I have finished the course, I have kept the faith; henceforth, there is laid up for me the crown of righteousness, which the Lord, the righteous Judge, will award to me in that day" (2 Tim. 4:7-8). What an excellent departure this was! I hope that we all shall be able to make such a declaration at the end of our race.

Although the departure of the Apostle Paul was most excellent, I still love the departure of Jacob, for his departure was lovely and pleasant. Paul's departure was simple. He had no wife and no children. At the time of his departure, he was alone in prison, and there were not many complications. With Jacob, however, there were a great many involvements.

Due to God's ordination and due to his own striving, Jacob became involved with various matters and people. For example, Jacob had four wives: Leah, Rachel, and the two maids. Although his heart was to have Rachel, he was cheated by Laban, who gave him Leah instead. Of course, Rachel was also given to him. In actuality, who was Jacob's genuine wife—Rachel or Leah? According to the record of Genesis, Jacob treated both Leah and Rachel as his genuine wife. He buried Leah in the cave of Machpelah where Abraham and Sarah, and Isaac and Rebekah were buried. By burying Leah in the cave of Machpelah, where the genuine wives of the fathers were buried, Jacob indicated that he recognized her as his real wife. Later, however, as he was departing, he made a sovereign arrangement for Rachel. By doing this, he was telling his descendants that he considered Rachel his real wife. Jacob's life was so involved that it is difficult to determine who his real wife was.

Jacob's four wives gave birth to twelve sons, each of whom was in a category of his own. If there had not been so many categories among Jacob's sons, it would have been impossible for the history of Israel, the history of the church, and even our own personal history to be represented by them. In the prophetic blessing pronounced upon Jacob's twelve sons in chapter forty-nine, we see a representation of the history of Israel, the history of the church, and of our personal history. In order to have such an all-inclusive picture, there was the need of an intricate involvement. Throughout his life, Jacob became involved not only with his wives and sons, but also with various geographical regions. He was born in the good land, but he journeyed to Padan-aram, and later returned to the good land. During the years of his retirement, he moved to Egypt with his family. Each of these moves produced more involvements. Jacob became involved even with Pharaoh, the most powerful person on earth at the time. Jacob had involvement upon involvement, including involvements with the Arameans and the Egyptians. This involvement is also seen in his burial in the good land. The Canaanites thought that it was an Egyptian funeral when it actually was a Hebrew one. A company of Egyptian horsemen and chariots attended the burial of a Hebrew gentlemen. Besides all this, Jacob was involved with God. What involvements Jacob had! If we put together all the portions of the Word that speak of Jacob's involvements, we shall rejoice before the Lord and say, "Praise the Lord! Hallelujah for the Lord's rich word!"

In spite of Jacob's manifold involvement, he departed from this life in an excellent manner. His departure was not only triumphant; it was also pleasant and excellent. No one wants to face death. It is always a sad thing for someone to die. Nevertheless, I am fond of the record of Jacob's departure. In this record we do not have a morbid picture, but a very pleasant painting. After reading this message, I believe that many will be convinced that, in certain respects, Jacob's departure was more inspiring than that of the Apostle Paul. More than three chapters are given to the account of Jacob's departure, but only a few verses are given to Paul's. Let us now consider the details of Jacob's departure, one by one.

(1) Asking Joseph to Put His Hand under His Thigh

Genesis 47:29 says, "And the time drew nigh that Israel must die: and he called his son Joseph, and said unto him, If now I have found grace in thy sight, put, I pray thee, thy hand under my thigh." This matter of having Joseph place his hand under Jacob's thigh has been a problem to many Bible students. Jacob did not say to Joseph, "Do your best to get a physician to heal me." Rather, he asked him to place his hand under his thigh. What is the significance of this? No doubt, it means to swear. But why did Jacob not have Joseph raise his hand if the significance of this act were only that of taking an oath? Instead of guessing, we should understand the Bible according to the facts contained in it. Under the guidance of the Holy Spirit, we can trace what happened to Jacob's thigh during his lifetime. On the eighth day after he was born,

Jacob was circumcised in a part of his body close to his thigh. Then after Jacob had been striving for more than ninety-five years, God came in to touch his thigh. Thus, Jacob experienced both circumcision and a divine touch. First, something was cut off from a place very close to his thigh. That was circumcision. Years later, Jacob experienced a divine touch that caused him to walk with a limp. If you look deeply into the significance of these two things, you will see that both have the same meaning. To be circumcised is to have our flesh, our natural life, cut off. Jacob had been chosen to inherit God's covenant. But his flesh, his natural life, was not useful for this. Rather, it was a hindrance.

Consider the case of Abraham. God's covenant was made with Abraham in Genesis 15. Abraham, however, used his natural strength with Hagar to fulfill God's promise. God was offended by this and stayed away from Abraham for thirteen years. Thirteen years later, God came back to Abraham and seemed to say, "Abraham, I am the all-sufficient One. I will keep My promise. Because I have promised to do something for you, I don't need you to use your natural strength to fulfill what I have promised. What you did with Hagar greatly offended Me. For that reason, I have stayed away from you for these thirteen years. Now I have come to tell you that in My presence you must cut off your natural strength." From that day onward, God's covenant of grace became the covenant of circumcision. The covenant of circumcision means that the covenant of grace cannot be fulfilled or inherited through man's natural strength. If we would inherit God's promise of grace, our natural strength must be circumcised. On God's side, this covenant is a covenant of grace. But on man's side, it has become the covenant of circumcision. God still intends to give grace to man. However, in order to receive God's covenanted grace, we must have our natural strength cut off.

Jacob's circumcision was a sign that he was not supposed to live by his flesh or natural strength. Nevertheless, after his circumcision, Jacob continued striving in the flesh. Although he had been circumcised, he lived as one who had not been circumcised. How much he exercised his strength to inherit God's promise! He used his ability to supplant and to scheme as if he had never been circumcised. Symbolically Jacob had been circumcised; but in reality he was not circumcised until he had been dealt with by God for many years and was in his nineties. For twenty years Jacob was under the hand of Laban, who nearly exhausted Jacob's strength. Eventually, Jacob was forced to leave Laban and return to the land of his father. As he was on the way home, God raised up circumstances to force him to go to Him. Laban was pursuing him, and Esau was awaiting him. Hence, Jacob was in a dilemma, wondering what to do. He seemed to say to himself, "What shall I do? If I go backward, Laban is there. But if I go forward, Esau is there. There is no place to which I can flee." At Peniel he sent away his wives and children and stayed alone to make a deal with God. That night Jacob was so strong in his flesh that he even wrestled with God. The Lord touched Jacob's thigh. That was Jacob's real circumcision. From that time onward, Jacob was lame.

As Jacob was departing this life, he did not have strength even to walk; he could only lie on the bed. As we have seen, Jacob's real circumcision took place when God touched his thigh. Now his lying on the bed was another genuine touch from God. After the first touch, Jacob could no longer walk in a normal way, but now he could not even get out of bed. His natural strength truly had been terminated. Thus, we may consider this as Jacob's third circumcision. At the time of his first circumcision, he was hardly affected at all. After the second circumcision, his thigh was touched and he became lame; however, he could still move. But now at the time of the third circumcision he had no ability to move at all. This was the time for him to trust absolutely in the grace of God. When you cannot do anything, when you are not able to move, and when you have no strength, that is the time for you to trust in God.

Because Jacob had no more trust in himself, he asked Joseph to place his hand under his thigh. This indicated that Jacob recognized that he had no strength to do anything for himself. The only thing he could do was trust in God. His son Joseph, the premier of the leading country on earth, certainly could do something for him. Whatever would be done for him after his death would be done by Joseph. Thus, Jacob asked him to place his hand under his thigh, recognizing by making this request that he had been dealt with by God to the uttermost. Jacob was declaring to the whole universe that he no longer had the strength to do anything for himself. Rather, he could only cleave to God's promise of grace. During his lifetime Jacob had learned one thing: that he could not do anything for himself. All he had done was in vain. Thus, he came to trust in God's promise of grace. To him, that promise was the promise of circumcision, of terminating his natural strength to inherit God's promise.

How vivid and beautiful is this first aspect of Jacob's departure! Here is a man who has learned by experience that it is all a matter of God's grace, not a matter of his doing. He realized that he had been circumcised, that he had been touched by God and was not able to do anything. I repeat, when Jacob was eight days old, he was circumcised. When he was more than ninety years old, he was touched by God and became lame. Now at the age of one hundred forty-seven he was confined to bed, unable to do anything. He surely needed God's grace, which at that time was represented by Joseph and was concentrated in him. Joseph was a type of Christ. Jacob's trust was in God's grace, which is focused in Christ. His confidence was no longer in his thigh. The thigh is the strongest part of our being, for by the strength of our thigh we walk and support ourselves. Jacob's thigh had been circumcised and touched. Because he had been fully terminated, he turned absolutely from his natural strength to God's grace in Christ. Joseph's hand, signifying the hand of God's grace, was not placed upon Jacob's thigh, but under it. This indicates that the strong hand of God's grace bore Jacob for the fulfillment of God's covenant of promise. It was not by Jacob's strength, but by the hand of Joseph, that Jacob was brought to the good land for his actual inheritance. It is not by our strength, but by the grace of Christ that we inherit God's promise.

(2) Considering Death as Sleep

Humanly speaking, no one wants to die. Jacob, however, viewed his death as sleep (47:30, Heb.). Although no one likes to die, everyone enjoys sleeping. It is so sweet to sleep, especially when we are exhausted. For one hundred forty-seven years, Jacob had been bearing a heavy burden and had had many involvements. After enduring so many problems, the time had come for him to rest, to sleep. Thus, he considered death as sleep. He might have said, "My grandfather Abraham is resting. Why should I still strive and bear burdens? I would like to sleep as well."

By viewing death as sleep, Jacob indicated that he believed in resurrection (1 Thes. 4:13-16). He was not a Sadducee, an ancient modernist who did not believe in resurrection. Those who sleep wake up after they have had adequate rest. When I wake up after a good night's sleep, I am refreshed. Jacob has been sleeping for thirty-seven hundred years. When the Lord Jesus was on earth, some of Jacob's descendants, the Pharisees and Sadducees, were arguing whether or not Jacob would wake up, that is, whether or not he would be resurrected. The Pharisees, the ancient fundamentalists, believed in the resurrection, but the Sadducees did not. The Lord Jesus, of course, believed in the resurrection. He even told the Sadducees that God was called the God of Abraham, the God of Isaac, and the God of Jacob, indicating that He is not the God of the dead, but of the living (Matt. 22:32). Jacob is still resting, waiting for the time of resurrection. Perhaps when we see him, we shall say, "Good morning, Jacob."

(3) Charging Joseph Not to Bury Him in Egypt, but in the Good Land

Jacob charged Joseph not to bury him in Egypt, but in the good land (47:29-30). Although he gained much in Egypt, he had no heart for that place. His heart was in the good land. Hence, he charged Joseph to bury him in the good land, in the cave of Machpelah, where his fathers had been buried, that he might inherit the good land. By charging Joseph in this way, Jacob indicated that he had faith in God's promise. He believed that one day the good land promised by God would be the portion, the inheritance, of his descendants. As Jacob was departing, he was a man full of faith. I hope that when we depart we also shall be those full of faith, not faith in something vain, but faith in what has been promised by God in His Word. There are many promises in the Bible for us to believe in. When we depart, we must depart in faith in God's trustworthy word written in the Bible.

The record of Jacob's departure makes no mention of his illness, of his will, or of the way he distributed his properties among his children. The good land was their inheritance, and God's promise was the will Jacob bequeathed to his children. Although the record of Jacob's departure says nothing of his illness or bequests, it gives a beautiful, vivid picture of his life in the presence of God. Truly Jacob was a man of God. As he was dying, he was not threatened by death. Rather, because he was full of faith and hope, he enjoyed his departure.

(4) Worshipping God on the Top of His Staff

As Jacob was dying, he worshipped God (47:31, LXX; Heb. 11:21). It is not an insignificant matter that a dying man would worship God. Jacob worshipped God on the head of his bed. As we have seen, his being confined to bed revealed that he had no more natural strength, that he could not move, and that his trust was completely in God. Hence, he worshipped God there.

The Septuagint translates the last part of 47:31 as "on the top of his staff." In writing Hebrews 11:21 Paul quoted, not the Hebrew text, but the Septuagint. Thus, Hebrews 11:21 says, "By faith Jacob, when dying...worshipped, leaning on the top of his staff." Spiritually speaking, this is very significant. The bed signifies that Jacob had no human strength, but the staff signifies that he was a person filled with the experience of God in his life. The staff was a symbol of Jacob's life of sojourning. In Genesis 32:10 Jacob said, "For with my staff I passed over this Jordan." Throughout his life of sojourning, God was continually with him. Therefore, at the end of his life, Jacob worshipped God on his bed, signifying that he had no strength, and on his staff, signifying that the God whom he worshipped had shepherded him throughout his life.

Jacob's worship of God was not without personal experience. He was not worshipping an objective God. When he was dying, he was worshipping the God whom he had experienced in a full way in a life of sojourning. This was a holy ending of such a matured sojourner. I hope that when we depart from this earth we shall worship God in this way, not worshipping One whom we have not experienced, but worshipping the One whom we have experienced throughout our lifetime. Jacob did not speak about God in a doctrinal way or worship Him in a formal way. He worshipped God according to his experience. The God whom Jacob worshipped was closely related to Jacob's staff, which was a testimony that Jacob was a sojourner on earth (Heb. 11:13) and that he was always under God's leading (Gen. 48:15). According to Hebrews 11:13, he was among those who died in faith expecting one day to enter into what God had promised.

To worship on the top of the staff requires putting the hands on the staff. Jacob asked Joseph to put his hand under his thigh, indicating that Jacob put his full trust in the hand of God's grace. But Jacob put his hands upon the staff, indicating that he recognized that he had always been under God's care of grace throughout his entire life.

(5) Remembering Rachel's Sorrowful Death

In 48:7 we see that as Jacob was departing he remembered Rachel's sorrowful death. He was faithful to her in giving her son Joseph a double portion (48:5-8, 20, 22). What Jacob did with respect to Ephraim and Manasseh in chapter forty-eight was done in remembrance of Rachel. Jacob's first son was Reuben, and his second was Simeon. His eleventh son was Joseph, the first son born of Rachel. Jacob's twelfth son, Benjamin, was also born of Rachel. His first two sons were born of Leah. Jacob, however, desired to make the two sons of Joseph, who was born of Rachel, his first two sons to replace Reuben and Simeon. In Jacob's heart, Joseph's two sons became his first two sons. In chapter forty-eight Joseph presented his two sons to Jacob, and Jacob said, "And now thy two sons, Ephraim and Manasseh, which were born unto thee in the land of Egypt before I came unto thee into Egypt, are mine; as Reuben and Simeon, they shall be mine" (v. 5). In other words, they would replace Reuben and Simeon. Jacob seemed to be saying, "Joseph, your sons Ephraim and Manasseh are no longer for you; they are for me, and I am for Rachel." The birthright among Jacob's sons was shifted from Reuben to Joseph through Jacob's desire to remember Rachel, who was continually on his heart. By doing this, spontaneously Jacob made Rachel his genuine wife. God honored what Jacob did and made it a fact by the allotting of the land at the time the children of Israel entered the good land.

Today among the human race there is no faithfulness between men and women. But in the case of Jacob we see Jacob's faithfulness and honesty toward Rachel. From the day he first saw her, he fell in love with her, and his heart never changed. Jacob was faithful, and God honored this faithfulness. Jacob made Joseph's sons, Ephraim and Manasseh, his first two sons years after Rachel's death. During all these years, Jacob never forgot her. He was still faithful in his love toward her. Genuine love between a man and woman is always honored by God. If you do not love a woman, you should not marry her. But if you marry her, you must love her, and love her with a love that is faithful and honest. In human society today, this kind of love has been lost. A man may love someone today and change a short time later. Nothing offends God's ordination more than such unfaithful love. If you marry a certain person, you must love her to the uttermost. How good it is to see a dying man who still remembered the one he loved! Jacob's love never changed. Some might have said to him, "Jacob, you are one hundred forty-seven years old, and you are about to die. Rachel has been dead for forty years. You don't need to be concerned about this. Why do you need to call Joseph in and ask him to give you his two sons to replace your first two sons? Jacob, simply rest on your bed until you die." Nevertheless, Jacob's faithfulness to Rachel in making Joseph's two sons his first two sons so that Joseph as his firstborn might inherit a double portion of the land is recorded in God's holy Word. Sovereignly, when the portions of the land were allotted under Joshua (Josh. 24), the portion Jacob gave to Joseph was allotted to Ephraim and Manasseh.

This means that what Jacob did was honored by God. A husband should never change his love for his wife. If you are faithful in your love for her, God will honor that faithfulness. This is the highest morality.

(6) Realizing That God Had Shepherded Him All His Life Long

In 48:15 Jacob spoke of God as the One who "shepherded me all my life long unto this day" (Heb.). I hope that all of us will be able to say at the time of our departure that our life was under God's shepherding. May we be able to say, "I was not a sheep without a Shepherd. The Lord has been my Shepherd my whole life long. Now as I am about to die, I am still under His shepherding. I do not choose my own way. He is leading me, and I am under His shepherding."

(7) Prophesying concerning His Twelve Sons

As Jacob was dying, he prophesied concerning his twelve sons (49:1-2). Jacob did not prophesy by saying, "Thus saith the Lord." Rather, he prophesied by being one with God to speak for God. Whatever Jacob spoke became God's word. Jacob was God's mouthpiece. This is the kind of prophecy we find in the New Testament. For example, in 1 Corinthians 7 Paul said that he had no commandment of the Lord, yet he would give his opinion as one who had received the mercy of the Lord to be faithful. Nevertheless, what he spoke was the word of God, for Paul was absolutely one with God, and what he said was God's word. The fact that Jacob could prophesy in such a way was a strong sign and manifestation that he was matured in life. Because he had become one with God, he was mature in life. Therefore, whatever he uttered was God's speaking. He did not claim that God told him to say certain things; neither did he declare, "Thus saith the Lord." He simply spoke, and whatever he said was God's word. God honored it and fulfilled it. God has certainly fulfilled the prophetic blessing pronounced by Jacob upon his twelve sons. This proves that he departed in the maturity of life. His departure reveals his maturity.

(8) Buried with High Honor

In 50:1-13 we have the record of Jacob's burial, which was more grand than a state funeral. When Joseph went to bury his father, "with him went up all the servants of Pharaoh, the elders of his house, and all the elders of the land of Egypt... And there went up with him both chariots and horsemen: and it was a very great company" (50:7, 9). This indicates that Jacob was buried in a stately manner, full of honor. Because Jacob was full of hope, expecting to be resurrected, he charged his son Joseph to carry out his burial in a way corresponding to God's promise. Only unbelievers, those who have no faith in God, neglect the matter of their burial. If we have faith in resurrection, we should make a good arrangement for our burial, an arrangement that will show others that we are not without hope. We expect to be resurrected in a glorious manner to meet the Lord.

The departure of the Apostle Paul was triumphant. However, the departure of Paul was that of a martyr, whereas that of Jacob was normal. Martyrdom does not reveal the normal departure of a man who loved God. We see such a normal departure in the record of Jacob. For this reason, although I appreciate the departure of Paul as a martyr, I love Jacob's departure more because it provides a picture of a normal departure of one of God's children. Regarding Jacob's departure, there is nothing sad or unpleasant. On the contrary, everything is encouraging and edifying. Whenever I read these chapters describing Jacob's departure, I am edified and say, "Lord, grant me the grace never to fear death. When death comes under Your arrangement, I want to take it just as Jacob did." This attitude, however, requires the maturity in life. Jacob, who had become Israel, was mature in life. Therefore, he could depart in such an excellent way.

About the Author

Witness Lee was born in 1905 in northern China and raised in a Christian family. At age 19 he was fully captured for Christ and immediately consecrated himself to preach the gospel for the rest of his life. Early in his service, he met Watchman Nee, a renowned preacher, teacher, and writer. Witness Lee labored together with Watchman Nee under his direction. In 1934 Watchman Nee entrusted Witness Lee with the responsibility for his publication operation, called the Shanghai Gospel Bookroom.

Prior to the Communist takeover in 1949, Witness Lee was sent by Watchman Nee and his other co-workers to Taiwan to ensure that the things delivered to them by the Lord would not be lost. Watchman Nee instructed Witness Lee to continue the former's publishing operation abroad as the Taiwan Gospel Bookroom, which has been publicly recognized as the publisher of Watchman Nee's works outside China. Witness Lee's work in Taiwan manifested the Lord's abundant blessing. From a mere 350 believers, newly fled from the mainland, the churches in Taiwan grew to 20,000 in five years.

In 1962 Witness Lee felt led of the Lord to come to the United States, settling in California. During his 35 years of service in the U.S., he ministered in weekly meetings and weekend conferences, delivering several thousand spoken messages. Much of his speaking has since been published as over 400 titles. Many of these have been translated into over fourteen languages. He gave his last public conference in February 1997 at the age of 91.

He leaves behind a prolific presentation of the truth in the Bible. His major work, *Life-study of the Bible,* comprises over 25,000 pages of commentary on every book of the Bible from the perspective of the believers' enjoyment and experience of God's divine life in Christ through the Holy Spirit. Witness Lee was the chief editor of a new translation of the New Testament into Chinese called the Recovery Version and directed the translation of the same into English. The Recovery Version also appears in a number of other languages. He provided an extensive body of footnotes, outlines, and spiritual cross references. A radio broadcast of his messages can be heard on Christian radio stations in the United States. In 1965 Witness Lee founded Living Stream Ministry, a non-profit corporation, located in Anaheim, California, which officially presents his and Watchman Nee's ministry.

Witness Lee's ministry emphasizes the experience of Christ as life and the practical oneness of the believers as the Body of Christ. Stressing the importance of attending to both these matters, he led the churches under his care to grow in Christian life and function. He was unbending in his conviction that God's goal is not narrow sectarianism but the Body of Christ. In time, believers began to meet simply as the church in their localities in response to this conviction. In recent years a number of new churches have been raised up in Russia and in many eastern European countries.

OTHER BOOKS PUBLISHED BY
Living Stream Ministry

Titles by Witness Lee:

Abraham—Called by God	978-0-7363-0359-0
The Experience of Life	978-0-87083-417-2
The Knowledge of Life	978-0-87083-419-6
The Tree of Life	978-0-87083-300-7
The Economy of God	978-0-87083-415-8
The Divine Economy	978-0-87083-268-0
God's New Testament Economy	978-0-87083-199-7
The World Situation and God's Move	978-0-87083-092-1
Christ vs. Religion	978-0-87083-010-5
The All-inclusive Christ	978-0-87083-020-4
Gospel Outlines	978-0-87083-039-6
Character	978-0-87083-322-9
The Secret of Experiencing Christ	978-0-87083-227-7
The Life and Way for the Practice of the Church Life	978-0-87083-785-2
The Basic Revelation in the Holy Scriptures	978-0-87083-105-8
The Crucial Revelation of Life in the Scriptures	978-0-87083-372-4
The Spirit with Our Spirit	978-0-87083-798-2
Christ as the Reality	978-0-87083-047-1
The Central Line of the Divine Revelation	978-0-87083-960-3
The Full Knowledge of the Word of God	978-0-87083-289-5
Watchman Nee—A Seer of the Divine Revelation ...	978-0-87083-625-1

Titles by Watchman Nee:

How to Study the Bible	978-0-7363-0407-8
God's Overcomers	978-0-7363-0433-7
The New Covenant	978-0-7363-0088-9
The Spiritual Man • 3 volumes	978-0-7363-0269-2
Authority and Submission	978-0-7363-0185-5
The Overcoming Life	978-1-57593-817-2
The Glorious Church	978-0-87083-745-6
The Prayer Ministry of the Church	978-0-87083-860-6
The Breaking of the Outer Man and the Release ...	978-1-57593-955-1
The Mystery of Christ	978-1-57593-954-4
The God of Abraham, Isaac, and Jacob	978-0-87083-932-0
The Song of Songs	978-0-87083-872-9
The Gospel of God • 2 volumes	978-1-57593-953-7
The Normal Christian Church Life	978-0-87083-027-3
The Character of the Lord's Worker	978-1-57593-322-1
The Normal Christian Faith	978-0-87083-748-7
Watchman Nee's Testimony	978-0-87083-051-8

Available at
Christian bookstores, or contact Living Stream Ministry
2431 W. La Palma Ave. • Anaheim, CA 92801
1-800-549-5184 • www.livingstream.com

10-142-001
ISBN 978-0-87083-915-3